D1499722

# THE ENGLISH PEASANTRY
## IN THE
## LATER MIDDLE AGES

# THE ENGLISH PEASANTRY
## IN THE
# LATER MIDDLE AGES

———◆———

THE FORD LECTURES
FOR 1973 AND
RELATED STUDIES

BY

## R. H. HILTON

CLARENDON PRESS · OXFORD
1975

Oxford University Press, Ely House, London W. 1

GLASGOW   NEW YORK   TORONTO   MELBOURNE   WELLINGTON
CAPE TOWN   IBADAN   NAIROBI   DAR ES SALAAM   LUSAKA   ADDIS ABABA
DELHI   BOMBAY   CALCUTTA   MADRAS   KARACHI   LAHORE   DACCA
KUALA LUMPUR   SINGAPORE   HONG KONG   TOKYO

ISBN 0 19 822432 X

© Oxford University Press 1975

*All rights reserved. No part of this publication may be reproduced,
stored in a retrieval system, or transmitted, in any form or by any means,
electronic, mechanical, photocopying, recording or otherwise, without the
prior permission of Oxford University Press*

HN
385
. H57

*Printed in Great Britain by
William Clowes & Sons, Limited, London, Beccles and Colchester*

*To*
*J. R. B. and J. E. C. H.*

LIBRARY
ALMA COLLEGE
ALMA, MICHIGAN

# PREFACE

A LECTURER is severely tempted to enlarge and perfect his lectures. The result may be a considerable improvement but there is also the danger of intolerable delay. I have decided therefore to publish my lectures more or less as they were given. Any additional material which appears here was omitted from the original lectures at the time of delivery because of the need to contain the lecture within the allotted hour. I thank the Electors to the Ford Lectureship for having invited me, and the audience for their patience in listening to them. I would also like to thank the Delegates to the Clarendon Press for agreeing to reprint a number of papers which are now difficult to obtain and which seem to me to fit in well with the theme of the lectures.

*December 1973*

# CONTENTS

## THE FORD LECTURES

## RELATED STUDIES

# THE FORD LECTURES

# I

## The Peasantry as a Class

In January 1313 an agreement was sealed between Thomas, Lord Berkeley, and the Abbot of St. Peter's monastery, Gloucester, concerning intercommoning arrangements between the tenants of the manors of Coaley (near Stroud) and Frocester in Gloucestershire, of which they were the lords. One sentence in the agreement tells us that the abbot and convent 'ont graunte qe le dit Monsieur Thomas e ses franks tenauns . . . e les peisauntz le dit Monsieur Thomas puissent communer ove tutes lur bestes en tut le champ de Southfield'.[1] This is the earliest use that I know of in English records of the term 'peasant', a word which was, in fact, seldom used. I do not wish to argue that the appearance of the word is all that significant, for it is not the word which matters but the social stratum which many different words designate. I give this quotation because some historians have doubted whether the word ought to be in the medievalist's vocabulary. Professor Beresford has expressed some scepticism about it and K. B. McFarlane, in his 1965 lecture 'Landlord versus Minister and Tenant' expresses a similar scepticism when he refers to the 'so-called peasantry'. On this occasion, it was indeed 'so called'.[2]

English historians' interest in the peasantry, or whatever word they have chosen to use, goes back at least a century if we choose

---

[1] *Historia et Cartularium Monasterii Sancti Petri Gloucesteriae*, i, ed. W. H. Hart, 1863, p. 147.

[2] M. W. Beresford, *Economic History Review (EcHr)*, 1958, pp. 156–7. In a review of W. G. Hoskins, *The Midland Peasant*, 1957, Professor Beresford quotes Disraeli—with approval?—'What can it signify whether a man be called a peasant or a labourer?' and ends the review with the question, 'Finally what is a Peasant?' K. B. McFarlane, *The Nobility of Later Medieval England*, 1973, p. 215.

to confine ourselves to those first making a serious study of this social group, such as J. E. Thorold Rogers or F. Seebohm.[3] Today, however, the peasantry has a new set of devotees among social scientists—economists, social anthropologists, and sociologists—who are concerned not with history but with the contemporary world. The reasons are not far to seek, or to guess at without seeking. The world today is still wrestling with the problems of decolonization and of the economic development of societies which have not yet undergone industrialization. These are societies where the majority of the population are peasants, and so peasants and peasant economy have become, as never before, subjects of wide practical and theoretical interest.

This is what lies behind the spate of works on the economics of underdeveloped societies, on individual peasant cultures, or on peasants in general. A bibliography of books and articles on the subject would seem endless, but a taste of the material can be obtained from collections which have appeared in students' readers, such as the American *Peasant Societies* and the English *Peasants and Peasant Societies*. Scholarly writing on the subject of modern and contemporary peasantries has indeed reached the point where the publication of a new periodical *The Journal of Peasant Studies* is envisaged.[4]

Under the pressure of this flow of material, medieval agrarian historians might well wonder in what shape their own subject survives. The sociologists and anthropologists have indeed made use of the researches of outstanding medieval historians such as P. Vinogradoff and M. Bloch, but rather as providers of illustrative material for their own theorizing than as analysts in their own right. It may be that there are good reasons for this. Perhaps Vinogradoff is not taken seriously as a theorist about peasant society because of his predominantly legal approach. Perhaps

---

[3] J. E. Thorold Rogers published the first volume of *The History of Agriculture and Prices* in 1866; F. Seebohm's *English Village Community* was published in 1883. Seebohm acknowledged a debt to H. Maine, whose *Ancient Law* was published in 1861.

[4] *Peasant Societies: A Reader*, ed. J. M. Potter, M. M. Diaz, and G. M. Foster, 1967; *Peasants and Peasant Societies*, ed. T. Shanin, 1971. The first number of the *Journal of Peasant Studies* appeared in 1973.

Bloch is thought to be too insistent on locating the peasantry within the framework of the medieval *seigneurie* to be considered relevant to a consideration of the modern—or the universal— peasantry. But it is well known that the historical dimension in social science is not always appreciated—the readers which I have cited contain no historical articles, perhaps as an act of deliberate policy.

In fact, historians have appreciated for some time that the history of the medieval economy, and therefore of the peasantry, might have lessons for the study of contemporary transformations. This, at any rate, seemed to be the thinking behind the organiza- tion of the programme of the Second International Conference of Economic History which was held at Aix-en-Provence in 1962. Another step towards the practical recognition of the lessons of history was taken in 1967 when the International Labour Office's research organization, the International Institute of Labour Studies, recognizing the ILO's hitherto rather predominating interest in industrial workers, organized a series of studies of peasants. The first of them was a historical seminar on peasant movements, including those of the Middle Ages.[5] If these develop- ments have meant that students of the peasantry are beginning to appreciate the importance of history, they have also led to an injection into historical work on peasants of new theoretical considerations not now derived from legal studies but from sociology and social anthropology. There is much that is fruitful to be gained by the historian from this work; much, too, that can be criticized.

Those whose vision of the world is no longer Eurocentric, as it has been for too long, and those whose vision of history rightly transcends the traditional divisions between the ancient, medieval, and modern epochs have been impressed by the apparent ubiquity of peasantries. Appreciation of this ubiquity, and apparent durability, in time and space, predisposes some to assume that 'peasant economy' or 'peasant society' has its own internal

---

[5] *Second International Conference of Economic History, Aix-en-Provence, 1962*, 1965; Henry A. Landsberger (ed.), *Rural Protest: Peasant Movements and Social Change*, 1974.

logic which, if not everlasting, remains constant, whether found in the ancient world, in medieval feudal society, in central and eastern Europe in modern times, or in the contemporary so-called 'third world'. It is not surprising that the Russian economist, A. V. Chayanov, who analysed the peasantry of his own country in the pre-revolutionary period should have been so influential, in spite of the inaccessibility of his most important theoretical writings until very recently. For in his *Theory of Non-Capitalist Economic Systems* as well as in his *Theory of Peasant Economy*[6] he seemed—in spite of his practical aims—to be offering a general theory of the economies of all peasant societies. And just as Vinogradoff, Savine, and Kosminsky had done in their different ways at an earlier period, he seemed to bring to the study of the medieval peasantry lessons to be derived from a contemporary peasant society which could be observed in its actual workings.

This is no place to go into Chayanov's theories which everybody may now study. It seems possible, however, that his emphasis on the importance of the demographic factor in rural society was already influencing certain European medievalists by 1950 through the reports of M. M. Postan to the Ninth International Congress of Historical Sciences in Paris. Chayanov was not quoted at this time, but the German version of his work makes its appearance in a footnote to an important demographic study of the peasantry of southern England, by M. M. Postan and J. Z. Titow, published in 1959.[7] The suggestion, limited by Chayanov to Russia, that the changing size of peasant holdings was due rather to the changing size of the family than to the success or failure of the peasant household on the market appears in M. M. Postan's introduction to a collection of medieval documents published in 1960. Although the arguments in his introduction could be seen entirely within the context of discussions between medievalists, and Chayanov was not quoted, there seemed to

---

[6] Both published under the title *The Theory of Peasant Economy*, ed. D. Thorner, B. Kerblay, and R. E. F. Smith, 1966.

[7] *IXth International Congress of Historical Sciences, 1950: Rapports*; 'Heriots and Prices on Winchester Manors', *EcHR*, 2nd ser. xi. 1, 1959.

be an element of Chayanov versus Lenin in the arguments used.[8]

Chayanov's discoveries about the relation between family size and the size of the holding are not necessarily applicable outside Russia,[9] suggestive though they may be. Nor of course are they the only elements in his analysis of the peasant economy which are worthy of the attention of medievalists. He insisted not only on the minimal importance of the market but also on the insignificance of hired labour. He introduced the interesting concept of an equilibrium struck between the satisfaction of the demands of the peasant family and the drudgery of labour, a concept which implied the non-costing of family labour in the household budget. This model of the peasant economy could easily lead, if adopted uncritically, to a picture of the peasant community as a world in itself, untouched by history. It is, however, fair to say that Chayanov himself did not take this extreme view, though he does suggest the category of 'family economy' as a social formation of similar status to slavery, feudalism, capitalism, and communism.

But if Chayanov posited the 'family economy'—that is, essentially, the peasant family economy—as one of the great historical social formations, this seems to be carried a stage further by Daniel Thorner, an economist with considerable practical experience as well as theoretical understanding of the peasantry. Thorner, who was very influential in making Chayanov's work known to Western scholars, enunciated a theory of peasant economy at that Second International Conference of Economic History to which reference has already been made. According to this theory any economy can be described as a peasant economy where (i) at least half of the total product of society is agricultural; (ii) where at least half of the working population is engaged in agriculture; (iii) where there is an organized state with

---

[8] *Carte Nativorum*, Northampton Record Society, Publs. vol. xx, 1960, pp. xxxiv–xxxv; V. I. Lenin in 'The Development of Capitalism in Russia', 1898 (*Selected Works*, i, 1936) strongly argued the case for social differentiation in the village resulting from production for the market and the exploitation of wage labour.

[9] See the remarks by W. Kula in 'La Famille paysanne en Pologne au XVIIIe. siècle', *Annales: économies, sociétés, civilisations*, xxvii, 1972.

a minimum number of administrative officials; (iv) where at least 5 per cent of the population lives in towns; (v) where the typical unit of agricultural production is the family holding, with family labour contributing more than half of the total productive effort. Although Thorner insists that there exist specific features that can distinguish one type of peasant economy from another, it would seem that this concept 'peasant economy' could embrace most of human history between 'tribal' (American, 'folk') society and the completion of industrial transformation in modern times. It could certainly apply to most European medieval states.[10]

It is hard to see, whatever the supporters of the concept of 'peasant economy' might say to the contrary, how this view of history which effectively merges all pre-industrial societies together, differs from that other interpretation of human history which describes all pre-industrial societies as 'traditional' societies. The attraction of this interpretation is that it rightly emphasizes the enormously significant, not to say traumatic, experience which industrialization has been for the peasants of early capitalist as well as of early socialist societies. It has at least two weaknesses: first that it tends to elide (as does the 'peasant economy' theory) the differences between succeeding types of pre-industrial society, and secondly, that since the differences which are minimized tend to be those between different types of social stratification, the facts about social stratification itself tend to be distorted.

The theories about traditional society owe a good deal to the stimulating work of André Varagnac.[11] One of the strong features of this work was that it helped to turn folklore, still largely in the 'collecting' stage of inquiry, into a scientific discipline by introducing the concepts of social anthropology. By gathering together a great range of evidence about archaic practices in the French countryside in the nineteenth and early twentieth centuries Varagnac presented a picture of a society which was essentially stratified into age groups, complete with the cult of the last of the age groups—the dead. This traditional civilization of the

---

[10] Dr. Thorner's paper to the conference is reprinted in Shanin, op. cit.; see also his article on 'Peasantry' in the *International Encyclopedia of the Social Sciences*, 1968.     [11] *Civilisation traditionnelle et genres de vie*, 1948.

countryside was defined as one 'persisting throughout the great periods of history, underlying those civilizations of the upper classes which follow one another in the firmament of history and of thought; but remaining *one* from a time difficult to fix, but which many competent authorities agree in placing in the Neolithic Age'.[12] Whatever the force behind these interpretations which stress the apparently unchanging and inviolate character of peasant or traditional society in the pre-industrial era, there is nevertheless a serious danger in submerging the other historical classes into an undifferentiated peasant sea. In minimizing the specific features of ancient, medieval, and early modern societies we not only risk overlooking the dynamic of change but also losing the separate class character of the peasantry.[13]

But it is not only by minimizing the role of other classes that the position of the peasantry and in particular the medieval peasantry is falsified. This is also achieved in a reverse sense by reducing the peasantry to a subordinate position in society, with no independent role to play. We find this in some currently fashionable theories about medieval and early modern societies whose stratification, it is said, was by 'orders' or 'estates' not by class.

There are two converging though originally (one supposes) entirely separate sources for this interpretation. Some historians seem to have accepted as true descriptions the prevalent social theories of the medieval world with which they are concerned. As is well known, the social theory elaborated in the Middle Ages, mainly by clerical writers, assumed that society was composed of estates which were defined according to their function. The oldest and longest-lasting of the theories proposed a tripartite division of society into those who pray, the priests, those who fight, the knights, and those who work, the peasants. This theory became so generalized that up to the seventeenth century it was a commonplace of the most banal of literary works.[14] But the

---

[12] Op. cit., p. 34.

[13] S. H. Franklin, in *The European Peasantry: the Last Phase*, 1969, p. 3, is right to criticize 'the vertiginous telescoping of history' into which less careful scholars than those I have quoted might be tempted.

[14] Ruth Mohl, *The Three Estates in Medieval and Renaissance Literature*, 1933; repr. 1962.

complexity of social organization meant that other orders had to be introduced without changing the essence of the theory. This essence was that the orders were organically interrelated; that the social order stood or fell by their mutual support in the performance of their respective roles; and that the functional division was of divine or natural rather than social origin. In other words it was not the product of history.

The most succinct description in contemporary terminology of a society such as that of Europe in the pre-capitalist era has been made by Roland Mousnier. This is how he sees the stratification of medieval and early modern, indeed of all non-capitalist societies. In such societies,

estates are distinguished from each other, not because of the income and consumption capacity of their members, nor because of their position in the production of material goods but because of the esteem, honour and dignity attached by society to social functions which have nothing to do with the production of material goods.[15]

This theory of *société d'ordres*, in so far as it is applied to the Middle Ages, appears to be based on the acceptance by the historian of the society's own evaluation of itself (or rather the evaluation by its ruling intelligentsia). It is reinforced by modern sociological theory, for one of the competing commonplaces of sociology is that social class is the product of the market and is therefore a characteristic of the era of industrial capitalism. Orders, estates, or status groups on the other hand are the characteristic forms of stratification in pre-market societies. The classic statement is by Max Weber:[16]

We may speak of a class when a number of people have in common a specific causal component of their life chances, in so far as this component is represented exclusively by economic interest in the possession of goods and opportunities for income and is represented under the conditions of the commodity or labour markets . . . in contrast to the class situation we wish to designate as status situation every typical component of the life fate of men that is determined by a specific, positive or negative, social estimation of honour.[16]

[15] *Les Hiérarchies sociales de 1450 à nos jours*, 1969, p. 19.
[16] *From Max Weber: Essays in Sociology*, ed. H. H. Gerth and C. Wright Mills, 1948 and 1970, pp. 181, 186–7.

Medievalists, working within the traditionally accepted medieval period up to the end of the fifteenth century, seem to have been less consciously influenced by those theories than the historians of the French and English pre-revolutionary *anciens régimes*.[17] Hence, in England, the mixture of neo-Thomism and Weber (which appears in Mousnier's writings) is found exemplified in P. Laslett's *The World We Have Lost*, with its curious, one might even say original, concept of a 'one-class society'. In this view there was only one *class* in seventeenth-century England, that of the ruling nobility and gentry. This social stratum was a class, rather than an estate, because it was composed of people with a common political consciousness, 'a number of people banded together in the exercise of power, political and economic'.[18] By this definition, of course, England could be described as a one-class society long before the seventeenth century. The ruled strata, on the other hand, in particular the peasantry, cannot be designated 'classes' by this definition and are therefore described as status groups.

It is somewhat ironic, in view of the fact that Dr. Laslett's book seems to be directed against current Marxist interpretations of seventeenth-century history, that in it he comes near to an aspect of Marx's own definition of a social class which has recently been strongly emphasized. It has, of course, often been stressed that Marx defined class in different ways on different occasions, but on some of these occasions he certainly suggested that for a social stratum to be fully a class (a class *for* itself as well as *in* itself) it must have a common class consciousness. It is of particular interest for us that one of the places in Marx's writings frequently cited to illustrate this definition of class concerns the peasantry. It comes from his *Eighteenth Brumaire of Louis Bonaparte*.

[17] I am thinking about consciously articulated theory rather than unexpressed assumption. The historians of the school of Father J. A. Raftis working at the Toronto Pontifical Institute of Medieval Studies come pretty near to expressing medieval organic society theory in a modern social anthropological disguise. See E. B. Dewindt, *Land and People in Holywell-cum-Needingworth*, 1972. One must also mention a work by M. Guy Fourquin who appears as a disciple of M. Mousnier in a polemical work, *Les Soulèvements populaires au moyen age*, 1972.

[18] P. Laslett, *The World We have Lost*, 1971, p. 23.

... in so far as millions of families live under economic conditions of existence that separate their mode of life, their interests, and their culture from those of the other classes and turn them in hostile opposition to the latter, they form a class. In so far as there is merely a local interconnection among these small-holding peasants and the identity of their interests begets no community, no natural bond and no political organization among them, they do not form a class ...[19]

Marx, however, makes clear that in writing so he is dealing not with the peasantry in general but specifically with the peasants of the post-revolutionary and post-Napoleonic epoch. Describing them as 'a simple addition of homologous magnitudes, much as potatoes in a sack form a sackful of potatoes' and as 'a nation of troglodytes', he distinguishes *this* peasantry, bound by debt to urban usurers, from the pre-revolutionary peasantry, bound by feudal obligation to aristocratic landed property. As one would expect in Marx, he insists on a historically changing not on an eternal peasantry.

I propose to define the peasantry as a class, as determined by its place in the production of society's material needs; not as a status group determined by attributed esteem, dignity, or honour.[20] Such a definition will indeed pick out certain features common to peasants in other epochs than the Middle Ages and in other places than Western Europe—common features which may lead us to make fruitful if dangerous comparisons. The definition must not, however, be too wide, as is the case with a recent statement by a well-known theorist of peasant society. Henry Landsberger describes peasants as 'persons obtaining their livelihood from agriculture and of low economic, political and cultural status relative to other groups in society'.[21] Such a definition could apply

[19] The quotation is used in Shanin, op. cit., p. 230 and by D. McLellan, *The Thought of Karl Marx*, 1971, p. 156.

[20] In spite of the support which historians who designate social strata in the medieval and early modern periods as status groups, not classes, claim to have from the social and political theory of the period, most medieval theorists in fact, describe the peasants' social role in economic terms, that is that they are the producers of the material goods necessary for the existence of the rest of society.

[21] *Framework for the Study of Peasant Movements* (International Institute for Labour Studies paper, 1966), p. 3; cf. Landsberger, op. cit., p. 10.

to ancient or American plantation slaves as well as to modern agricultural workers. It is a definition which denies the specific character of peasantries as a distinctive social class in history as well as in contemporary reality.

The essential elements of a useful definition of this stratum of cultivators and herdsmen are:

(i) They possess, even if they do not own, the means of agricultural production by which they subsist.

(ii) They work their holdings essentially as a family unit, primarily with family labour.

(iii) They are normally associated in larger units than the family, that is villages or hamlets, with greater or lesser elements of common property and collective rights according to the character of the economy.

(iv) Ancillary workers, such as agricultural labourers, artisans, building workers are derived from their own ranks and are therefore part of the peasantry.

(v) They support super-imposed classes and institutions such as landlords, church, state, towns by producing more than is necessary for their own subsistence and economic re-production.

The definition of these common characteristics permits fruitful illuminations in the course of comparing peasantries of different epochs and places, though the illumination of obscure places in the history of one peasantry by the comparative method must be distinguished from the delighted recognition of similarities which though gratifying may add little to our understanding. It is more important, perhaps, to stress again the specific characteristics of peasantries in different historical epochs. If the peasants of France differed profoundly from each other on either side of the historical divide created by the Revolution and the Code Napoléon, there is all the greater contrast between the peasantries of medieval Europe and the peasantries of the neo-colonial world under the political and economic pressures of the great powers and the international companies. Medieval peasantries must be understood not only as 'peasantries' but in the context of the institutions and culture of medieval feudal society, indeed in

the context of specific phases in the development of feudal society.
For example, their relations with their lords are expressed in the
terms of specifically European concepts of loyalty and dependence, through homage and fealty. Enserfment, which has, of
course, been the common lot of many peasants all over the world,
assumed its particular medieval forms through the circumstances
of the transition from the ancient to the medieval world. The
ideas of medieval peasants were shaped not only by their own
material circumstances but by the sermons and penitential pre-
scriptions of the Church. They were also strongly influenced by
the concepts of customary law, not least concerning free and
servile status and tenure.

    We know next to nothing directly about such ideas held by
medieval peasants as would enable us to judge whether they were
conscious of their existence as a class 'for themselves' or whether
they simply accepted an outwardly conferred role. Perhaps these
two are not in fact alternatives. Under certain circumstances, the
acceptance of a traditional role could develop into a consciousness
which was antagonistic to other social classes. For example, the
concept that the peasants laboured for the rest of society was
interpreted at a time of acute social conflict, by one of the Tuchin
bands in central France, to imply that any captives with soft
uncalloused hands should be killed outright.[22] The failure of the
French nobility, especially after 1356, to perform their accepted
social role of protection seems to have been as important a reason
for the hatred which the Jacques had for them as the fact that they
made forcible levies on the peasants for the replenishment of their
castles.[23]

    In England there appear two elements in the ideas of the
peasant class which suggest some nascent form of class consciousness. First, villein tenants selected from current legal concepts a
doctrine of free status which becomes more and more detached
from that of freedom of tenure. This is already found in the thirteenth century, often enveloped by the technicalities of pleadings

[22] M. Boudet, *La Jacquerie des Tuchins 1363–84*, 1895.
[23] Froissart and Jean de Venette both emphasize this disillusion with the nobility, R. H. Hilton, *Bondmen Made Free*, 1973, pp. 131–2.

for the privileges of ancient demesne. By the second half of the fourteenth century, and particularly in 1381, it has become a ground for agitation, a social and political slogan. Secondly, in 1381 the spokesmen for the peasant (and artisan) rebels, momentarily at any rate, seem to have abandoned the traditional social doctrine of the tripartite society. The evidence is of course fragmentary and uncertain, but they seem to have arrived at a concept of a popular monarchy, a state without nobles, perhaps even without churchmen, in which the peasants and their king are the only social forces and in which common law has been broken to be replaced by a new law created by the peasants themselves.[24]

— It is generally assumed that the material conditions of medieval peasant life would hardly allow the development of a common consciousness over anything but the most restricted area, but the concept of medieval peasant culture as entirely local and enclosed must not be exaggerated. Relationships between town and country were such that there was a constant interchange of people, countrymen migrating to take up skilled and semi-skilled jobs in the towns, townsmen with unsevered country connections returning to take up family holdings, or simply moving away from urban poverty and restriction. Even without migration, small town markets brought in peasants from the surrounding villages to buy from local craftsmen as well as to meet pedlars and greater merchants from the cities. In the fourteenth and fifteenth centuries soldiers returning from or on their way to wars must have spread news about the wider world to a large number of villages. The itinerant and sprawling households of nobles and ecclesiastics must also have reduced the isolation of the communities through which they passed and on which they depended for supplies. Even if many parishes had rectors or vicars whose presence was only occasional these men nevertheless acted as links between local, regional, and wider communities. They, the stipendiary priests whom they employed in their absence, and many chantry chaplains brought the international culture of the Church into the village, in however a diluted a form.

Regional differences, whose importance is now so much

24 Hilton, op. cit., pp. 227–30.

stressed, no doubt produced variations in peasant practices, social organization, and mentality. The communities of nucleated villages in champaign country contrast with the hamlets of wood-land areas. Mountain and plain, arable and pasture, cereal pro-duction and the cultivation of olive and vine all contribute con-trasting determinants of thought and action. It is surprising, therefore, that in the history of European movements there should have been a few strongly marked common themes found in all parts of the continent in spite of great variations in the natural environment. To give one example only, there could hardly be a greater contrast than that between the vine and olive cultivation on the shores of Lake Como and the grain and stock farming of the English midlands. Yet the quarrel in the ninth and tenth centuries between the tenants of the monastery of St. Ambrose, Milan, at Limonta bears extraordinary resemblances to those found in many thirteenth century English villages over peasant claims to ancient demesne privileges—the objection to increased labour services and other forms of servile obligation, the initial reliance on asserted freedom of status as a protection against exploitation, the insistence on the right to guaranteed fixed status and conditions because of a previous tenurial link with the sovereign, now lost through the alienation of the estate.[25]

However, similarity of response to similar forms of oppression does not constitute evidence for a common class consciousness. If this appears at all in medieval peasant movements, it is in rare flashes, and normally very localized. For the most part, in so far as one has evidence at all, the ruling ideas of medieval peasants seem to have been the ideas of the rulers of society as transmitted to them in innumerable sermons about the duties and the charac-teristic sins of the various orders of society. To what extent those ideas were mingled with those derived from the ensemble of archaic beliefs and practices which entered into the religion of rural communities is unknown, and perhaps unknowable.[26]

[25] Op. cit., pp. 66–70.
[26] There are some interesting examples of medieval practices in E. Hull, *Folklore of the British Isles*, 1928, e.g. pp. 84–6; but dating is a serious problem with most folklore material. Much of it is not securely dated before the eighteenth century

The following lectures, in contrast with the present discussion, focus narrowly in time and space. The microscopic view is essential if generalizations about peasants are to have a satisfactory evidential basis. The evidence is mainly drawn from the documentation of thirty or forty villages in the counties of Stafford, Worcester, Warwick, and Gloucester. These are villages which were mostly parts of large estates whose administrators kept full records. Those estates which have contributed most contained villages scattered throughout two, three, or all four of the counties. The Church estates are prominent, those of the Bishops of Coventry and Lichfield and Worcester, Worcester Cathedral Priory, the Benedictine Abbeys of Burton, Evesham, and Pershore, the Cistercian Abbeys of Bordesley and Stoneleigh, the Premonstratensian Abbey of Halesowen, the Bridgettine nuns of Syon. The biggest lay estate, that of the Beauchamp Earls of Warwick, has left some records but fewer than one would have expected. Other lay properties include the royal manors of Bromsgrove and Feckenham, the Somerville manor of Alrewas, the manor of Shuckborough, owned by a family of the same name, and a few smaller properties with scantier records.

Evidence from the public records naturally supplements that from private archives. This includes the records of the royal law courts, especially the class of Ancient Indictments. The most important of the public records which have been used has been the Poll Tax of 1380-1, famous for its role as the precipitating cause of the 1381 rising. The returns of the tax collectors have had a dubious reputation. Most taxes in the Middle Ages were badly assessed and collected, and that of 1380-1 has been shown to have been particularly inadequate in those respects. However, it is unique in the amount of information which is given about the occupations of those people who were assessed, and even about the composition of tax-paying households. Returns for this tax

as readers of such works as J. Brand, *Popular Antiquities*, 1813, or the publications of the Folklore Society will realize. (Cf. E. S. Hartland's *County Folklore—Gloucestershire*, Publs. of the Folklore Society xxxvi, 1895, which relies heavily on S. Rudder's *New History of Gloucestershire*, 1779.) See K. Thomas, *Religion and the Decline of Magic*, 1971, for the medieval background to sixteenth- and seventeenth-century belief.

exist for a large number of villages in the Gloucestershire Cots-wolds and South Staffordshire. Whatever the inadequacies of the returns they cannot be ignored by the social historian.

I have decided to confine my inquiry into the peasantry of these west Midland villages roughly to the century after the first visitation of the bubonic plague. This period seems to me to have a unity which makes it possible to give a coherent interpretation of various aspects of peasant life. As I see it, this was a period of considerable self-confidence, even assertiveness among tenants and labourers alike, an assertiveness which was not checked by the defeat of the 1381 rising. In this period the grip of traditional forms of lordly power over tenants was faltering and was not yet adequately replaced by newer forms of domination, for example through the Justices of the Peace. The faltering grip was not only reflected in the withering away, however uneven, of villeinage but in the general decline in the level of customary rents and other obligations.

There were symptoms during this period, if not of a peasant class consciousness, at any rate of political awareness. This was quite apparent in 1381, and reappears later, especially in the 1440s, showing, among other things, a loss of respect for the traditional élites. Perhaps this political awareness did not go very far because there may at the same time have been a weakening of the co-hesion of village communities. This would be due to factors beyond the control of any class in English society. One factor was the decline in population which led to a slow but clearly identifiable regrouping of settlements, a movement sometimes known as the desertion of villages. There may be an element of archaeological illusion here (the large number of insufficiently interpreted earthworks). Another factor was the decline of tradi-tional manorial organization in so far as this focused on the management of the demesne. But there may be an element of documentary illusion here (the decline in the amount of informa-tion recorded in manorial records).

This, then, may be interpreted as a period intermediate between the disappearing stringencies of the feudal estate organization dominated by the lords' professional bailiffs and the new stringencies of landlords and their lessees in the late fifteenth and the sixteenth centuries. It would therefore be a period when the forces within the peasants' economy—the village economy— were more free from both old and new style landlords than at any other time. The 'historic process of dissolution'[27] of medieval society had begun with the dissolution of the ties of serfdom but the separation of peasants from their land, whether by processes of social differentiation or by force, had not yet happened.

[27] K. Marx, *Pre-Capitalist Economic Formations*, ed. E. Hobsbawm, 1964, p. 104.

# II

# The Social Structure of the Village

OUR understanding of the social structure of the late Middle Ages is sometimes more influenced by the impression we receive from the imaginative literature of the period, such as that of Chaucer and Langland, than by the record sources which have been left behind by administrative or judicial action at local or central government level. We have been warned off too facile a use of literary evidence. Some students of Middle English literature, concerned with aesthetic judgements or with inner spiritual meanings, resent the use of such poems as *Piers Plowman* as a 'grab-bag' of illustrations of social history.[1] We may respect such critics without being deflected from our purpose, which is different from theirs. More serious for the social historian is the argument that medieval literature, even that which impresses by the vividness and apparent actuality of descriptive material in it, presents us with a picture of unchanging traditional social types and attitudes. It is not a mirror of contemporary society but a make-up of past, highly stylized images.

The social thinking as well as the social imagery to be found in imaginative works of the fourteenth and fifteenth centuries is profoundly influenced by the ancient theory of the tripartite division of society. Some scholars have traced this theory as far back as the Sanskrit and ancient Irish law codes.[2] Whether this is so or not, it is certain that Aelfred, King of Wessex in the eighth century, and Adalbero, bishop of Laon in the eleventh century, thought in those terms[3] and from then on it is a powerful com-

---

[1] R. W. Worth, *Piers Plowman and the Scheme of Salvation*, 1957, p. 22.

[2] Cf. J. Batany, 'Des 'trois fonctions' aux 'trois états', *Annales ESC* xviii, 1963. M. Dillon and N. Chadwick, *The Celtic Realms*, 1967, pp. 92ff.

[3] W. J. Sedgefield, *King Alfred's Old English version of Boethius, De Consolatione Philosophicae*, 1899, Chap. xvii. J. P. Migne (ed.), *Patrologia Latina*, vol. 141,

monplace, disseminated not only in literary works but in sermons. An English preacher of the fourteenth century describes the functions of the orders of society for his audience in these traditional terms:

Knights and other gentles with hem shuld sett her business abowte the good governance in the temporality in the time of peace and also about divers points of arms in the time of war ... priests should principally intermet to learn the law of Christ and lawfully to teach it ... and lower men shuld hold them content with the questions and the subtlety of their own labour.[4]

John Gower regarded it as a generally accepted view—'we know that there are three estates in which everyone in the world serves according to custom'.[5] Caxton thought it worth while (1483–5) to translate and print Raymond Lull's *Book of the Order of Chivalry* (1276–86),[6] a work containing essentially the same image as that employed by Aelfred and Adalbero.

In a culture permeated over a long period of time by traditional imagery, the constituent elements of that imagery are not necessarily repeated with the same emphasis. But what determines which elements will be selected at any particular time from the total fund of available images? Clearly it must be contemporary concern, which is always changing.

From the fourteenth and fifteenth centuries we have many literary works of varying quality which depict different aspects of rural society. Two social types appear, quite clearly delineated, presented sometimes together and in contrast with each other, sometimes singly. They are the ploughman and the labourer. The term ploughman means here not an employee but the husbandman who possesses a plough-team as well as a more or less substantial holding of land. The labourer is the hynd, the swain, a landless wage-labourer or a cottar. As we shall see, the emphasis in

---

1880, cols 774–88: 'Carmen ad Robertum Regem', ll. 275–96; and G. Duby, *L'An mille*, 1967, pp. 74–5.

    [4] W. O. Ross, ed., *Middle English Sermons*, EETS O.S. 209, 1938, p. 224.

    [5] J. Gower, *Vox Clamantis*, Bk. III (*Latin Works of John Gower*, ed. G. C. Macaulay, vol. iv, 1902; translated by E. W. Stockton, *Major Latin Works of John Gower*, 1962).

    [6] *The Book of the Ordre of Chyvalry*, EETS O.S. 168, 1926.

the literature assumes significance in the light of other evidence about rural social strata at this time, even though these two types have been present in the Western European countryside for centuries.[7]

William Langland picks out the ploughman for supreme emphasis, and the labourer merges into a background occupied by a whole range of other social types. In later versifying the two are often found together, the ploughman hierarchically superior even if not always valued higher. Gower, for instance, regards the ploughman as at the root of contemporary social discontents. He is sluggish, grasping, rejects the servitude which is ordained by God, is consumed with envy for the leisure of the rich and powerful. More frequently, the Langland tradition which exalts the ploughman is followed. In *Pierce the Ploughman's Crede* (late fourteenth century) the poor ploughman, out at work in the field with his wife and his children, is the very type of social virtue. It is he who can better teach the Creed to the poet than the learned and the religious. In *The Ploughman's Tale* the same author, speaking as the ploughman, complains of the clergy 'they have the corn and we the dust'. In a later fifteenth-century poem, *God Spede the Plough*, the husbandmen are presented as those who 'mayntayn this worlde'. Yet the product of their labour is unfairly divided, with the parson, the king's purveyors, the tax-gatherers, the lord's rent collector, the court officials, the friars, and the lawyers.[8]

The ploughman appears as a figure of central importance, even when he is not admired. Cain, a figure depicted with considerable power in the *Towneley Plays*, is shown as a hardworking ploughman, unwilling to yield the tithe of grain which he has sweated to

[7] The ploughman and the labourer correspond exactly to the *laboureur* and the *manouvrier* in France. The division between the owner of a plough-team and the cottar is clearly seen in Domesday Book and in the earlier continental *polyptyques*. Cf. G. Duby, *The Rural Economy and the Life of the Countryside in the Medieval West*, 1968 (English edition), pp. 31, 115.

[8] *Pierce the Ploughman's Crede*, ed. W. W. Skeat, EETS O.S. 30, 1867; *The Ploughman's Tale*, ed. W. W. Skeat, 'Chaucerian and other pieces,' supplement to *The Works of Geoffrey Chaucer*, 1897; *God Spede the Plough*, ed. W. W. Skeat, EETS, O.S. 30, 1867; not to be confused with the poem of the same title in R. H. Robbins, *Historical Poems of the Fourteenth and Fifteenth Centuries*, 1959, p. 97.

produce. His boy, the plough-team driver, describes him as 'a good yeoman'. In the second shepherd's play in the same cycle, the leading character among the shepherds, harassed as he is (according to his own complaint) by 'gentlery men', is also a land-holding husbandman, for it comes out in the course of the play that he has his own cart and his own plough. Another ploughman treated satirically rather than admiringly appears as the 'hero' of *How the Ploughman Learned his Paternoster*. His command of all the skills of husbandry has brought him the rewards of an accumulation of gold and silver and a well-stocked larder.[9]

The labourers share little of this sometimes ambivalent admiration which the poets express for the ploughmen. They are uppish and self-assertive because they are indispensable. The ploughman of *God Spede the Plough* bemoans the fact that he must pay his servants wages 'or else full still the plough may stand'. The third shepherd in the second shepherd's play of the *Towneley Plays*, who is as clearly a servant as the first shepherd is an employer, ripostes to the complaints made by the other two shepherds.

> But here my trouth, master, for the fayr that ye make
> I shall do thereafter wyrk as I take;
> I shall do a lyttyl, sir, and emang ever lake . . .

Little wonder that the labourers are treated with hostility, expressed most often indirectly by the poets through the mouths of their ploughmen heroes. Since some of this literature is Lollard or anti-clerical in outlook the contempt for labourers is sometimes expressed indirectly, one line of attack on the clergy being because of their upstart origin. In the *Ploughman's Tale*, the ploughman says that monks of low social origin should be put back into the class to which they truly belong, that of the labourers, 'threshing and dyking fro town to town, with sory mete and not half enow.' The ploughman in *Pierce the Ploughman's Crede* criticizes pro-motion into the clerical order of 'beggars brats' and says that they should stay in the ranks of the ditch-cleaners, feeding on beans and bacon rind.

---

[9] *The Towneley Plays*, ed. G. England and A. W. Pollard, EETS e.s. 71, 1897, pp. 10–16, 117; 'How the Ploughman learned his Paternoster' is in *Reliquiae Antiquae*, i, ed. T. Wright and J. Halliwell, 1841.

The conventional attitude to servants is expressed by the sermon-writer. They should not only be 'well willed' and 'serviceable' but 'dreadful' as well; good behaviour, in other words, is guaranteed by fear. This is also Gower's view. The only way in which labourers can be controlled and lords preserved is by terror. He writes not only in a period of general rebelliousness but when demands made by labourers were at their most extravagant—in the eyes of employers. Gower complains that these men cannot be hired by the year or even by the month, but with difficulty by the day, that instead of being satisfied with the water they were brought up on they demand good food and drink. They are without the power of reason. In fact, they do not believe in God.[10] His condemnation of the labourers is even more drastic than his attack on the ploughmen. He is, of course, writing in a literary tradition in which each order of society is castigated for its particular vices, and consequently his views are less revealing about the special position of the labourer than those opinions which are explicit or implicit in the 'ploughman' literature, where the labourers' shortcomings are contrasted with the virtue of the husbandman.

These writers' preoccupations with the contemporary strains in the social fabric do not include concern for the issue of freedom and serfdom. The classification of tenure and status in manorial documentation as between free and villein was still important, as indeed were the practical consequences of this distinction in the life of the peasant population. The demand for freedom was a weighty slogan in 1381, and from time to time continued to be so, even in hardly appropriate circumstances, as in Norfolk in 1549. But the freedom–serfdom dichotomy may have been moving into the background, for it is in fact seldom mentioned in literary and other sources. True, in some poems such as *Mum and the Sothsegger* it appears, but here one suspects mostly for alliterative effect in the list of types whom the poet asks for advice about plain speaking—'fre men and frankeleyns . . . bondemen and bourgeois . . . citezeyns and souvrayns . . . bachiliers, banneretz, barons . . .' In literature—and even in statute law—society by now

---

[10] *Middle English Sermons*, p. 59; Gower, op. cit., Bk. v, chap. 10.

is normally classified functionally and economically rather than by legal status.[11]

A normal contrast in literature is between 'lords and common people'—thus Daw Topias, in his debate with Jack Upland. Caxton in his translation of Lull writes of kings, princes, lords— and common people. In the *Tale of Beryn* the classification is similar: clergy and knights and 'lewde sotes'.[12] Country people are referred to as 'tillers' or husbandmen, normally without distinction of status. When the sumptuary laws, preoccupied as their authors were with fine social distinctions, were drawn up, the distinction between freedom and servility was not mentioned. Leaving urban types on one side, we find the following groups in the key sumptuary law of 1363: those with goods worth 40s.; and 'people of the estate of servants in husbandry, that is carters, ploughmen [ploughholders], ploughdrivers, oxherds, cowherds, shepherds, swineherds, dairymen, threshers etc.' The 1390 statute against poachers with their dogs (suspected too of conspiracy) refers to men with land worth less than 40s. a year, artificers, labourers, and servants. A 1463 sumptuary petition has the following hierarchy: yeomen, those with 40s. a year from land, servants in husbandry, common labourers, and artificers.[13]

One of the most interesting of the few survivals of the terminology of freedom and unfreedom in current speech at the turn of the fourteenth century was the word 'franklin'. Perhaps the best-known example, Chaucer's franklin in the *Canterbury Tales*, is rather misleading. The description of his social and political role, as well as of his way of life, puts him firmly among the county gentry,[14] among that majority who did not bother to assume the expense of knighthood. It is true that, in the instruc-

[11] *Mum and Sothsegger*, ed. M. Day and R. Steele, EETS o.s. 199, 1936.

[12] 'Jack Upland and the Reply of Daw Topias' in *Political Songs and Poems*, ii, ed. T. Wright 1861; *The Tale of Beryn*, ed. F. J. Furnivall and W. G. Stone, EETS e.s. 105, 1909.

[13] *Statutes of the Realm* i, 37 Edward III, c. xiv; ii, 13 Richard II, I, c. xiii. *Rotuli Parliamentorum*, v, pp. 504–5.

[14] I find G. H. Gerrould's arguments in 'The Social Status of Chaucer's Franklin', *PMLA*, xli, 1926, more convincing than those of R. M. Lumiansky in 'The Character and Performance of Chaucer's Franklin', *University of Toronto Quarterly*, xx, 1930–1.

tions to tax assessors of the second poll tax of 1379, Parliament equated franklins as far as payment was concerned with lesser squires and farmers of demesnes or tithes.[15] Nearly a century later Sir John Fortescue, in his *De Laudibus Legum Anglie* (perhaps committing somewhat of an archaism) wrote of them as men with economic resources which would enable them to lead village society in the absence of a resident knight or squire.[16]

It may be that the terminology used by Parliament to divide the population into taxation classes had the effect of persuading assessors and collectors to classify as 'franklins' persons who in current parlance might be differently named. The fragmentary 1379 poll tax return for southern and eastern Warwickshire names over 30 franklins, some assessed at 6s. 8d., most at 3s 4d., and several of them described as 'petty' franklins, assessed as low as 12d.[17] It is not often that one can find parallel evidence which permits a fuller description of one of those individuals. However, one of the franklins assessed at 3s. 4d. was from Canley near Coventry. He was Richard Cloude, a member of an old-established and well-documented freeholding family on the estate of the Cistercian Abbey of Stoneleigh. His holding probably amounted to at least 150 acres.[18] He may well have resembled the franklin in *Mum and the Sothsegger*, the possessor of 'a frankeyleyn-is fre-holde al fresshe newe' with 'the gladdest gardyn that gome ever had' and 'a faire hous with halles and chambres'.[19] Later, no doubt, such a man might be described as a 'yeoman', though at this time that word still retained much of its old military meaning of armed attendant.[20]

Whether the franklin was playing a substitute role for the gentry at the end of the fourteenth century or not, an examination of a better-preserved set of Midland poll tax returns of 1380–1,

[15] V. H. Galbraith, ed., *The Anonimalle Chronicle*, 1927, pp. 126–9.
[16] ed. S. B. Chrimes, 1942, Chap. xxiv.      [17] PRO, E179/192/23.
[18] *Leger Book of Stoneleigh Abbey* (*SLB*), ed. R. H. Hilton. Dugdale Society, 1960, The Cloude holding had a curious history, ibid., pp. xix, xx.
[19] ll. 945 ff.
[20] For the holdings of Midland yeomen in the 16th century, an analysis based on probate inventories, see W. G. Hoskins, 'The Leicestershire Farmer in the 16th Century', *Essays in Leicestershire History*, 1950.

those for eastern Gloucestershire and south Staffordshire, strikingly illustrates the lack of resident gentry in the majority of villages.[21] Out of some seventy-five villages in south Staffordshire only nine had resident gentry. Out of 135 villages in Gloucestershire, in the Cotswolds, and the Avon Valley only thirteen had resident gentry. Even bearing in mind the possible deficiencies of evidence, and recognizing that ecclesiastical institutions such as monasteries would naturally not establish a personal presence, the figures are striking. However important lordship was in general in the late medieval countryside, in many villages the lord was not present as part of the visible structure of local society.

This is not to say, of course, that the relations between lord and tenant, expressed in the payment of rent and in the jurisdictional subordination of the mass of customary tenants, was not still a crucial issue in the countryside. It remains a key issue in agrarian history, well represented in the historiography of the subject. The theme of the yeoman, franklin, and demesne farmer, that is of the peasant upper stratum, is another important theme, but also fairly well represented in the writings of historians. What is less well known, because of the scarcity of the evidence, is the composition of the average cultivator's household. By comparison with what we know about the composition of his landed holding we are almost completely in the dark, although the literary references which I have quoted suggest that the place of the labourer was assuming considerable importance.

I propose to approach this problem by combining the use of two well-known types of evidence, the third poll tax returns of 1380-1 and the manorial evidence, primarily the records of the manorial courts. The defects of both of these sources, particularly for the investigation in hand, are well enough known. In the first place they both emphasize, for their own reasons, the importance of the landholding male head of household. In the second place, they underestimate the importance of the labourers and servants. In the third place they underestimate the number and importance

---

[21] The Gloucestershire returns are unprinted: PRO, E179/113/31, 31A, 35A. The Staffordshire returns are printed in *Collections for a History of Staffordshire*, xvii, 1896, ed. W. Boyd. See also M. Midgley, ibid., 4th series, vi, 1962.

of women. I shall return to these themes in subsequent lectures, but the distorted figures of the poll tax returns may be exemplified at this point. According to these returns there were in Staffordshire 108 males for every 100 females and in Gloucestershire 113 males for every 100 females. Although the excess of males over females was not as great as it was according to the Essex tax returns (121 males to 100 females), it was still rather large, especially in Gloucestershire, and can hardly be explained for example by an immigration of unmarried men seeking work. The normal excess of male to female births being 105 to 100, the large excess of males suggests systematic tax evasion, at any rate in Gloucestershire, which we can in any case prove by more direct evidence.[22] It may have been easier to conceal the ages of girls over 15 (the tax exemption minimum), perhaps because young males already had to be included in the tithings. It may also have reflected the concealment of servants, a high proportion of whom were female.[23]

The household which was at the centre of gravity of the social and economic life of the village—and very likely at the physical centre too—was that of the 'tiller' or 'ploughman' of the poets, the 'husbandman' of statute and legal process, the holder of the whole or half yardland in the manorial extents. The landed basis of the household's existence varied in acreage—between perhaps a dozen and forty or fifty acres of arable—from household to household, from village to village, and from time to time during the period of the household's existence.

Who belonged to this household? Numbers in it fluctuated from time to time, just as the acreage of the holding fluctuate, though we must not assume a causal relation between the two. At its greatest extent it could contain the grandparents, or even, as we shall see, an unrelated older generation surviving from a

---

[22] The sex ratio is not as simple as C. Oman thought it was, *The Great Revolt of 1381*, new ed., 1969, p. 28. See T. H. Hollingworth, *Historical Demography*, 1969, p. 376. In Staffordshire a comparison of the 1377 and the 1380–1 returns suggests that in a few villages there was no more evasion at the latter than at the former date. The 1377 returns are edited by M. Midgeley, op. cit., But see Appendix II to Oman, op. cit.

[23] See below, p. 32.

previous family's tenancy. There could be a married couple of the next generation, that is the son and his wife or a daughter and a son-in-law. There could also be one or more unmarried persons, male or female, of the same generation, offspring of the grand-parents. Then there would be the children of the married couple. And finally one or two living-in servants. At its smallest extent it could consist simply of a widow, or a widower, or an unmarried male or female. These last would soon be married through social and seigneurial pressure; so might the widow and the widower if young enough. A nuclear family would be beginning again the cycle which could result in a household of three generations.

The importance of grandparents in a period when people achieved early maturity, early marriage (probably), and early death, should not be underestimated. A sermon *exemplum* helps to illustrate this. In this story a son and his wife take over the family holding. At first the grandfather is fully maintained at his son's board. After a time his rations and clothing are reduced; then he is made to eat with the children. Finally he is put into a 'little house at the utmost gate'. The old man is not defeated. He pretends to have a coffer full of coin and, playing on his son's hope to inherit, is restored to the house and to full board.[24] The story illustrates the breakdown of the customary practice by which grandparents were properly supported even when they had handed over the conduct of the holding to the next generation. Arrangements in the manor court to safeguard their position illustrate what were their customary expectations, normally (one presumes) respected without a court order being necessary. Such arrangements are well enough known by students of manorial documentation, and are not confined to the period which interests us.

Two examples of these arrangements occur in the court records of the Beauchamp manor of Elmley Castle in 1412.[25] In one, John Bonde, tenant of a messuage and half a yardland, surrendered the holding into the hands of the lord for the benefit of the heir Nicholas Bonde. The court established the following

---

[24] *Middle English Sermons*, pp. 89–90.
[25] Worcester County Record Office (WRCO), B.A. 899:95.

conditions for his future. John was to have his right to a place for his bed in the chamber, with freedom of access; an annual livery of four bushels of wheat and one quarter of barley, properly winnowed and cleaned; a space for tying up a beast; and further sustenance (*sustentacione*, presumably other food and clothing).[26] This is a straightforward provision for a relative, if not a father (the relationship is not stated). In the other case a more unusual, though not unique, provision is made. William Dyryng surrendered his messuage and half yardland called Dyryngs place for the use of his heir Richard. Richard then surrendered the holding to the use of Richard Dervell, later to become a farmer of the demesne, and his wife. But the elder Dyryng, William, was still guaranteed, in the agreement made with the Dervells, a room above the hall with freedom of access, four bushels of wheat and four bushels of barley, payable by the Dervells. The two successive surrenders must have been made fairly near to each other in time, for they were reported to the same court session.[27]

The presence, therefore, of grandparents in the same household as the succeeding generations, or even of the older generation of previous tenants, would be a normal feature. Furthermore, this family cohesion would still further be strengthened by the development, in customary tenures, of the three- or multi-life lease to named persons, usually man, wife, and one or more offspring.

The living-in servants and other lodgers in the peasant households present considerable problems. There is little doubt that, in general, many households employed servants or *famuli*. Such persons are frequently presented in the manorial courts for various trespasses in the woods, cornfields, meadows, and fisheries, but it is not absolutely certain whether they were in fact living in the household of the person whose servants they are said to be. Nor is the same problem cleared up when servants or lodgers are presented (as at Shuckborough in 1411 and 1413) for not being properly sworn into a tithing.[28] Persons described as servants could also be the offspring of the family. The poll tax returns make this

[26] Court of 14 October, 14 Henry IV.
[27] Court of Monday on the Eve of the Finding of the Holy Cross, 13 Henry IV.
[28] PRO, SC2/207/71, 72.

clear with the frequent description of a taxpayer as *filia* (or *filius*) *et serviens eius*, coming after the name and designation of the head of household and his wife.[29]

In other words, one gets an impression from the court rolls of a fair number of household servants, but no precise indications of the spread of these servants throughout the households of the village. Here we have to turn to the much-criticized returns of the 1380–1 poll tax. Whatever the shortcomings of these returns, they have long been known as evidence, especially for the East Anglian counties, of social developments affected by the growth of rural industry.[30] It can be shown for instance that between 50 per cent and 70 per cent of males in East Anglian villages were employees designated as servants or labourers. Totals themselves are not, however, relevant for our present purpose. But the Gloucester-shire and Staffordshire returns indicate which servants were attached to particular households and which were not. It would appear that in these counties the assessors went from house to house enumerating those who lived there and were liable to tax. This can easily be shown from a comparison of a rental of the Gloucestershire village of Sherborne with the poll tax list. There was nearly a thirty-year gap between the two documents (the rental being dated 1355) but the rental's significance for this comparison is that the holdings are listed in it according to the location of the messuage-place in the village, rather than, as is normal, according to tenurial classification. The messuages are described as being either in the East End or the West End of the village working from east to west along the main street. The comparison of the lists shows that a substantial number of families had survived between 1355 and 1380. They are found in the same order in the tax list as in the rental, together with persons attached to the household.[31]

---

[29] An interesting case of a father punishing the abductor of his 'daughter and servant' in 1386 is in the Appendix to R. H. Gretton's *Burford Records*, 1920.

[30] Essex and East Anglian poll tax returns are printed in Oman, op. cit., and by Edgar Powell in *The Rising in East Anglia*, 1896.

[31] The Sherborne Rental is part of the muniments of Lord Sherborne, which are now in the Gloucester County Record Office (GCRO). The Sherborne tax return is in E179/113/31. See 'Winchcombe Abbey and the Manor of Sherborne',

But even though we may, in general, suppose that those servants whose names are entered after the names of their employers were living in the employer's household, we have only minimum figures. It seems certain from supplementary returns made by the Gloucestershire collectors that there was in some places a massive concealment of servants, not, as Oman concluded from the Essex evidence, of unmarried females. Some of the Gloucestershire returns indicate this quite clearly. These consist of lists of names arranged village by village. At the end of each list is written the phrase *omnes isti sunt laborarii et servientes*. All are assessed at the full rate, 12*d.*, whereas it is not uncommon, in those returns where cultivators' households are also listed, for servants to pay less while their employers pay more than 12*d.* The names of some villages, however, are given without an attached list of taxpayers. The explanation given (as in the case of four villages in Rapsgate Hundred) is as follows: 'Presentatores de eisdem villatis dicunt separatim per sacramentum eorum quod ad primam sessionem plene presentaverunt.'

In other words these are the records of a second visitation of the tax collectors. Whether there was further concealment at the second inquiry or not, the fact is that some of the villages had understated the number of servants by 50 to 100 per cent. At Kempsford, for instance, the first assessment listed about 30 servants out of a taxed population of 118. A further 39 servants were revealed by the second inquiry, 19 of them being women. Unfortunately, those returns hinting at the scale of evasion are fragmentary. Evidence for many villages is missing. Some villages were acquitted. Others show less evasion than Kempsford, which in any case was one of the biggest villages in the county. Nevertheless, we must accept that any figures of servants and labourers revealed by the tax returns are very much minimum figures.[32]

Owing to the fragmentary nature of the second returns, we cannot even guess what number of missing servants we should add to the figures in the original returns. From the original returns

by R. H. Hilton in *Studies in Gloucestershire History* ed. by H. P. R. Finberg and in *University of Birmingham Historical Journal*, 1949.

[32] The second returns are E179/113/31A.

it would seem that the proportion of households with a living-in servant or servants was not high. In about eighty Cotswold villages there might have been one household in eight with a servant or servants. But the living-in servants by no means exhaust the employed population in the village. In these same villages we find groups of single persons entered up at the end of the list after those household entries which include, as well as the heads, the wives, children, other relatives, and living-in servants. The single persons are sometimes given an uninformative surname, but they are most frequently designated as ploughmen, carters, or herds-men; carpenters, thatchers, or slaters; or 'taskers',[33] that is, general labourers. Such persons are present in this area at about seven for every seventeen households of cultivators. It is no easy problem to relate this group to the household structure, of which they seem hardly a part. Some may, of course, have been cottagers. Others may have lodged in houses in the village, though in this case it is not quite clear how they escape being included in the personnel of the household. It could be that as lodgers not in-volved in work on the holding they would not be included.

The calculation for a whole region of average numbers of servants and labourers in relation to total population or to house-holds means little because considerable variations from village to village are thereby concealed. In the little group of adjacent hamlets in the north Cotswolds known as Pinnock, Ford, and Hyde there were eleven households of cultivators and a shepherd. In another hamlet a few miles away, Farmcote, there were eight households of cultivators and six single men. Three of these were described as ploughmen, one of whom employed a servant. It is unlikely that they were ploughmen-husbandmen in the sense discussed above but they may have been employed by Hailes Abbey which was nearby. At Buckland, in the Avon valley at the foot of the Cotswold scarp, there were thirty households of cultivators. Of these thirty, half had an adult son or daughter; five had living-in servants. Then there were sixteen persons designated as cultivators of whom nine were women. These may have been single-person households—temporarily. There was a separate

---

[33] For 'taskers' see E. W. W. Veale (ed.), *Great Red Book of Bristol*, i, 1933, p. 129.

group bracketed as *servientes*, eight married couples, six single men and two women. Three of them were carters and two were shepherds. This large village was a manor of St. Peter's Abbey, Gloucester, which may account for the fact that one of the servants was a hayward and the other a bailiff.

Always bearing in mind the tendency of this evidence to underestimate the number of servants, it would seem that where peasant households had servants, they rarely numbered more than one or two. The big concentrations tended to be in lords' households, whether demesne servants or pure domestics. The servants of Robert Somerville, Esq., at Aston Somerville in the Avon Valley were workers on the demesne—two dairymaids, two shepherds, two ploughmen, a labourer, and a carter. On the other hand at Church Eaton, Staffs., the squire, Thomas of Brompton, had seven household servants not described occupationally. The parson of the rich and disputed living in the same village had thirteen servants. Otherwise, in this fair-sized village there was not much wage labour. There were about thirty other households, eighteen being cultivators and four cottagers. Only four of the cultivators and two tradesmen had servants; four of these servants were sons or daughters of the household. But there were also ten labourers apparently working independently.

The Staffordshire returns show the distinction between living-in servants and independent labourers more clearly than do those of Gloucestershire. Persons described as servants are nearly always attached to households. Labourers are never so attached. Servants usually pay less than the full quota of 12*d.* Labourers also sometimes pay less than the full quota, but mostly they pay the full rate. They are often married, and sometimes have their own servants. Although many of the servants living in are female there is a surprisingly large number of independent female labourers. These statements are exemplified in the return from Brewood and its six associated hamlets of Chillington, Horsebrook, Somerford, Engleton, Hatton, and Dunston.[34] The total taxed population was 249. There were 45 peasant households and some 40 artificers and retail tradesmen. There were 15 servants all

---

[34] Part of the estate of the Bishop of Coventry and Lichfield.

attached to households. None of the 35 labourers were attached to households. Twelve of them were married. Nine of them were women.

My examination of the social structure of the village has ended where it began, with a focus on the role of labourers and servants in peasant communities. There is more to be said about this subject, particularly in the next lecture. Meanwhile, I must explain if not excuse the emphasis which I have placed on the evidence of the poll tax returns. This is the only source which, inadequate though it clearly is, enables us to assess the situation quantitatively. The fact is that, although servants and labourers do occasionally appear in the manorial records, this appearance is fleeting. If they are not tenants, as most of them are not, they do not appear in the rentals. If the lord is still working his demesne, their appearance in the manorial accounts, unless they happen to be manorial *famuli*, will be anonymously within a group of employees costing so much, at so much a day, for bringing in the hay, or the corn, or whatever is the task. But as the demesnes are leased out, they cease to be recorded in the accounts. They do not even appear in the manorial court records, except for occasional delinquency, for the business of the court is dominated by the peasant householders. This can be seen clearly by comparing court rolls of the manor of Alrewas with the contemporary poll tax return. The servants, of whom the tax return names twenty-five, hardly ever appear in the contemporary court proceedings.

Something useful can, however, be said on the basis of an examination, mainly of the tax returns, with such ancillary manorial and literary evidence as we can find. Many servants, especially women, were closely integrated into the life of the peasant household; some servants, indeed, though regarded and described as such, were members of the family. But many villages contained a significant if not numerous group of independent labourers, some of them married, many sufficiently well off to pay the full tax rate.[35] This no doubt reflects the high earnings of

[35] In some counties there was no differential rating, but in Staffordshire the richer must have agreed to help the poorer. The only concern of the exchequer was that the total sum returned should amount to 12*d.* per taxpayer.

the period, which also explains the self-assertiveness of the labourers during this period, short-lived though it may have been. The attitude is perfectly reflected in the statement by the shepherd's servant in the second shepherd's play of the Towneley cycle:

> Whereto shuld I threpe?
> With my staf I can lepe
> And men say 'lyght chepe
>     Letherley for-yeldys'.

# III

## The Peasants' Economy

MUCH that has been written about English agrarian history in the late Middle Ages has been focused on the economy of the estate. To understand the estate is, of course, the key to a vital area of social, even of political history. This is not now my concern. I wish to get away as far as possible from the estate, whether of great or petty lords, and to consider the problems of the village economy. These are many, and I will refer initially only to some of the more important. Some of these problems are peculiar to the period with which I am concerned, others are important for earlier periods as well.

A question of particular importance, which some historians may think has been solved—though I do not—is whether the peasants' economy was significantly market-oriented. This is a problem of central importance for the investigation of all peasantries, medieval or not. If the peasants' economy was market-oriented, can we get any idea how widely it was involved in small-scale commodity production? This inevitably leads us to ask to what extent social and economic developments in the direction of capitalism are to be seen. For instance, was labour itself becoming a commodity? What was the nature of the internal stratification of the peasant community? Did families acquire large holdings because they had many mouths to feed or in order to produce grain and livestock for the market, and so to accumulate wealth?

Let us rehearse the generally acknowledged trends in the century after the bubonic plagues between 1349 and 1375. In England there was a relative abundance of land and movable resources compared with the labour whether of tenants or workers. However we interpret urban developments in this period, not even the strictest stagnationist denies the growth of craft industry in the countryside. If we believe that in spite of the plague mortality certain centres of urban production were also growing then we can assume a growing market for agricultural products. Since we are focusing our attention on the west Midland region let us briefly consider what constituted this market. Bristol and Coventry, both important manufacturing and commercial centres, were, after York, the two biggest provincial towns in England. Gloucester and Worcester were fair-sized county towns, and Worcester indeed was moving up the urban league table. Thriving urban centres of lesser size included Lichfield, Cirencester, and Warwick; and smaller market towns were fairly thick on the ground.[1] Rural industrial growth in metals and textiles can be seen in south Staffordshire, north Warwickshire, north Worcestershire and the Cotswolds, and mining was still active in the Forest of Dean.

The workers of the region shared the increase in real wages which was general throughout the country, especially from the 1380s onwards, and in so far as those were paid in money, the market for all commodities would be enlarged. At the same time rents and seigneurial dues were falling. It is true that the government, the nobility, and gentry adopted administrative and judicial means to combat high wages and low rents, but they were not able to halt the trend. The result must have been an increase in the incomes of the main rural groups, whether tenants or labourers or both.

This is the changing background against which we must examine age-old and new features of the peasants' economy. It was essentially based on the holding which supported those households whose outlines were briefly sketched in the previous lecture. The characteristic evidence which depicts these holdings is the manorial rental, containing the names of the tenants responsible for acquitting to the lord the rents and services owed. The description of the holding itself can be quite detailed, but as is now well known the actual working holding of the tenant could

---

[1] W. G. Hoskins prints a useful appendix showing the ranking order of the main English towns in his *Local History in England*, new ed., 1973.

be rather different from that written in the rental, owing to the amount of temporary leasings of portions of holdings and of demesne land. In addition it is possible that rental evidence gives too much of an impression of the separateness of the individual holdings. We all know, of course, that medieval villagers had to co-operate with each other over common pastures and at harvest periods, and this introduced a collective element in the village economy which modified the individualist features of economic activity. But, as we shall see, there was a shifting network of inter-household economic arrangement which must also have considerably modified the separateness of individual village households.

All the same, we have to start off with the individual holding, though we have to realize, too, that the concept of an 'average' holding is one which we must regard as dubious for at least two reasons. Firstly, the holdings in the late medieval village were unequal, as they had demonstrably been as early as the eleventh century. This was an inequality of holdings which seems to have been a constant feature of all peasant communities. Secondly, within each of the broad categories of rich, middle, and poor peasants there was a considerably fluidity of size and composition of individual holdings. This fact is perhaps less appreciated than the better-known tripartite categorization of the tenant population; and it means that precision about the exact measurement of holdings as they were distributed among the various groups of tenant at any given time is not as significant as the rental evidence would suggest.

The tripartite division of holdings into rough categories in our period and in most of the old-established villages with which we are dealing goes as follows. The broad middle range of holdings is composed of yardlands and half yardlands fluctuating between a dozen and thirty acres of arable with appurtenant pasture and other rights, including of course the messuage place in the village and perhaps a croft nearby. There is a smaller, but perhaps growing, group of holdings with between thirty and a hundred acres of arable, occasionally even more. This was partly the consequence of relative land abundance. Another consequence of relative land abundance was that the group of small-holders and cottagers, still in some places the largest of the three groups, was relatively declining in size. There was considerable regional variation. In the wooded Arden country, if the late fourteenth-century rental of Stoneleigh Abbey possessions covering about eight villages south of Coventry is to be taken as representative, small-holdings still constituted nearly half of the total.[2] In Cheltenham and district nearly a third of the peasant holdings were small.[3] But in the villages owned by Evesham Abbey in the Cotswolds around Stow-on-the-Wold it would seem that less than one in ten of the total were small holdings.[4] Of course, the three categories fluctuated in size. The trend at this period toward the diminution of the small-holding group and the increase in the number of large holdings seems fairly certain. The three broad categories, however, remain.

Nevertheless, there was considerable impermanence, within the categories, of the size and composition of individual holdings. This was partly because, as has been mentioned, peasants enlarged or contracted their holdings by means of short-term leases among themselves. At this time when landowners were often leasing out all or part of their demesne lands piecemeal, holdings could be temporarily enlarged by similar short-term lettings of demesne arable, meadow pasture, or even woodland. Peasant holdings could reach a considerable acreage in this way, but often for a limited period of time. However, it must be stressed that there is little evidence to show that ageing tenants disposed of portions of their land as their children grew up and left home. An analysis of the size of holdings at the time of the tenants' death suggests either that they died in full possession of the holding or that, if old and impotent, they had already handed over the complete tenancy to an heir, retaining only the right to share hearth, bed, and board.[5]

    [2] *SLB.* The second part of this document consists of a detailed rental of the estate dated 1392.

    [3] Cheltenham rentals in the PRO are SC11/216, 217, 218, 220.

    [4] PRO, SC11/248, a rental of 1373.

    [5] This statement is based on an analysis of all the holdings at the death of the tenant recorded in the court rolls of the estates with which I am concerned in these lectures.

Accumulated properties in land and livestock (at this time, one suspects, a function of active production for the market) did not necessarily survive after the active tenant's death. In Midland villages, whether because of the lack of heirs or because of the very considerable mobility of the peasant population, between a third and a half of holdings went outside the family after the death of the head of the household. Additionally, there are indications that the villagers themselves frowned on accumulation. At Ombersley, an Evesham Abbey manor composed of fifteen scattered hamlets on the east bank of the river Severn between Worcester and Stourport, the tithingmen of the manor were asked in 1415 to make a declaration of custom concerning three holdings which a tenant named John Patrik, recently deceased, had accumulated. The tithingmen said that such an accumulated holding should be divided between the offspring of either sex. In the event, John Patrick's son Richard got one of the holdings; the widow got the other, with reversion at her death to Richard; the married daughter got the third holding.[6]

Although we often know in fair detail about the landed composition of peasant holdings from rentals, we seldom have any opportunity to see the internal workings of these holdings—how the land was cropped, what sort of equipment there was, how much livestock. Peasants did not keep records as lords' reeves or bailiffs had to do for the working of the demesne. About the only insight we get is when a holding was confiscated and its workings exposed in the manorial records. I have already written about one of these cases, a reeve named Walter Shayl on the Bishop of Worcester's manor of Hampton Lucy in Warwickshire.[7] He fled from the manor in 1377 probably because of a heavy debt of £20 and more which he owed to the lord. His working holding illustrates the advantages which a manorial official had, and also the way in which a rental, if it had been compiled before the flight, would have misrepresented the situation. Walter had the family yardland, but he was also cultivating another yardland which was officially *in manibus domini* for lack of a tenant. His sown acreage therefore was quite considerable, 35 acres. Sixteen

[6] WCRO, BA 3910, 24 vii. m. 2d.    [7] Below, p. 201.

of these acres were under winter crop (8 of wheat and 8 of rye) and 20 acres under spring crop (7 of pulse, 12 of drage, and 1 of oats). He was paying very little rent, as reeve, but in other respects his economy would presumably be that of other well-to-do peasants. The grain that was gathered from his holding was accounted for with the grain from the demesne. The figures indicate that the yield per acre from his holding was in some cases less than half the yield of the demesne.

Another confiscated holding can be described in more detail. This had belonged to a certain John Mashon, an Ombersley tenant who seems to have been on the run in 1414 as a horse thief. He had a cottage in Ombersley village, a messuage and half yardland in Suddington, a third of a croft from the demesne and two extra acres from the two common fields. There were 19½ acres under crop, 14 acres being winter sown (12 acres wheat, 2 acres rye) and 5½ acres of spring crop (3 drage, 2 vetch, and half an acre of mixed vetch and oats). One of the acres sown with wheat was sub-let to another tenant. The crop was valued—perhaps under-valued—at 50s. The valuation was by neighbours, one of whom bought it. We are also given details of the live and dead stock which are not often available for peasant economies. There were two oxen, a cow, a calf, four hogs, twenty geese, and a cock with four hens. There was half a bacon in the larder. Apart from small household and stable utensils there was a wagon, a winnowing fan, a riddle, a plough with iron attachments, three cartloads of firewood, and three vats with five quarters, five bushels of malt. The holding was reissued to a local family. The wife only got the cow, the calf, the poultry, and the firewood.[8]

If, as is often supposed, wheat was a cash crop for peasants, it played a considerable part in the economy of these two holdings. There is little in the description of Mashon's movable goods to suggest that the livestock had anything but an ancillary role in an essentially cereal-producing economy. But these two cases cannot

---

[8] WCRO, BA 3910, 24 v. m.1. A servile tenant at Bishampton at his death in 1417 had, in addition to his customary holding, land in free tenure which the lord seized. It was cropped as follows: 3½ acres wheat; 5 acres barley; 2½ acres peas. The free land also included a virgate of meadow, and an enclosed pasture. PRO, SC2. 210/17 m. 7.

be used for further generalization. In any case we know that in some parts of the region peasant sheep-raising was important.

All the evidence suggests that the village economy based on the peasant households was considerably monetized. Upward obligations in the form of rents, seigneurial dues, and state taxes were mainly acquitted in money, with the exception of heriot. Heriots, especially when combined with the mortuary payment to the parson, constituted a heavy levy in kind especially in Staffordshire and north Worcestershire.[9] Even here, the heriot was often sold back for cash to the widow or to the heir, thus becoming equivalent to a cash levy. The lateral connections of the peasants' economy, that is outside the village, were market-oriented and therefore monetized. Unfortunately, these are not measurable, for there is no source for estimating sales from the peasant household. The only evidence is that of prosecutions and litigation recorded in the manorial court rolls. From these we have evidence about transactions that we could have guessed at. In the early fifteenth century there were peasant timber sales in the Cannock forest area.[10] The frequent issue of licences to sell foals in the Halesowen records indicate that horse, and indeed fatstock sales, were important for the villages and hamlets which made up this large manor on the Worcestershire–Shropshire–Staffordshire boundary. An ordinance issued by the Abbot of Halesowen in 1363 gives us indirect evidence of the importance of sales out of the manor, for it forbade sales of grain and other victuals by customary tenants other than in the Monday market which was held in the Abbot's little borough of Hales, on pain of confiscation of goods found in other markets.[11]

Two prosecutions at Wolverley in north Worcestershire (a manor of Worcester Cathedral Priory) in 1373 indicate the nature of some peasant livestock deals, for they show separate disputes over joint trading in sheep and cattle for shared profits. A presentment at Alveston in Warwickshire, another Priory Manor,

[9] See below, p. 234.
[10] Staffordshire County Record Office (SCRO), D. 1734/2/1/176, fols. 2, 5, 6, 10 *et seq.*
[11] Birmingham Reference Library: Halesowen Court Rolls (HCR), 346355 (example of licence to sell foals); 346345 (ordinance).

in 1435 shows the same thing. Richard Henbroke of this place was presented for overcharging the village pastures with beasts which he was fattening for the market (*impinguendos pro mercato*).[12] Prosecutions for trespass with sheep flocks are not uncommon, and the scale undoubtedly implies that these animals were being grazed for commercial purposes. I need only mention presentments at the Priory manor of Cropthorne in the Avon valley in 1398 of two such flocks of sheep estimated at 300 and 200 sheep each; and a flock of 400 sheep in 1398 at Winshill near Burton in the Trent valley, a Burton Abbey property. I mention these cases because of the valley location. The Cotswolds were not the only part of the region where peasants raised sheep.[13]

Transactions of a monetary character within the village are prominent in the court-roll evidence. Naturally, there is more litigation between suitors to the court from the same manor than litigation between villagers and outsiders. The greater volume of internal transactions of which this litigation is evidence does not therefore necessarily mean that economic relations within the village were more important than connections beyond the village. Nevertheless inter-peasant pleas of debt, detention of chattels, and broken agreements are sufficiently numerous in court records covering the whole of our region to indicate that the buying and selling of commodities between inhabitants of the same village or groups of hamlets within the same manor was an important feature of the peasants' economy.

Pleas of debt and detention of chattels are our main evidence for the sale of goods, where A sues B for non-payment of money for goods bought. It is noticeable that throughout the region these pleas are predominantly concerned with sales of livestock of all sorts, sheep, pigs, and cattle. These constitute more than a half of all sales that I have noted. Sales of grain and hay are much less frequent, and still less frequent is evidence for the sale of manufactured goods, although there are a few cases of sales of

[12] Worcester Dean and Chapter MSS. (WD & C), E 26, Tuesday after Epiphany 47 Edward III; E56, Wednesday after St. Luke Evangelist, 14 Henry VI.
[13] WD & C, E41, 3rd October, 22 Richard II; SCRO, D.1734/2/103 Pt. VI, Discovery of Holy Cross, 21 Richard II.

cloth and commodities made of iron. These proportions are, of course, no more than indicative. The transactions which are represented by court action because they were not brought to a conclusion satisfactory to both sides must be only a small proportion of the total.

The one commodity which had the greatest internal sales was ale. The evidence for this is presentments by official ale-tasters of brewers who broke the provisions of the assize of ale. These statutory provisions would presumably be interpreted by the stewards of manorial courts according to the articles of inquiry at views of frankpledge, of which a local example is to be found in the Stoneleigh Abbey Leger Book.[14] This list directs inquiry into the numbers of brewings; the breaches of the assize by sales of ale not tasted by the taster; sales measured by cups or bowls not officially sealed by the manorial authorities; sales of unhealthy (red) ale; sales made before or after the showing of the sign for sale to take place. It has often been suspected that presentment and amercement of brewers was simply a form of licensing, a suspicion which is certainly justified by the regularity of individual presentments and the total lack of information about which provision of the assize was being broken. The presentments indicate that in most manors quite a number of tenants—in the region of a dozen or a couple of dozen—were regularly brewing. Most of them, however, were presented for only a few brewings, usually under ten. But side by side with this majority of modest brewers we find one or two in each village who were obviously brewing on a fairly large scale. A good example is John Chater of Shuckborough in south Warwickshire who between 1387 and 1400 was presented at each court session for between fourteen and thirty brewings, compared with the one or two brewings of most other tenants. Neither he, however, nor any other big brewers who make their appearance from time to time seem to be building up permanent businesses. Chater's wife seems to have taken over about 1400, Chater himself made a short come-back, then other brewers came

---

[14] *SLB*, pp. 98–100. This list of articles is much more detailed than that in *Statutes of the Realm*, i, 1810, pp. 246–7. It must have been drawn up after the passage of the Statute of Labourers, 1351.

to the fore.[15] This failure of permanent accumulation seems to match the impermanence of the multiple holdings.

One of the most striking features which illustrate the monetary aspect of the village economy is the amount of inter-peasant indebtedness. The evidence is not easy to interpret because the court records very often simply state that A impleads B in a plea of debt, stating the sum of money claimed, but not giving information about why the money was owed. Court records vary a good deal in the paucity or otherwise of information. Many pleas do contain an account by the plaintiff of the circumstances. These most often concern wages not paid, goods taken but not paid for, or various service contracted for which have been performed but not paid for. Occasionally we find examples of loans of cash (*moneta prestita*)[16] which have not been repaid, but not surprisingly this explanation is rare. The evidence about the origin of most debts is of course useful to the historian in throwing light on various types of transactions between peasants. But even the evidence about debts whose origin is not explained is of interest for our inquiry into the monetization of the local economy. For example, would one not expect, in a primarily natural economy, to find peasants borrowing and lending grain amongst themselves? Our records do in fact show that this sort of transaction was taking place. But out of over a hundred unexplained pleas of debt in our court rolls only 7 or 8 per cent concern loans in kind, that is, in grain. The rest are pleas about money, and could of course include straight money loans.

The sums of money vary greatly. It is possible that the sums claimed are larger than those actually involved in the original transaction, though there would not be the same reason for inflating the claim as in the case of claims for damages which were often pitched ridiculously high and if granted were normally drastically reduced by the court. Disagreements between plaintiffs and defendants did not usually reveal the same sort of gap as is found between damages claimed and granted. Some of the sums

[15] PRO, SC2. 207/70 mm 4–8d; 207/71 mm 1–3d.
[16] WRCO, BA 3910, 24 No. 11 (Ombersley 1413).. But there are many cases which clearly concern cash loans without this phrase being employed.

claimed by creditors were nevertheless quite substantial if one bears in mind that the normal daily wage was 4*d.* The majority (40 per cent) of the claims were for sums between 1*s.* and 5*s.*; 10 per cent were less than 1*s.*; 20 per cent between 5*s.* and 10*s.*; 16 per cent between 10*s.* and 26*s.* 8*d.* 7 per cent over 26*s.* 8*d.* There are few references to security for loans in the modern sense of this term, though in a number of cases where large sums were borrowed, land was pledged by the borrowers. Henry Alwyne and his wife, of Alrewas, Staffs., in 1360 borrowed 11*s.* 8*d.* and pledged half an acre of meadow and half an acre of arable; and again 3*s.* 8*d.* on a pledge of 7 acres of arable and meadow.[17] There is no indication here of the land being transferred to the lenders. This, however, was done at Horton, Staffs, in 1398 where a man transferred a messuage and 20 acres to a lender for 3 years for a loan of 12 marks.[18] There is no reference to usury, though this was apparently known at the local level, for one of the Stoneleigh frankpledge articles of inquiry reads: *De usuariis mutuantibus pro certo lucro.*[19]

The evidence for a considerable volume of monetary transactions within the village should not lead us to overestimate the movement of the village economy in a capitalist direction. The apparently advanced development of small-scale commodity production seems to be taking place in a situation in which there was still an element of the transfer of use values from household to household. But since the evidence is still mainly from litigation in the manor court, the element of cash nexus will be exaggerated rather than minimized. Inevitably money enters into relationships between households and it will not do to sentimentalize them.

A land market involving permanent alienation is not prominent. We are here considering land held by customary tenure where sales take the form of surrender into the hands of the lord by A to the use (*ad opus*) of B. The amount of such sales varies of course from village to village and from time to time. Drawing on the

---

[17] SCRO, D. o/3, Saturday after St. Swithun, 34 Edward III.
[18] SCRO, D. 1490/33/4, Great Court of Thursday after St. Denys, 22 Richard II.
[19] Not in the frankpledge articles in the *Statutes of the Realm*.

court roll evidence available from our region during the period with which we are concerned I calculate that this type of transaction accounts for rather less than 10 per cent of all movements of land. Furthermore, it seldom involves complete holdings, but most often a few detached acres of arable or meadow.

Sub-letting by one peasant household to another seems to have been more frequent than sales, as it always had been, long before our period begins. We have already seen an example of it in the lease by the felon, John Mashon, of one acre of wheat land. However, owing to the easing of seigneurial restrictions on sub-letting, the court roll evidence reveals less of what was going on. It is true that the Abbot of Burton was still trying to control sub-letting in a precept of 1368 and an ordinance of 1381, but the more general manorial attitude was probably that of Worcester Cathedral Priory, some of whose tenants, from at least the 1430s onwards, were getting general licences to sub-let included in the terms of their leases.[20] Consequently the evidence for sub-letting from this period is not so much from manorial prosecutions for illegal sub-letting as from litigation between lessor and lessee. It is a minor element in court business. In so far as the evidence lets us see what was happening this sub-letting was mainly of odd acres, enclosures, and crofts; the terms were either for so many crops from land, or for periods of years ranging from one to ten.

More prominent and revealing of inter-household traffic than the sub-letting of land are cases which can be grouped under the following headings; hiring or non-commercial borrowing of facilities; service contracts; hire of labour. These activities suggest something approaching an interpenetration or a blurring of the distinction between separate household economies.

We could perhaps include under 'hire of facilities' very short-term leases of pasture and herbage, distinguishable from the longer-term sub-lettings of arable. An example is shown by a dispute in 1414 at Ombersley between Thomas Chapman and

---

[20] SCRO, D. 1734/2/1/102, Saturday after Apostles Philip and James, 42 Edward III; ibid./103, St. Luke Evangelist, 4 Richard II; e.g. W.D. & C., E60, Sedgeberrow, Thursday after St. Denis, 22 Henry VI. However, the Priory still amerced those guilty of illegal sub-letting.

William Atte Bone over the pasture of one of Henry's oxen on William's land.[21] Arrangements to hire or borrow animals are fairly common, especially cows in milk. We find examples of this at Halesowen, Alrewas, and Branston near Burton.[22] The normal rate seems to have been 2s. 6d. to 3s. a cow per annum. This sort of transaction seems highly commercial, but other borrowings may have had little to do with profit-making. This was frequent enough to be used for literary effect. The shepherd-ploughman in the second shepherd's play of the Towneley Cycle complains— among other things—about 'swanes' who borrow 'my wane, my plough also'.[23] At Halesowen in 1372 Richard Rondulf, who had leased a bit of pasture to Philip Hypkys also had to sue Philip for the return of a ploughshare and a coulter. In 1382 on the same manor Thomas Schyrlet and Richard le Tourneur were in dispute over the hire of a plough and a muck cart.[24] Even the manorial officials could be involved in these borrowings. The Prior of Worcester's bailiff at Harvington in 1401 was short of a plough-team driver. He made an arrangement with a local tenant to borrow the tenant's own driver in return for a loan of the demesne plough with its six-ox team.[25]

This hire of facilities merges into peasants' employment of their neighbours to do jobs on contract. A case at Wetmore, Staffs., in 1372 indicates that one peasant was hiring another to come along with his cart to carry muck. In 1379 at Shobnall, also on the Burton Abbey estate, Robert of Bradley sued John Lomburhurde for failure to fulfil an agreement to bring a cart to carry peas for him. It is worth noting that John Lomburhurde was tenant of a yardland.[26] This sort of carriage contract is found elsewhere, as are ploughing arrangements. In 1376 there was a plea at Alvestone concerning the breach of an agreement, whereby

[21] WCRO, BA 3910, 24 v. m.2.

[22] HCR, 346327 dorse; SCRO, D. o/3, Saturday after St. Lucy, 34 Edward III; ibid., D. 1734/2/1/102, Saturday of St. Mary Magdalene, 42 Edward III.

[23] Op. cit., p. 117.

[24] HCR, 346350; 346359.

[25] WD & C, E42, Thursday after Translation of St. Thomas Martyr, 2 Henry IV.

[26] SCRO, D. 1734/2/1/102, Wednesday after St. Martin, 46 Edward III; ibid., /103, St. Nicholas, 3 Richard II.

one man had agreed to bring along two oxen to harness to another's plough.[27] Widows are found making this sort of arrangement with neighbours. In 1372, Tibot of Austrey, Warwicks., and her daughter made an arrangement with William Bonde that he should come along at the appropriate time and help to get her hay in. She sued him because he had gone off to help somebody else.[28] In 1375 Emmot of Heye at Newnham, Worcs., in the absence of her sons overseas, tried to get a man to cultivate and manure two acres for her, with one-third of the crop as payment.[29] In 1416, a widow from Ombersley, Margery Foster, hired a customary tenant from the hamlet of Hadley to come to plough and manure her land.[30] Not that it was only widows who relied on this sort of help. Thomas Schyrlet, the Halesowen tenant whom we have already met, hired another tenant in 1384 to harrow his land. In 1387 and 1390 we find Thomas himself carting and ploughing for another tenant.[31]

Another type of contractual arrangement between neighbours which is somewhat difficult to distinguish (perhaps should not be distinguished) from the hire of such facilities as herbage, was that by which one man put his animals under the care of another, probably with his own herds or flocks, and on his own pasture. This is fairly frequent, shown for instance in litigation at Burton concerning broken agreements for the custody of a mare (1367) and pigs (1380).[32] Here the grievance was the non-payment of the fee. At Pattingham Richard le Herdeman was sued for losing another's cow that had been put in his custody (1368).[33] At Elmley Castle, Thomas Shepherd was being sued sixteen years after the event, by a man whose sheep he had agreed to look after, one of which he lost.[34] These arrangements are not easily interpreted, for in two of these cases the surnames of the defendants suggest the

[27] WD & C, E28, Tuesday after Translation of St. Oswald, 50 Edward III.

[28] SCRO, D1734/2/1/102, Saturday after Epiphany, 46 Edward III.

[29] WD & C, E27, Monday of St. Denis, 48 Edward III.

[30] WCRO, BA 3910, 24 vii. m.3.

[31] HCR, 346363 A; 346366 A dorse; 346369 B.

[32] SCRO, D1734/2/1/102; date of court illegible, but between October and December, 41 Edward III; ibid., 103, St. Gregory, 4 Richard II.

[33] SCRO, D. 1807, roll 26d, St. Peter ad Vincula, 42 Edward III.

[34] WRCO, BA. 899: 95/11d, Friday before St. James Apostle, 22 Richard II.

specialist village herdsman; he was, however, not necessarily solely a salaried official, but could be more in the nature of an entrepreneur. Something approaching a professional fattener of stock is suggested by a Halesowen case of 1381, when Roger Folkesham sued John Barker for failing to look after five of his bullocks in winter, for failing properly to feed an ox put out for a fixed period, and for failing to put two bullocks and a cow on good pasture.[35]

Do these cases indicate that neighbours were helping each other, or exploiting their needs for a cash profit? The distinction may not be clear, but in the context of the pre-capitalist village community, it might be right to stress the element of mutual help whilst at the same time appreciating that this could imperceptibly develop into a largely commercial relationship. The same ambivalence is to be found with regard to the hire of labour.

Although I have presented literary evidence which seemed to indicate a feeling of division between the ploughman–husbandman and the hired labourer, it is doubtful whether we should as yet consider them as separate classes. Their antagonism could be compared rather to a family quarrel than to the hostility arising from a social gulf.[36] After all, as we have seen, children of the household were often classified as servants within the household. Children from one household were also put out as servants in another. William Ketel, member of a well-documented peasant family in Halesowen, put out his daughter or daughters to service in other households, and sued the employers for breach of contract. He accused Henry of Teynhall in 1373 of beating one of his girls and of not giving her a reasonable dinner as originally stipulated. The two men came to a settlement. Two years later William Ketel sued William in the Moor to whom he had put either the same or another daughter in service. The employer,

[35] HCR, 346359, Wednesday after St. Oswald the King, 4 Richard II; Wednesday after Conception, 5 Richard II.

[36] Compare the declared hostility during the peasants' war in Germany in the early sixteenth century between the peasants of Messkirch and the day-labourers, who, as was pointed out at the time, were their sons and sons-in-law. D. Sabean, 'Tenure et parenté en Allemagne à la fin du moyen âge', *Annales ESC*, 1972, p. 904.

he said, had not given the girl her two tunics a year.[37] The family from which the daughter came was not necessarily poor. At Elmley Castle in 1458, Guy Frensshman, apparently a newcomer who married a local widow, had bought 10s. 4d.-worth of malt— a considerable quantity—from Thomas Gybbe, for which Thomas sued him. But Guy was also suing Thomas, in the same year, for 2s. wages and 2s. for clothes owed to his wife's daughter Joan.[38]

In the village context, service of this sort seems not to have involved derogation. In Alrewas in 1359, John the son of Henry Reve was admitted, at his father's death, to the family holding, a yardland. Although John was of age, he may still have been too young or perhaps too simple to manage the land, so he surrendered it for a twelve-year term to William Adcoke, during which period he was to be Henry's servant.[39] This is hardly surprising when we see tenants putting their children as servants to other tenants. In any case, even if a labouring class was gradually emerging, the small-holding wage worker was still to be found, not necessarily taking work to supplement the income of the small holding, but taking land to supplement earnings as a servant. This at any rate could be the interpretation of an issue at Overbury in 1378 of four acres of demesne meadow to Alice, a servant; or of a report at Cleeve Prior in 1399 that William, the servant of Thomas Juggement, was holding six acres of demesne *sine titulo* which was to be seized;[40] or of permission to John Tandy, *werkmon*, at Ombersley in 1417 to take two cottages as a sub-letting from one of the tenants.[41]

This ambivalent labour situation fits in to the picture of a village economy which in a sense was transitional. It would be ridiculous to think of a village idyll of organically related groups. But it is clear too that the competitive element between household

---

[37] HCR, 346352, Wednesday of St. Andrew Apostle, 47 Edward III; 346353, Wednesday after St. Agatha, 49 Edward III.

[38] WCRO, BA. 899:95/29, 28 October, 37 Henry VI.

[39] SCRO, D. 0/3, Saturday of St. Edmund the Bishop, 33 Edward III.

[40] WD & C, E41, Overbury, Tuesday before Conversion of St. Paul, 22 Richard II; Cleeve Prior (Marston), Wednesday after Translation of St. Thomas, 23 Richard II.

[41] WRCO, BA 3910. 24 viii, Thursday after Michaelmas, 5 Henry V.

economies was modified by a system of mutual adjustment, operating partly through a market situation. Nor was the gulf between employer and labourer profound. The social gulf that was still the most important was that between the peasant and the lord.

# IV

# Conflict and Collaboration

IN the last lecture I suggested that conflicts between employers and wage earners could not have been a significantly divisive element in the life of the rural communities in the fourteenth and fifteenth centuries. Our evidence suggests that at any rate up to the middle of the fifteenth century and probably well beyond, the *de facto* control of village affairs by the chief tithingmen and the jurors (sometimes but by no means always the same people) was rarely questioned. These village notables were, as is well known, invariably drawn from the leading families, that is the long-established and territorially well endowed.[1] They operated in the manor court, of course, under the supervision of the lord's steward, but their influence and power in local affairs must not be underestimated. When their authority was questioned, as very occasionally happened, it was represented as an offence against the whole community. At Shuckborough in south Warwickshire in 1387 two tenants refused to subscribe to certain ordinances, probably by-laws concerning common pasture or harvest regulations—we are not informed. Their offence, which was punished by amercement, was emphasized by the use in the court record of the phrase familiarly attached to by-laws, that they were 'made for the common profit with the assent of all'.[2] However hierarchically structured the village may have been, this phrase suggests that it was still an interlocked community.

As always, there were many causes for friction between individuals. We would not be likely to underestimate this aspect of village life in view of the dependence of the operation of the manorial court, whose records we use, on the machinery of presentment of offences and pleas between individuals. Tres-

[1] A fact most recently documented by E. B. Dewindt, op. cit.
[2] PRO, SC2. 207/70, 15 May, 10 Richard II.

passing beasts in other men's corn and grass and petty theft—
or borrowing—among neighbours are the common currency of
court business in the fourteenth and fifteenth centuries. Most often
these ended in amercement, sometimes in the intervention by the
community through the court. In 1420 two tenants at Ombersley
were quarrelling over the use of a grinding-stone and iron spindle
in the boundary between their two holdings; the court, advised
by the seventeen tithingmen, instructed them to share.[3] In fact all
those disputes over buying, selling, borrowing, and hiring which
provided us with our evidence for the nature of the household
economy should be enough to warn us against having any senti-
mental picture of a harmonious village idyll. But conflicts within
the village were between individuals or families, not between
social groups.

On some issues, the village notables acted strongly. This must
normally have been in collaboration with the lord's authority,
though by no means necessarily as a result of the initiative of the
lord, his council, or his steward. As one would expect, non-
conformity with the expectations which the village community
had of its members as cultivators led to intervention. At Moor in
Worcestershire, as a result of presentment by the homage in 1374,
William Heyne forfeited his half yardland for not maintaining it,
and his children were refused their inheritance. Four men at
Pattingham in Staffordshire were accused in 1394 of enclosing
their arable land, thereby depriving the members of the community of their pasture rights on the fallow. At Cleeve Prior in
1435, nine tenants were presented for not cultivating their holdings.[4] This is the sort of action inevitable in an agricultural system
characterized by the intermixture of unfenced parcels of arable.
This control by and for the community of land-holding families
went a good deal further than technical matters. Outsiders were
excluded from village affairs—this in spite of other evidence
showing considerable openness and mobility of the population.

[3] WRCO, BA 3910, 24 v, Thursday after close of Easter, 8 Henry V.
[4] WD & C, Monday after Ascension, 48 Edward III. He had allowed the holding *adnullari et adnichilari*; SCRO, D. 1807, 10 May, 18 Richard II; WD & C,
E55, Monday after St. Dunstan, 13 Henry VI.

Nor can it be assumed that this exclusion was simply an expression of the lord's claims for exclusive jurisdiction. At Oxhill in 1396 it was the tenants who agreed among themselves not to get outside help in internal disputes over trespassers, agreements, and contracts; we find a similar village ordinance at Broadway in 1422, issued by the steward at the request of the tenants.[5]

This practical control over outside contacts by the court, which must have represented the interests of the tenants as much as those of the lord, is illustrated by a number of cases. A penalty of 40s. was imposed in 1377 at Wolverley on man who arranged an arbitration, a *dies amoris*, and brought in outsiders leading to the oppression of his neighbours. In 1398 at Elmley Castle two tenants were amerced 12d. each for impleading another tenant in another court. Teddington tenants were in trouble on two occasions for bringing in help from outside to settle internal quarrels. In 1402 it was outsiders from Cheltenham and in 1415 it was tenants of the Earl of Warwick who were brought in to the prejudice not only of the lord of Teddington, the Prior of Worcester, but of the other tenants. A man in Ombersley in 1418 was amerced 20s. for vexing tenants in other courts. The high amercement in this case was due to the fact that other terror tactics employed by him had led to one of his neighbours abandoning his holding.[6]

Villagers were jealous of the intrusion of strangers within the boundaries of concern of the village community, an attitude which was manifested within the community by an almost obsessive concern for privacy and confidentiality. The presentment by the Oldbury tithingmen in 1421 of a woman who hid under a wall to listen to her neighbours' secrets could of course be matched in many other villages, and is even provided for in articles of the view of frankpledge a century and more earlier.[7]

---

[5] PRO, SC2. 207/60, Saturday after St. Martin, 20 Richard II; SC2. 210/27, 3 October, 1 Henry VI.

[6] WD & C, E 29, Friday after Epiphany, 1 Richard II; WRCO, BA 899. 95, day before Annunciation, 21 Richard II; ibid., BA 3910, 24 v, Tuesday after St. Mark Evangelist, 6 Henry V; WD & C, E43, Friday after conversion of St. Paul, 3 Henry IV; E47, Overbury, 30 January, 3 Henry V.

[7] e.g. that printed in *Statutes of the Realm* i. Above, p. 45. The Oldbury case is HCR 346394, Wednesday before St. Ambrose, 9 Henry V.

Nor is the concern for the privacy of the deliberations of notables all that unusual. We find it certainly in urban records. At the village level we find it at Halesowen in 1388 when a member of the manorial jury was presented for telling people about the opinions (*consilium*) expressed by jurymen in private discussion. A member of the Broadway jury in 1432 was even presented for revealing his own contribution to the discussions of the Broadway portmoot.[8]

Pressure by the village community through its notables, or by the notables acting on their own behalf, was exercised in a variety of other ways. Unpopular characters were run out of the township. Agnes Flower, a servant in Shuckborough, was involved— so said the jury of presentment—in various fracas and petty thefts during the course of the year 1390. Eventually they declared her 'not worthy to remain in the lordship'. Her employer, a leading tenant of the manor, incurred a penalty of 6s. 8d. for keeping her on after the expulsion order.[9] There were few areas of life in which the notables could not interfere. The homage of Halesowen made an inquiry into the allocation of rooms in the house of a dead tenant, John of Lapal. They decided that his heiress, Christina, was to have the hall, the rooms on the lower side, and the best household utensil. The widow, who must have been a second wife, was to have the rooms on the upper side of the hall and the rest of the household utensils.[10] In Ombersley, the corresponding role to that of the Halesowen homage was filled by the heads of the tithings from the various hamlets. They, too, were asked to make a declaration about custom in 1415. The rightful heir to a holding in the hamlet of Brockhampton was discovered to be living in a holding in Hampton near Evesham (also a manor of the Abbot of Evesham) which he had acquired by marriage. To qualify for the Brockhampton holding he must come to live on it, and leave Hampton. This he refused to do.[11]

The village community—or its leading personalities—could be

---

[8] HCR 346367A dorse: Wednesday after Tiburtuis and Valerian, ii Richard II; PRO, SC2/210/27, 28 April, 10 Henry VI. The portmoot survived as a tithing from the attempt by the Abbots of Pershore to create a seigneurial borough.

[9] PRO, SC2. 207/70, Tuesday after St. Leonard Abbot, 14 Richard II.

[10] HCR, 346345, Wednesday of St. Nicholas, 37 Edward III.

[11] WCRO, BA 3910. 24 vii, Thursday after St. Faith, 3 Henry V.

oppressive towards individuals within it. One finds little or no protest against this control. But it was also capable of solidarity against measures from above, in particular from the manorial lord. The turbulent decades between about 1360 and 1400 were marked by many occasions of friction which generated action based on this solidarity. The background, as is well known, was that of increasing seigneurial financial embarrassment following the population collapse of the three decades after the first visitation of the plague. There were many ways in which lords of manors attempted to solve their problems, including wage regulation on a national level, but also including local and sporadic attempts to exploit the monetary possibilities of lord's rights over customary tenants.

One of the most important of these rights was the control over the marriage, or movement outside the manor, of single women and widows, a control which yielded a money income so variable as to suggest that it must have been felt as arbitrary and therefore irritating or oppressive. In the vast majority of cases the payment is recorded as being made by the women themselves, although merchet was traditionally paid by the father. The level varied a good deal from estate to estate, and from year to year on the same estate. On the Worcester Cathedral estate it ranged between 6s. 8d. and 13s. 4d. At Pattingham, Staffs, it varied between 5s. and 10s. The court record of this place indicates negatively some of the criteria for the assessment of the fine, for in 1356 Alice Bacon was only charged 3s. 4d. to leave the manor because she was old and feeble.[12] On the Gloucester Abbey estates in the 1350s the level was lower though still arbitrary, ranging from 3s. to 5s. At Halesowen the post–Black Death rate was relatively low, 2s. to 4s., and tending to rise in the 1370s. The renunciation by single women here of their inheritance rights may have been a factor in reducing the fines. These lower rates are also found on the lay estates of the Beauchamps (Elmley Castle) and the Crown manor of Bromsgrove. When one remembers that at this period a man's daily wage was only 4d., a fine of even 3s. 4d. would be quite heavy, let alone twice, thrice, or four times that amount.

[12] SCRO, D. 1807, Raising of Holy Cross, 30 Edward III.

Another indication of heavy and arbitrary money exactions which would exacerbate relations between lords and tenants is to be found in the entry fine charged on heirs and others succeeding to holdings. It is generally believed that entry fines tended to fall as rents fell, and if one established an average in the decades after 1350 this might seem to be the case, for many holdings which had been for some time in the lord's hands without takers were eventually let out for no fine or for only a low one (such as a couple of hens). The occasional heavy fine seems now, and no doubt seemed then, to be out of line with normal expectations. In 1369 a half yardland in Halesowen was let for a fine of £5 and three years later 16s. was charged for entry to a two-acre holding whose normal rent was 12d. A half yardland with a cottage at Blackwell leased to a woman for life fetched a fine of £4 3s. 4d. in 1370. Fines in lieu of heriots for holdings at Cheltenham at the turn of the century—mostly half yardlands—were £6.[13]

There seems little doubt that this irregularity reflected hard individual bargaining in which tenants would no doubt feel that they were the weaker party in the face of the lord's prestige and power. Two interesting examples of the bargaining process are to be found at Overbury in 1377. John Love wanted a vacant holding but was unable to pay the £3 entry fine demanded. Agnes Bentley offered to pay the fine if he would marry her daughter Alice. Unfortunately, it was known that he had already had sexual relations with one of Alice's kinswomen and by the rules of consanguinity this ruled out marriage. He had to retire from the bidding. Another couple put in, but were unable to raise the fine by the due date. Eventually, two men who had a hereditary claim on the holding surrendered this claim to their married sister who was allowed to take over, but at a fine of £6. The other case begins with a proclamation in the manor court, asking for bids for a reversion to a yardland held for life by Margery Love, possibly the mother of John Love just mentioned; John Hafron came forward as nearest heir, and was offered the

---

[13] HCR, 346349, Wednesday after St. Martin, bishop, 43 Edward III; ibid., 346350, Wednesday after Ascension, 46 Edward III; WD & C, E25, Thursday before St. Peter in Cathedra, 44 Edward III; PRO, SC2, 175/26 m.2.

reversion—if he bid highest. He was told to wait until after dinner. Henry Hyde his brother next asked to be considered and likewise was told to come after dinner. The next bidder was the husband of Alice, sister to John and Henry, who was also told to wait until after dinner with the same promise that he should have the holding if he bid higher. The life tenant now surrendered, and for £6 combined fine and heriot her son John succeeded.[14]

This problem of growing friction between landlords and tenants in the decades between the Black Death and the end of the century, and particularly before 1381, poses the question of peasant attitudes to the performance of labour services, sometimes regarded as the most outstanding feature of servile subordination, and certainly a cause for dispute in the pre–Black Death period. After 1350, the direct cultivation of the demesne by landowners was on its last legs; most of the big estates in the west Midlands had abandoned direct cultivation by the end of the century, in some cases earlier.[15] All the same, there are considerable evidences of unwillingness to do labour services, particularly boon services for haymaking, harvest, and ploughing. These quarrels over the performance of boon services are found quite widespread in the 1360s and 1370s on such estates as that of Burton Abbey in Staffordshire, of the Bishop of Worcester and of Worcester Cathedral in Worcestershire, Warwickshire, and Gloucestershire, on the Worcestershire and Warwickshire estates of the Beauchamps, and on the estates of the Cistercian Abbey of Bordesley at Tardebigge, Worcestershire. Tenants' labour resources were just as attenuated as those of the landowners. The diversion of

---

[14] WD & C, E29, Friday after Finding of Holy Cross and Thursday after Deposition of St. Wolfstan, 1 Richard II.

[15] John Smyth, in his *Lives of the Berkeleys* (ed. Sir J. Maclean, 1883), written in the middle of the seventeenth century, was the first historian to appreciate the importance of 'the change' which he attributed largely to the peasants' revolt: ibid., ii. 5. The Berkeley estates were scattered over the Severn valley and the Cotswolds. The Bishop of Worcester and the Cathedral Priory of Worcester were leasing out most of their demesnes by the turn of the century as were the Beauchamps. Coventry Cathedral Priory had leased out most by 1410. Pershore Abbey was a little later. Evesham and Gloucester Abbeys lack documentation, but may have been similar to Pershore. Burton Abbey also seems to have kept demesnes in hand until the early fifteenth century.

labour at crucial times of the year was much resented. The attitude was summed up by a tenant at Shipston-on-Stour in 1377 who was said to have persuaded his fellow tenants not to go before their lord the Prior at Worcester to answer for refusal to hoe the demesne because, he said, it was nothing but stupidity.[16]

On manors where labour services were not an issue, the tensions built up over other matters as well as over the arbitrary exploitation of the financial side of seigneurial rights. It is not easy to measure this build-up and one's impressions tend to be rather subjective, but in the various hamlets which made up the manor of Halesowen there seems to have been an abnormal amount of poaching, theft of or refusal to hand over tithe grain, quarrels about the level of multure between millers and tenants, not to speak of manifestations of discontent directed elsewhere than at the lord or his officials, such as attacks on royal tax collectors.[17]

These, however, were individual skirmishes. As one might expect in the years around 1381 there were also recorded clashes between lord and peasant suggesting that matters were moving in places towards village rebellion. The conflicts on the estate of Worcester Cathedral Priory over the performance of labour services led in July 1379 to a general seizure of all the goods and chattels of the servile tenants of the estate on all manors.[18] The situation remained disturbed for several years. The Prior excused himself at the beginning of July 1381 from attending the Benedictine General Chapter at Northampton on the grounds that the Cathedral tenants, free as well as servile, together with other adherents to their cause, were using the excuse of a supposed manumission of serfs (a rumour no doubt of the Mile End manumissions a month previously) to withhold services and prepare

---

[16] *Ipse dixit quod non esset nisi stulticia*, WD & C, E28, Blackwell, Monday after Epiphany, 1 Richard II.

[17] Examples of attacks on royal tax collectors, HCR, 346348, Wednesday of St. Luke the Evangelist, 42 Edward III; ibid., 346353, Wednesday after St. Denis, 48 Edward III.

[18] WD & C, E30, Blackwell, Tuesday before Translation of St. Thomas, 2 Richard II. The seizure which the Prior justified in the record *ex certis causis et litteris ipsum moventibus* was repeated in subsequent courts held in other manors.

for insurrection.[19] Whether or not the insurrection came we do not know. Something must have happened because in January 1385, again on the pretext of a withdrawal of services, there was a further seizure of all servile tenants' chattels. The justification for this seizure, written into the court records, was that it was 'by the requirements of the laws and custom of the Kingdom of England.'[20] This probably refers to the doctrine of the lord's ownership of the chattels of his villeins. It seems likely that there was no seizure of chattels in practice. This would probably have been beyond the capabilities of the estate officials and in any case would have been self-defeating if it had interfered with peasant cultivation. The declared seizure was probably made so as to provide the basis for swift and arbitrary action against individuals without due process of manorial custom.

A hint of a similarly tense situation is found in the records of a court of the manor of Halesowen held on 1 September 1380.[21] All tenants of the manor were declared to be in mercy except for those who had fined (in effect, bought their peace) and two other named persons. This general announcement is not further explained, but as we shall see it fits into a pattern of discontent on this manor. More explicit, and very similar to the Worcester Priory action, is a record on court rolls of the Abbot of Gloucester's manors of Aldsworth, Coln Rogers, and Upleadon in 1412. Before the record of the normal business of each court is the statement 'At this court, as at all preceding courts, all the lord's bondmen (*nativi*) with their goods and chattels are seized into the lord's hands and so remain.'[22] Unfortunately these records are isolated. There are none revealing the earlier phases of this situation and none survive for other manors. One suspects, however, that these manors, two in the Cotswolds and one in the Forest

[19] W. A. Pantin (ed.), *Chapters of the English Black Monks*, iii, Camden Society, 1937, p. 205.

[20] WD & C, E32, Blackwell, Monday before St. Hilary, 8 Richard II. In the margin is written *seisina generalis*.

[21] HCR, 346357, Wednesday after St. Giles abbot, 4 Richard II.

[22] GCRO, D936a. M.4, Upleadon, Monday after St. Leonard; Aldsworth, Saturday before St. Luke Evangelist; Coln Rogers, Wednesday after St. Luke Evangelist, 14 Henry IV. The order was repeated in the following year.

of Dean, were not the only ones affected. Apart from the evident social tensions of the period the only attributable cause for this situation is the policy of the dominating Abbot Frocester (1382–1412). According to the abbey chronicle, Frocester was a considerable spender, on building work in the cloisters; on books, vestments, and plate; and on flocks of sheep and building work on the estate.[23] Money like this did not come out of the air. Ultimately it must have come from the tenants.

We know nothing else about what happened on the Abbot of Gloucester's estate, but the troubles at Halesowen moved towards a typical village rebellion in the October of 1386. This was the time when tenants of the manor were expected to do fealty and various other services to the lord. But in the hamlet of Romsley, under the leadership of two of the bondmen, all the tenants refused to do fealty, declaring that they did not intend to be bondmen of the Abbot any more. They were still in rebellion in the following March and it was not until after Easter that one of the two leaders was captured and imprisoned, where he died. The others—his fellow leader and the woman who was said to be behind it all—disappeared.[24] It is an interesting comment on the value of the manorial court records that none of these events is in any way referred to in them. Our knowledge of the revolt comes from a record of proceedings before the justices of oyer and terminer, of which the Abbot kept a copy.

This suggests that the survival of information about affairs of this sort is subject to many hazards, quite apart from the physical survival of documents. Many cases of local discontent must have escaped record in the manor court rolls—or in the more continuous records of Chancery. We are fortunate when the one makes up for the deficiencies of the other. By the end of the fourteenth century, for instance, the private records of the Hospitallers of Temple Balsall are no longer extant. But the central records confirm that in Warwickshire, too, the social tensions to which we have referred were present. The tenants here were refusing to perform services and in particular to pay the heavy heriot of one-third of the dead tenant's chattels. According to letters close, presumably recording complaints from the Hospitallers, the tenants were meeting in unlawful assemblies and swearing oaths to resist the Prior. There is an element of conventionality about the accusation, but the reality of collective resistance may well have been there.[25]

In the history of European peasant movements in the Middle Ages there is a considerable range of action from quiet pressure backed by financial inducement offered for concessions, to open rebellion. The balance of forces between lord and peasant varied from time to time and for different reasons. The rising demand for land in the twelfth and thirteenth centuries might in certain circumstances give the lord who controlled its supply the whip hand. But at the same time the accumulated cash reserves of peasant producers for the market could be used to buy concessions, as we see in the history of the Italian and French rural communes.[26] In England in the century after the Black Death there is every indication that the balance had swung perceptibly if not decisively in favour of tenants. One has only to look at the long-term trends in rents and wages, down and up, to see this. Long-term trends, however, in a society in which social power was an economic force, are not simply the result of supply and demand of the factors of production. We shall suggest that the collective will of some of the main actors in the social situation had no little effect.

C. C. Dyer has already produced a well-documented example of what seems to have been a conscious decision between the 1430s and 1450 by tenants of the Bishop of Worcester that they would not pay tallages, recognitions, and other fines, aspects of the total volume of payments by peasants to lords which were clearly derived by the lord through the exercise of his functions as the holder of a seigneurial franchise rather than as a landowner. The implication is that the seigneurial dues were considered in

[25] *Calendar of Close Rolls (CCR), 1392–6*, p. 280; *CPR 1391–6*, p. 429. B. A. Lees, *Records of the Templars in England*, 1935, pp. cxiii–cxiv.
[26] Hilton, op. cit., pp. 74–85.

some way less legitimate than the land rent. At the same time rent arrears were piling up on this as on most other estates in the fifteenth century. At what stage the normal medieval dilatoriness in making any cash payment on time merges into what could be called a 'rent strike' is impossible to say, but that stage seems to have been passed on these and on other estates.[27] Nor was it a phenomenon known only to estate administrators. To what else could this phrase by an early fifteenth-century moralizing verse writer refer?

> Lordis wete nevere what comouns greves
> Til hir rentis begin to ses.[28]

The situation on the Worcester bishopric estate was not unique. We have, during this period, other examples not merely of attempts by tenants to put pressure on their lords, but of success in these attempts. Furthermore, the lords concerned were socially quite divergent in type.

John Hampton, the lord of Kinver, seems to have been under pressure from tenants in the five villages of his lordship on the Staffordshire–Shropshire border at the turn of the fourteenth century. This is indicated by the fact that, having found mainpernors, forty-one of these tenants were released from outlawry proceedings and the term of imprisonment which followed a refusal to do services. Nothing more can be said about the nature of the dispute, but an isolated document thirty-four years later suggests that John Hampton and his tenants, following this period of conflict, had come to an agreement which was confirmed at this later date by his two sons, John the younger and Boyce (Boicius). The agreement no longer exists but the confirmation in the form of a sealed copy of the record of a court held after Easter week in 1434 has survived. According to this confirmation all labour

---

[27] *Past and Present*, No. 39. For rent arrears at the beginning of the late fourteenth century in Leicestershire see W. G. Hoskins (ed.), *Studies in Leicestershire Agrarian History*, 1949, p. 39; B. J. Harris shows peasant resistance as the main factor in rent arrears on the Duke of Buckingham's estate in Wales and the Marcher counties at the end of the fifteenth century in *Past and Present*, no. 43, 1968.

[28] J. Kail (ed.), *Twenty-six Political and Other Poems*, i, EETS o.s. 124, 1904, no. III, ll. 101–2.

services, heriots, and payments for permission to marry were
commuted for an annual sum of 37s. from all tenants, a little over
1s. a head since there were thirty-five tenants in 1434. Since the
labour services alone consisted of ploughing, weeding, harvest,
haymaking, and carriage obligations it seems likely that the
commutation involved a reduction of the total obligation, and a
success therefore for the tenants.[29]

A rather more impressive success was achieved during much
the same period of time by some of the tenants on the estate of the
Beauchamp Earls of Warwick. These were the men of Lighthorne, a big village entirely in the hands of the Earl, who was also
the patron of the parish church. It is about seven miles from
Warwick, the centre of Beauchamp power. It is also near to the
junction of the Fosse Way and the Warwick-Oxford road, not
badly situated from the market point of view. In the 1390s the
Earl was still cultivating a demesne of some 250 acres and grazing
a flock of 600 sheep and lambs. The work was done entirely by
hired labourers, the tenants' labour services, mainly haymaking,
being relaxed without payment *quousque mundus relevetur*. In 1398
the demesne was leased to John Blockley, the rector, and the
tenants on a ten-year lease, the consequence seemingly of Thomas,
Earl of Warwick's attainder. In September 1401, however, after
the estate was restored, John Blockley reported a fall of one-
twelfth in the rents due from the customary holdings, a situation
accepted by the widowed countess and her council—repeating the
gloomy phrase used earlier in the rent collector's accounts,
*quousque mundus melius relevetur*.[30]

There are many subsequent gaps in the manorial documentation. In 1410 the phrase *quousque mundus relevetur* is still used to
excuse the relaxation of services and decay of rents has doubled.

[29] *CPR 1396–9*, p. 365; *1399–1401*, pp. 44, 522; *CCR 1399–1402*, pp. 109, 291
I transcribed the sealed copy of the court-roll from a MS. brought some years ago
to the University of Birmingham School of History. I do not know its present
location and therefore print the transcript in the Appendix. The Hamptons held
the manor at farm from the Crown; John the younger was an esquire of the king's
body, was well supported by annuities from crown lands and may have been an
absentee landowner.
[30] Stratford-on-Avon Record Office (SRO), Willoughby de Broke MSS.
672 a–d, 674, 674a, 675, 676a.

By 1435 this item has doubled again. In 1437 a further increase in the decay of rent item is explained as being partly due to holdings being in the lord's hands for lack of tenants and partly due to a reduction of rents, the occasion for which is explained in a 'renewed' rental attached to the account. This gives a list of tenants' names and holdings, with the old rents and the new, reduced rents. At the head of the rental we are told that the Earl has instructed Thomas Huggeford and Nicholas Rody, the steward, to reduce ('moderate') the rents. The reason given is that the tenants had complained that the rents were so heavy that they could not keep alive. This was why so many holdings were in the lord's hands for lack of tenants. In addition the king's subsidy, the fifteenth, was levied so often that they had protested to the Earl that unless rents were reduced they would have to quit the manor so as to be able to gain a living.[31]

The real reductions they achieved amounted to 5s. out of the rent of 15s. 6d. for the yardland, and this was maintained for the next forty years. For after the Warwick estate had passed through the hands of Richard Neville and George, Duke of Clarence, the Lighthorne tenants still kept their reduced rent, even though the estate accounts of 1480 still showed the full rent of 15s. 6d. a yardland charged on the receipt side, but with the negotiated allowance recorded on the expenses side and still attributed to the negotiation of Huggeford and Rody in 1437.[32]

The tenants of Lighthorne won their case and maintained their gains in the face of one of the most powerful lords of fifteenth-century England. The nuns of Syon who had eventually acquired the English property of the alien Abbey of Fécamp were perhaps easier opponents.[33] The course of events by which their agricultural tenants in Cheltenham and five adjacent villages gained rent reduction was similar in outline to that which we have described. Those in dispute with the Abbess were about 120 peasants holding

---

[31] Ibid. 676, 685a.

[32] R. H. Hilton (ed.), *Ministers' Accounts of the Warwickshire Estates of the Duke of Clarence, 1479–80*, 1952, pp. 85–6.

[33] Sir John Cornwall, Lord Fanhope and his wife, who was aunt to Henry V, were first granted the property after its confiscation. G. Hart, *A History of Cheltenham*, 1965, pp. 23–4.

in base tenure, mostly with half yardlands or the equivalent. In addition to their old fixed money rent, the rent of assize, they owed a further sum for commuted labour services which were valued at £10 0s. 7¼d. under the name of 'work silver'. The evidence is fragmentary, consisting mostly of rentals. It is the accounts rendered by the Abbess's bailiff, however, which, like the Lighthorne accounts, reveal quite incidentally a crisis in the relations between the lady and her tenants. From a pardon granted to the bailiff at the end of the financial year 1451-2 it appears that the tenants had been withholding the payment of work silver since 1445. Negotiations were already in train at least as early as the September of 1451 for a reduction of the work silver payments. We know this because of expenses paid to the Abbess's chief steward, John Vampage, a Pershore lawyer, and to other members of her council during the five days of negotiation with the tenants.

The negotiations were evidently unsuccessful. At any rate they were not concluded until the following September as result of the arbitration of Ralph Botiller, Lord Sudeley, chosen as a mediator by the Abbess and the tenants. It would seem that he paid two visits before the matter was settled, the first time in July when he arrived accompanied by twenty-four mounted attendants and stayed for a day. At this meeting, apart from the Abbess and the tenants, there were four of the Abbess's advisers, Robert Clinton, Thomas Compier, Richard Burton, and Henry Newedyk. They were accompanied by nine mounted attendants. The second visit was in September, when Botiller arrived with forty-six mounted attendants to meet the negotiating parties and the Abbess's group of advisers. These negotiations lasted five days and concluded with a reduction of the work silver payment from £10 0s. 7¼d. a year to £6 13s. 4d. The expenses of the arbitration amounted to four times the amount by which the payment was relaxed.[34]

The remarkable feature of these negotiations between the Cheltenham tenants and the Abbess of Syon is the seriousness

---

[34] Among a number of fifteenth-century rentals the nearest in time to the episodes described is that of 28 Henry VI, PRO, SC11.217. The accounts are PRO, SC6. 852/24, 25.

with which their demands were treated. Not only was the arbitration conducted by one of the most powerful lords of the region,
but the document embodying the final settlement was witnessed
by an impressive array of local gentry, headed by the Prior of
Deerhurst and Sir Thomas Botiller, with a group of esquires
having such old-established aristocratic family names as Tracy,
Pauncefot, Burdet, Cassy, and Giffard.[35] It may well be that
there was a non-peasant pressure group among the tenants in
base tenure. As early as 1430 John Throckmorton, Esq., had a
share in some of the agricultural holdings in Cheltenham which
owed work silver. Later in the century, the lawyer and judge
William Grevile, who in an undated rental is listed as a Cheltenham free tenant, had also accumulated quite a collection of lands
held in base tenure. This, however, was after the confrontation of
1451-2, one of the results of which might have been to make base
tenure land more negotiable.[36]

The sharpness of antagonism between lord and peasant in the
second half of the fourteenth century seems to have been resolved
to some extent during the first half of the fifteenth century by
concessions to tenants. This could be interpreted very broadly in
terms of the changed land labour ratio which put tenants at a
considerable advantage. Other issues, social and even political,
might be involved. One might ask, for instance, whether the
frequently commented-on collaboration between gentry, yeomen, husbandmen, and artisans in Kent and Sussex at the time of
Cade's rebellion was confined to the south-east or whether the
political antagonisms of mid-century did not lead to some wooing
by the gentry of the upper ranks of the peasantry in other parts of
England.

It could be argued that there was nothing new about the presence of husbandmen in the retinues of the county gentry as they
pursued their factional quarrels throughout the countryside. Any
reader of fourteenth-century indictments before the king's justices
will know this. The following of Sir Humphrey Stafford of
Grafton near Bromsgrove in 1450 in his feud against the Har-

---

[35] Printed by J. E. Thorold Rogers, op. cit. iii, 1882, pp. 739-40.
[36] PRO, SC11. 218, 216.

courts provides an example of this.[37] The interesting variation, as in the Cade rising, seems to be when the gentry are no longer in the lead. Who *was* in the leadership of local or regional disturbances is, of course, not always clear, given the well-known tendency of the gentry to disclaim responsibility for movements which were a failure.

A typically confused situation in which gentry involvement, though certain, was nevertheless ambiguous, occurred in south Worcestershire in 1418. In that year, according to the indictment, a group of husbandmen from the village of Ablench in the hills to the north of Evesham attacked and broke up the Abbot of Evesham's mill in his manor of Lenchwick, destroyed cart-harness in the nearby manor of Norton, cut off the tails of his cart-horses and drove them through Evesham town and so threatened abbey officials and tenants that they left his service. The men from Ablench were not alone. They were backed by Nicholas Burdet whose home was in Ablench and by his more prestigious father, Sir Thomas Burdet of Arrow near Alcester in Warwickshire. The Abbot of Evesham was Roger Yatton, a big builder and spender like Abbot Frocester of Gloucester.[38] His need for money might have resulted in pressures on the tenants and others (for a number of Evesham townspeople joined in the riot). The focus seems to have been the Abbot's mill and it may be that the enforcement of a milling monopoly was involved. The Burdets were already involved in hostile litigation with the Abbot over land. In the end the Burdets escaped, possibly on a technicality, and the Abbot decided not to pursue them further.[39]

The popular feeling against the government which led to rebellions in Kent, Sussex, and Wiltshire had but faint echoes in the west Midlands. The property of the Abbot of Gloucester was despoiled in 1449 because the Abbot had been an ambassador for the government and was suspected of arranging a sell-out to the French. The attack was not serious and seems simply to have

[37] R. L. Storey, *The End of the House of Lancaster*, 1966, pp. 57–8; *CPR, 1446–52*, p. 461.

[38] W. D. Macray (ed.), *Chronicon Abbatiae de Evesham*, 1863, pp. 304–10. Litigation with the Burdets is mentioned on p. 309.

[39] PRO, JI.1.1038/3; *CPR 1416–22*, p. 147.

given scope to the traditional antagonism between the townsmen of Gloucester and the foresters of Dean.[40] John Brome, an unpopular Lancastrian in Warwick and its vicinity, was mobbed in 1450.[41] The nearest approach to a popular rebellion against the government came, not in 1450 against the Lancastrian regime, but in 1463–4 against the newly established Yorkist government.

This movement is almost unknown. A description of one phase was printed by C. L. Kingsford in his edition of the Annals of Gloucester.[42] Here we are told that there was a rising of the community of the shire who entered the town of Gloucester and beheaded John Dodyng, one of the town's bailiffs. These rebels invaded the town again and searched for other unpopular burgesses without finding them. At this point the Earl of Warwick tried to pacify the rising by granting their petition, of which no details are given. It was not until King Edward came with a retinue of armed nobles that the rising was suppressed, certain men *de plebi communitatis* being hanged and beheaded, their heads being displayed on the town gates. *Et facta est tranquilitas magna.* This episode might have related only to the tensions within the town and county which were revealed in 1449. These had erupted again in 1460 when the men of Gloucester (the *populum*) and the gentry of the surrounding countryside were pitted against the foresters of Dean in a dispute ostensibly concerning rival claimants to the office of Prior of the Gloucester house of Augustinian canons known as Lanthony Secunda. A feature of minor interest in the story is that the Earl of Warwick gave refuge to the party in the monastery which was supported by the *populum*.

But the whole story assumes a different aspect in the light of an indictment giving details of a much wider movement in late January and early February 1464, focused on a considerable area of the west Cotswolds, and the Vale of Gloucester, from Winchcombe through Stroud to Tetbury and Old Sodbury.[43] This is

---

[40] C. L. Kingsford, *English Historical Literature in the Fifteenth Century*, 1913, Appendix (The Annals of Gloucester), pp. 355–7.

[41] *Warwickshire Antiquarian Magazine*, iv, n.d., pp. 179–88. For the Brome family see C. C. Dyer, 'A Small Landowner in the Fifteenth Century', *Midland History*, i, 1972.

[42] *Loc. cit.*     [43] PRO, KB9/33.

described, in the no doubt exaggerated language of indictment, as if it were a *levée en masse* of men under arms summoned by the lighting of beacons and the ringing of bells in the parish churches of the region. Most of the persons named in the ten separate indictments by the various hundred juries avoided being brought to trial before the Earl of Warwick and his fellow justices at Gloucester. Of those who appeared, two were hanged, one was kept in custody, and six were pardoned. Five of the others had to obtain sureties. The only man accused of inciting to rebellion as opposed to being under arms against the king was Robert White, formerly of Ware, Herts., a weaver, also known as Robert Touker, touker (i.e. fuller). He was also accused of being a Lollard, spreading heretical opinions, and saying that it would not be unlawful to deprive archbishops and other churchmen of their temporalities, in order to endow 15 earls, 1500 knights, and 300 esquires for the defence of the kingdom. In the end, however, he was simply hanged for high treason and felony, and one suspects that the Lollardy accusation was simply an extra smear without foundation, echoing a fragment of an old Lollard programme, quite irrelevant here.

For the rest, the leading persons in the agitation consisted of a yeoman, four husbandmen, five labourers, thirteen craftsmen —and twelve merchants. The gentry component was provided by two members of the Bridges family—Thomas Bridges of Stroud and John Bridge of Coberley. Apart from the reference to the petition presented to the Earl of Warwick at Gloucester in October 1463 there are no indications of any expression of grievances, that is if one discounts the Lollardy accusation against Robert White. One of the indicted persons, Thomas Phelps of Ree in Quedgeley parish, a chapman, appears two years later in a list of Lancastrians who had once been pardoned and then withdrawn from the land to support Queen Margaret.[44] No one else on this Lancastrian list figures in the Gloucestershire rising, so that although there are hints of dynastic commitment, the most that one can say is that when there was trouble in high places popular discontent embracing a wide social spectrum, but

---

[44] *Rotuli Parliamentorum*, v, 1783, p. 511.

not necessarily under the direction of the supposed natural leaders of the people, was liable to manifest itself. There is no telling what led Robert White, weaver, and Robert Llewellyn, yeoman, to the hangman, but they and the others might have had the same reasons for insurrection in 1463 as the men of Kent had in 1450. There are no indications that they were knit together by the bastard-feudal loyalties which bound local men to Humphrey Stafford of Grafton in 1450 or to his son in 1486.[45]

[45] The Humphrey Stafford of Grafton who was in rebellion against Henry VII in 1486 was said to have been supported by yeomen, husbandmen, graziers, labourers, and craftsmen from a considerable area of north-eastern Worcestershire, especially from the Bromsgrove area. PRO, KB9/138.

# APPENDIX

*A deed of 1434 by which John Hampton, Lord of Kinver, commuted for a money rent all the servile dues and services of his customary tenants*

Kynvar
: Ad curiam tentam ibidem die Lune in crastino octave Pasche anno regni Regis Henrici Sexti post conquestum duodecimo.

Hassecote
: Willelmus Welot, Thomas Hawes, Johannes Rolffe, Ricardus Lyne, Willelmus Perot et Johannes Hawes de eadem.

Storeton
: Johannes Yate, Willelmus Bate, Johannes Lyrcocke, Tibot atte Yate, Thomas Alden, Thomas Dowte, Johannes Comber, Thomas Bate, Thomas Dasshefen et Johannes Webbe de eadem.

Compton
: Thomas Lytholl, Thomas Pylle, Thomas Toye, Johannes Watkys, Ricardus Hulle, Ricardus Britte, Willelmus ffieldmon, Henricus Newnam, Margareta Jones, Johannes Hulle, Mariena Mollesley de eadem.

Over Dunnesley
: Thomas Hulmon, Ricardus Lyne, Agnes Hugge et Thomas Comber de eadem, custumarii (.....)[1] ersis consuetudinibus Johanne Hampton, armigero, Domino de Kynvar de terris et tenementis suis ibidem debitis et ex antiquo consuetis, videlicet pro arruris, sarculacionibus, mescionibus in autumpno, ffalcacionibus, factura et collectione feni et cariagio eisudem. Item pro fine filiarum suarum maritando ac pro duplice herieto, videlicet medietatem porcorum et apium, capitagio garcionum necnon medietatem cuiuslibet integri panni scissi post obitum cuiuslibet tenentis ibidem.

Overende de Kynvar
: Necnon Thomas Comber, Johannes Bedell, Johannes Brodhull et Johannes Taillour pro diversis consuetudinibus dicto Domino de terris et tenementis in le Over ende de Kynvar debitis et consuetis, videlicet pro teddyng et rakyng fenum in pratis diversis, tredyng tassas in grangia domini ac pro fine filiarum suarum maritando necnon pro duplice herieto, videlicet medietatem porcorum et apium et medietatem cuiuslibet integri panni non scissi post obitum cuiuslibet tenentis ac pro capitagio garcionum ibidem, concordaverunt cum eodem Domino unanimi

[1] MS. torn.

assensu et in plena curia ibidem pro consuetudinibus predictis sibi et heredibus suis imposterum quietis relaxassandis concesserunt eidem domino et heredibus suis unum annualem redditum triginta et septem solidorum annuatim ad festum Nativi Sancti Johannis Baptiste de terris et tenementis predictis percipiendis. Et pro hac recognicione, fine et concordia, dictus dominus ac Boicius Hampton, frater eius et heres aparens concesserunt pro se et heredibus suis quod predicti tenentes et heredes sui quieti sint et exonerati de consuetudinibus predictis adeo libere et quiete prout iidem tenentes et antecessores sui quondam concordate fuerunt cum Johanne Hampton seniore, patre Johannis Hampton, armigeri, modo domini ibidem. Et ulterius predicti tenentes concedunt pro se et heredibus suis quod ipsi et heredes sui non capient aliquod de eodem domino et heredibus suis pro officio prepositi imposterum faciendo. In cuius rei restimonium Sigillum Johannis Corbyn, tunc senescalli ibidem presentibus est appensum, etc.
Seal.

# V

## The Small Town as Part of
## Peasant Society

In one of those mysterious letters which the rebel priest of the 1381 rising, John Ball, is supposed to have addressed to John Nameless, John the Miller, and John Carter, the warning is given 'bee war of gyle in borough'.[1] In spite of the constant recruitment of country people into the towns to make up for greater urban mortality, this phrase echoes an ancient distrust. Indeed to the west Midland villager, even if he never went to London, such large towns as Bristol and Coventry must have presented a strange aspect, with their crowds and closely packed houses, shops and stalls. Nor, if he were a villein, would he be welcomed into the community of the town. Town air did not necessarily make free. Those who wished to become burgesses of Bristol had to be already of free condition.[2]

But what about those numerous small urban centres, most of them probably with fewer than 500 inhabitants, which were recognized in medieval nomenclature as being different from the villages? These were the *villae mercatoriae* or *villes marchandes* of the official documents, places whose leading inhabitants (to quote the *Nonarum Inquisitio* for Gloucestershire of 1340) were men *non viventium de agrorum cultura et stauro ovium*.[3] How distinct were they, functionally and in occupational structure, from the villages? Did they have a separate cultural identity? Or were they, on the other hand, hardly distinguishable from the overwhelmingly agrarian society within which they were set? Was the small town an integral part of peasant society?

[1] E. M. Thompson (ed.), *Chronicon Angliae*, 1874, p. 322.
[2] F. B. Bickley (ed.), *The Little Red Book of Bristol*, i, 1900, p. 37.
[3] *Nonarum Inquisitiones*, 1807, p. 419.

It is now something of a commonplace that even sizeable medieval towns had a rural atmosphere. Such towns as Cambridge, Coventry, Nottingham, Warwick, and Leicester, to mention only a few, can be shown to have been contained within a rural envelope of arable fields, meadows, and pastures, over which members of urban communities had grazing rights even when they were not tenants of the arable.[4] Conflict over access to the common pastures was even in some places a hot issue in urban politics. One has only to think of the controversial figure of Laurence Saunders in late fifteenth-century Coventry.[5]

Even stronger reasons might be given for supposing that the smaller towns had a marked rural character. Many of these were seigneurial boroughs, that is small communities of burgesses set within agricultural parishes which often bore the same name and owed allegiance to the same overlord.[6] Some of the best-known small towns of the west Midlands fall into this category. The wool mart of Northleach in the Cotswolds belonged to the Abbot of St. Peter's, Gloucester; Tewkesbury, the river port at the Avon–Severn confluence was a possession of the Earls of Gloucester; Stratford-upon-Avon on a commercially strategic river crossing was founded by, and had as its lord, the Bishop of Worcester; Burton-on-Trent, playing a similar role further north, belonged to the Abbot of Burton. The list could be considerably extended. Can one, however, clearly distinguish, in places like this, the function and status of the typical inhabitant of the intrinsic settlement (as the little town was often called) from those of the

[4] F. W. Maitland, *Township and Borough*, 1898; *Victoria History of the Counties of England (VCH), Warwickshire*, viii (*The City of Coventry and the Borough of Warwick*), 1969; pp. 199–203, 483–6); P. M. Butler, 'The Common Lands of the Borough of Nottingham', *Transactions of the Thoroton Society*, liii, 1950; C. J. Billson, 'The Open Fields of Leicester', *Transactions of the Leicestershire Archaeological Society*, xiv, 1925–6.

[5] Well described by Mary Dormer Harris, who edited the *Coventry Leet Book* (EETS O.S. 134, 135, 138, 146, 1907–13), on the evidence of which the story is based. See her *Life in an Old English Town*, 1898, chapter xii, and *English Historical Review*, ix, 1894; *VCH Warwickshire* viii, 1969, 'The Common Lands', by R. B. Rose.

[6] H. P. R. Finberg, 'The Genesis of the Gloucestershire Towns', *Gloucestershire Studies*, 1957.

dweller in the forinsec, or foreign, as the area of agricultural activity was known?[7] What is needed is evidence about economic activity, and in particular about the occupations of the inhabitants. Inevitably, for the century after the Black Death, we turn to the evidence of the returns of the third poll tax, and get some surprises.

Stow-on-the-Wold, or Stow St. Edward, in Gloucestershire, was founded by the Abbot of Evesham at an unknown date, in the late eleventh or early twelfth century, at one edge of the big rural parish of Maugersbury. This is and was a typical rural market town, less well documented than one might hope, a reflection of the poor documentation of the estate on which it was situated. However, two records of the 1340s throw a little light and not a few shadows on the situation. It was one of three smaller towns in the county in 1340 (not counting Bristol and Gloucester) which contained merchants rich enough to be taxed separately, the others being Tewkesbury and Cirencester. But in 1347 a complaint was made which suggests that there was a strong element in the town that lived by agriculture. In that year the men of the village of Maugersbury complained in a Parliamentary petition that eleven men cultivating arable land were dwelling in Stow, storing their grain and wool in the town, and being assessed to the subsidy of a fifteenth therefore to the detriment of the subsidy payers of Maugersbury. Does this suggest the merging of town and country, the matter which is at issue?[8]

If we compare the list of names in the 1380–1 poll tax list of Stow with an almost contemporary Maugersbury rental we find an overlap of three or four names only,[9] between the town and the village. Fortunately the occupational description of the inhabitants of Stow is fairly complete. The taxed population was 166, so, depending on how much tax evasion there was and what

[7] Could the juridical separation of the foreign create, at this level, 'non-feudal islands in the feudal seas', as suggested in M. M. Postan, *English Economy and Society 1100–1500*, 1972, p. 212?

[8] *VCH, Gloucestershire*, 1965, pp. 142 ff; see also reference in note 3 above; *Rotuli Parliamentorum*, ii, 1783, p. 177.

[9] The Maugersbury rental is an Evesham Abbey estate document, PRO, SC11 248, dated 47 Edward III.

we think was the proportion to the total population of young people under fifteen, there could have been 250 to 300 people in Stow. There were twenty-eight separate crafts and trades in the town, but the heads of only four households were cultivators of the soil. It is not, of course, to be supposed that persons described as having other than agricultural occupations had no land. A brewstress, a dealer in sheep-skins,[10] a smith, and a merchant were among those Stow persons having holdings in Maugersbury or the other nearby Evesham Abbey manor of Swell. Nevertheless, the picture of late fourteenth-century Stow would seem to be one of a mainly industrial and commercial community.

The poll tax returns for Gloucestershire cover a number of other small towns with varying historical backgrounds, but whose occupational structure was similar to that of Stow. Chipping Campden, like Northleach a well-known wool mart, was not a new foundation and was feudally under divided lordship. The taxed population was 299—a total of more than 500? The inhabitants were engaged in thirty-five separate occupations. There were two cultivators and one ploughman—this was the total full-time agricultural component. Winchcombe was an ancient royal borough, much diminished in importance since the eleventh century. It had a taxed population of 201 (total 350–400?) who were distributed over thirty-five separate occupations. There were only two cultivators. Fairford, part of the Gloucester earldom, and no new town, was smaller than the others with a taxed population of only 111 (150–200?). A few names are illegible. Fourteen separate occupations can be deciphered, none of them being cultivators. Finally, three of the Gloucestershire towns in these returns have defective returns. The easiest to read is the return of the old Roman capital of the Cotswolds, Cirencester. The number of taxed persons was about 550 (nearly 1,000?). Although partly illegible, forty-three separate occupations can be counted, none of them being agricultural. Tetbury, a Braose lordship, and Lechlade, owned by the Holland family in 1380, have partly illegible returns, but no cultivator appears among those which can be deciphered.

[10] 'Velbrugger' that is fell broker.

The legal status of borough and manor, of the intrinsic and the foreign, varied a good deal from place to place. The economic and social character of these small urban communities seems to have been very similar and to have contrasted sharply with that of the nearby settlements. The distribution of occupations is much the same in all of the towns, showing a balance between services and manufacturing. Looking more closely at individual occupations there is a clear preponderance of retailers of food and drink and of articles of clothing (shoemakers and tailors in particular). Individual manufacturing crafts are less important, whether metal, leather, wood, or textiles. There is no indication of any manufacturing specialism, not even in cloth-making, and not even in Cirencester, the biggest of these centres. If there is anything which differentiates the occupational structure of one town from another it is not the balance of one commercial or manufacturing skill against another but the ratio of hired hands to self-employed craftsmen. If we are to rely on the description of occupations in the returns (which may be considered risky) the range is between Winchcombe, where only 20 per cent of those taxed were servants or labourers, and Chipping Campden and Fairford where the proportion ranged from 60 to 70 per cent. This seems to some extent to have been a reflection of the scale of enterprise. In Chipping Campden the famous wool merchant William Grevel had six servants. A smith had six, an innkeeper five, a draper four; and the two cultivators had four servants each.

In order to point the contrast between the almost entirely industrial and commercial character of these small towns, nothing could be easier, still using the 1380–1 tax returns, than to demonstrate the almost entirely agricultural character of the surrounding villages and hamlets, most of which were, of course, much smaller even than the smallest towns. More effective, perhaps, is to show how it was possible for a village to be as big as a small town and still to be a purely agricultural settlement. Kempsford was bigger than Fairford in 1380–1, judging by the number of taxpayers (118), but its occupational structure was quite simple: there were twenty-nine peasant households, seven persons employed in 'service' occupations, one weaver, and 28 servants and labourers.

Sherborne had more tax payers (176) than Stow-on-the-Wold. All of the taxpayers were classified as cultivators, though some were in fact also described as servants and labourers and a few had craft surnames. Urban characteristics were not necessarily correlated with size.

It may be that the tax returns underestimated the agricultural element in the small town by giving part-time cultivators the designation of the industrial or commercial occupation which took up the greater part of their time or produced the greater part of their income. This is a more likely distortion than the omission of names. Those omitted, as we have seen, tended to be servants. We turn therefore to other types of evidence, which unfortunately do not give us a direct check on the occupational evidence in the tax returns because this other evidence survives only for places in the west Midlands for which the tax returns are missing. The best evidence, of course, for the continuous life of a small town is the same as that from which we reconstruct village history, in other words, such byproducts of administration as rentals of property and the records of the courts leet and baron.

Some records of this type are extant for the riverside town of Pershore. We are presented here with something of a challenge in that an existing history of the town states that the inhabitants were mainly engaged in agriculture.[11] It is true that there was an agricultural element mainly connected with the demesne of the Abbot of Westminster on the outskirts of the town. The Abbot of Westminster was co-lord with the Abbot of Pershore, but by the fifteenth century the bulk of the real property in the main part of the town belonged to the Abbot of Pershore. It is the records of the Abbot of Pershore's courts which provide us with the best continuous history of the town, with gaps, between 1375 and 1509.[12]

Lists of Pershore tenants at the end of the fourteenth century

---

[11] *VCH, Worcestershire*, iv, 1924, p. 154.

[12] PRO.SC2. 210/71–81; the portmoots for Westminster tenants are recorded in Westminster Abbey MSS. 21976 ff. R. A. L. Smith in his unpublished thesis (London M.A. 1939) on 'The Estates of Pershore Abbey', p. 172, pointed out how Pershore Abbey had mainly bought out the Westminster interest in the town by the end of the fourteenth century.

show that an overwhelming majority of them were tenants of messuages, shops and cottages with gardens, rather than of land in the fields. The court records, apart from containing a good deal of evidence about the government of the town, have the usual details about real property in the town as it changed hands through death, surrender, and sale. During the course of the fifteenth century most of this property was the same as that found in the fourteenth-century lists, consisting, that is, of shops, gardens, and messuages. There was some arable land in the fields, but during the period covered by the rolls only 5 per cent of the properties dealt with were agricultural. And by no means all of those dealing in agricultural land were full-time cultivators. In 1382, for instance, a tenant of four acres in the Pershore fields was a carpenter; in 1393 there is a reference to a cardmaker being hired to mow barley.[13] If there was a distinct rural atmosphere about late medieval Pershore it would arise from the considerable number of gardens behind cottages in the town's principal streets and from the fact that many householders kept some livestock, especially pigs. Keeping pigs, however, does not make a peasant out of a shopkeeper. The essential difference must have been not only that the town-dweller was linked directly or indirectly to the market, but that his work was not determined by agricultural rhythms, but by the quite different (though not unconnected) tempo of the market. Judging by these criteria, Pershore, like the little Cotswold towns, would have a character essentially different from that of the agricultural villages and hamlets of the neighbourhood.

Similarly, Cheltenham borough (*burgus*) in the early decades of the fifteenth century, closely associated as a portion of the same lordship with such agricultural settlements as Cheltenham township (*villata*) and the adjacent villages of Arle, Alstone, Westal, Sandford, Bafford, Charlton, and Boddington, was clearly differentiated from them functionally. There was virtually no social or economic overlap between the fifty-five burgage and

[13] PRO, SC2.210/71, Friday after Easter, 5 Richard II; the surname of the aggrieved employer was 'Barbour' and the amount of land, 6 selions and 7 'londesendes'; ibid. 210/72, Saturday after Easter, 16 Richard II.

acre tenants of the borough and the half-yardlanders and small-holders of the villages.[14] The burgesses' occupations are by no means all indicated in the rentals, but those given are clearly urban, or non-agricultural–tailor, farmer, weaver, smith, shoemaker. Economic activity is shown in a J.P.s' session of 1422, for the whole lordship. The session was mainly concerned with presentments of traders and craftsmen for charging excess prices. There were from Cheltenham, six butchers, a tanner, eight shoemakers, three innkeepers, a fishmonger, three bakers, and six weavers. Out of the whole lordship there is only one presentment, from Arle, of an agricultural labourer, a thresher, for taking excess wages.[15] Cheltenham borough was a little market, the centre, as we shall see, of a local grain trade and a provider of services and manufactured commodities.

Stratford-upon-Avon, like Stow on the Wold, was carved out of a big rural parish which came to be known as Old Stratford. This act of creation by the Bishop of Worcester probably took place at the end of the twelfth century.[16] Fifty years later a rental of the bishopric demonstrates its continuing functional separation from the rural hinterland.[17] For the fourteenth and fifteenth centuries our evidence, though abundant, is one-sided, consisting principally of the records of the borough's Guild of the Holy Cross. This guild was the effective social and political organization behind the legal front provided by the bishop's borough court. By the end of the fourteenth century it had absorbed the other fraternities in the town and was a considerable owner of urban real property. Although not comprehensive, its rentals, accounts, and deeds undoubtedly provide a cross-section of burgess property interests, for its holdings were given by or bought up from the members of the borough community so as to

---

[14] PRO, SC11.220, no date given but surely earlier than suggested in the PRO list, probably earlier than 1450.

[15] PRO, SC2. 175/26. m. 5.

[16] The foundation charter referred to by W. Dugdale in his *Antiquities of Warwickshire*, 1730, p. 680, is lost but Mr. T. H. Lloyd has found a sixteenth-century copy, WCRO, BA.2636.009: 1, no. 43696, fol. 93.

[17] Marjorie Hollings (ed.), *Red Book of Worcester*, 4 vols., 1935–50, pp. 491–7; discussed by E. Carus-Wilson in *EcHR*, 2nd ser. xviii, 1965.

yield an income for the maintenance of the Guild chapel, the Guild chaplains, and the annual feast. There is virtually no investment by the Guild or by its burgess benefactors in agricultural property apart from a small amount of arable land in Bridgetown and Clifford on the south side of the Avon; The rental lists tenements, burgages, shops, barns, and some (but not many) gardens. The 500 or so deeds dated from the late thirteenth to the fifteenth century which passed with the Guild property into the hands of the sixteenth-century corporation cover a much wider range of burgess property interests than is shown in the rentals. Some deeds suggest very occasional burgess interest in portions of arable in parts of Old Stratford near the borough boundary and in the village of Shottery. But nothing modifies the overwhelming impression of an urban community of traders in grain, live-stock, salt, wine, and honey, modified by a manufacturing element primarily of weavers and fullers of woollen cloth.[18]

This suggestive evidence from old settled areas in the southern part of the west Midlands region has survived in a form which allows some conclusions about the function of certain small towns. Unfortunately, the 1380–1 poll tax returns for Staffordshire do not include this type of settlement, although the much larger cathedral town of Lichfield is recorded. There were clearly modest urban settlements in this county, of which Tamworth was one, which were similar in character to those we have discussed.[19]

---

[18] The rentals of guild property begin about 1328 and continue through to the sixteenth century. SRO, Stratford Corporation Records, Division XII, 120 ff. By 1451 the guild was getting rents from between 70 and 80 properties in the town, bringing in about £28 rent. Div. XII, 123. See also T. H. Lloyd, *Some Aspects of the Building Industry in Medieval Stratford-on-Avon*, Dugdale Society, 1961.

[19] Henry Wood, *Medieval Tamworth*, 1972, is based on the court records, selectively used. Although Mr. Wood makes the general statement that medieval towns were closely linked with the adjacent countryside—an incontrovertible statement—he says that agriculture in Tamworth was the main source of employment (pp. 58–9). But the occupations for which the leet records are evidence in the fourteenth and fifteenth centuries are as follows: dyer, smith, weaver, soaper, saltworker, merchant, carpenter, mercer, cobbler, chaplain, clerk, leech, tailor, skinner, cook, butcher, dryster (sic), locksmith, coverlet-maker, organist, baker, ironmonger, saddler, laundress, cartwright, draper, huckster, traunter. The only occupation with an agricultural connotation is hayward. Evidence of the ownership

The outstanding characteristic of these small towns, to sum up, was that in spite of their size they shared with much bigger towns and cities a sharp functional differentiation from the agricultural hinterland. Their inhabitants were overwhelmingly concerned with commerce and manufacture and the weekly market was the focus of their lives. On the other hand they were not specialized communities, for their purpose was to provide a general range of services and manufactured goods for the people in the surrounding villages.

It must not be imagined that this was the only possible pattern of small-scale urbanization. Since I have emphasized so much the evidence of the poll tax returns for occupational distribution, perhaps I may refer again to the well-known returns for Essex and parts of East Anglia.[20] These have provided evidence for those historians who have attempted to measure the growth of the late medieval woollen textile industry. It has often been described as a village or rural industry, and so in a sense it was. But this development could also be described as one which, in contrast to the situation I have been describing for parts of the west Midlands, reduced the distinction between town and country. For industrial growth in the villages did not simply result in peasants and artisans living side by side. It also introduced ancillary trades and manufactures, especially in victualling, clothing, and building which would turn a place into something more like a town than a village.[21] As Professor Carus-Wilson has shown, this industrial growth was beginning to happen after 1450 in the Stroud valley, associated in fact with a drainage of population from such Cotswold towns as Cirencester.[22]

of animals, whether pigs or sheep, hardly proves that there was an important agricultural element in the town's economy. See J. Gould, 'The Medieval Burgesses of Tamworth; their Liberties, Courts and Markets', *Transactions of the South Staffordshire Archaeological and Historical Society*, xiii, 1971–2, 31–2.

[20] Essex returns in C. Oman, op. cit.; Suffolk returns in E. Powell, *The Rising of 1381 in East Anglia*, 1896; for some unpublished East Anglian returns see my *Bondmen Made Free*, pp. 171–4.

[21] Cf. the remarks of A. R. Bridbury, *Economic Growth; England in the Later Middle Ages*, 1962, pp. 44–5, 47, 79.

[22] 'Evidences of Industrial Growth on Some Fifteenth Century Manors', in *Essays in Economic History*, ed. E. Carus-Wilson, ii, 1962. One could not pretend,

It was also happening in another area of economic growth within our region, that still wooded country which straddled south Staffordshire, north Worcestershire and north Warwickshire. This area was partly covered by the 1380–1 poll tax return and presents a picture of the transformation of village life, though not so far advanced, such as we have seen in East Anglia. The bishop of Coventry and Lichfield's manor of Rugeley, for instance, had the following occupational structure. There were thirteen peasant households, but thirty-four craftsmen (mostly in metal trades) and thirty-four servants and labourers. In Brewood and its half-dozen adjacent hamlets the process of industrial development involved less of that concentration which was associated with the urban environment. But all the same the proportion between peasants and craftsmen was about half and half. In Penkridge there was still a slight majority of agriculturalists, twenty-three peasants to thirteen persons in textile and metal crafts and seven in victualling trades. But this was also a place where there was a market and a fair and—not appearing of course in this lay tax return—a royal collegiate foundation of canons.[23]

In spite of its thirteenth-century status as a *villa mercatoria*, its burgesses and its two ruling bailiffs, Birmingham also character- ized this different pattern of small town development. It was an area in the late Middle Ages of relative population growth, suggesting a continuation of that drift from the old settled areas south of the river Avon towards Coventry and beyond which was already to be seen as early as the end of the thirteenth century.[24] It was a transit centre for the Welsh cattle trade and probably of iron from the north Worcestershire and south Staffordshire

however, that Stroud became a town in the Middle Ages, or that Cirencester ceased to be one. All the same, Cirencester in 1524 paid only rather more than twice the subsidy it was assessed at in 1334 (£57 as against £25) whereas the subsidy paid by Bisley, the area of the Stroud Valley development, increased thirteenfold (£64 as against £5).

[23] D. Styles, 'The Early History of Penkridge Church', *Historical Collections for Staffordshire 1950–1951*, 1954.

[24] J. B. Harley, 'Population Trends and Agricultural Developments from the Warwickshire Hundred Rolls of 1278', *EcHR*, 2nd ser. xi, 1958. In Warwick- shire alone, between 1332 and 1524, the percentage of the county's taxpaying population living in the Birmingham area more than doubled (2·3 to 4·8 per cent,

forges. But even in mid-sixteenth century the town itself with its pastures and its leading men in the grazier-butcher and tanning trades was by no means so 'separate' from agricultural as we have seen much smaller towns further south to have been.[25] If, however, we look beyond the Birmingham parish boundaries we find a rural hinterland as different from the old settled arable areas of the Avon and Severn valleys, south Warwickshire and the Cotswolds, as Birmingham was different from Stratford-upon-Avon. This was a rural hinterland of forest small-holders, free in status, mobile, poor and therefore inclined towards industrial by-occupations. We lack systematic evidence of these occupations but analysis of the many deeds of land transfer dated between the thirteenth and fifteenth centuries shows a great majority of smiths among such occupational designations as are given.[26] Birmingham's untidy growth like that of East Anglian industrialized 'villages' was the consequence of the industrial development of the whole region. The neat separation of small market towns from the surrounding countryside which we first noticed at Stow-on-the-Wold was the mark of a predominantly agrarian economy with minimal industrialization.

In countries such as France and Italy where the notarial registration of agreements was essential, the historian of town–country economies and social relationships is at a considerable advantage, even when there is no record of daily trade in and out of the town resulting from records of market or entry tolls.[27] The historian of the small town in England has neither source and consequently the precise measurement of its trade with the surrounding villages is impossible. One can but guess at the nature

while the downward trend in the south of the county, noticed by Dr. Harley between 1086 and 1278, continued—the percentage living in Kineton Hundred in 1332 was 27 per cent as against 17 per cent in 1524. I have calculated these figures from the two tax returns.

[25] W. B. Bickley and J. Hill, *A Survey of Birmingham made in 1553*, n.d. Cf. *VCH, Warwickshire*, vii.

[26] Birmingham Reference Library Collection of Original Deeds. These are well calendared, but include a mixture of manorial documents as well as charters.

[27] For an example of a small town history in the late Middle Ages based on notarial registers, see J. Birrell, 'Berre à la fin du moyen âge', *Cahiers du centre d'études des sociétés méditerranéennes*, no. 2.

of the relationship from evidence which at best gives only a static picture. Let us look at Winchcombe and its hinterland. This decayed old borough probably fulfilled a very localized function which can be guessed at by comparing the occupational structure of the town and the surrounding villages in 1381.

Winchcombe's tax return is contained in the return for the surrounding villages in the same hundred. There were thirty-two villages within no more than a five-mile radius comprising a recorded taxed population of 1,418 as against Winchcombe's 201, both of which we know to be considerable underestimates, hopefully at a similar rate. The little town and the villages seem to have complementary economies. Winchcombe, as we have seen, had an almost entirely non-agricultural population. Occupations were distributed as follows: 42 per cent were in clothing or victualling trades, 28 per cent were craftsmen in leather, wood, and building, 14 per cent were textile craftsmen, and the rest were merchants or in transport. In the thirty-two villages the population consisted almost entirely of households of cultivators, servants, and labourers in husbandry with a scattering of about forty-five building workers and smiths. We cannot know, of course, to what extent Winchcombe's urban economy had connections beyond these nearby villages. It might be drawn to some extent into the estate economy of its Benedictine Abbey, though the grain from the outlying manors which came to Winchcombe bypassed the market and went to victual the monks and their dependents directly. The wool from sheep grazed on the estate probably went to Northleach.[28]

Centres like Northleach and Chipping Campden had a wider role than that of Winchcombe in that they were not merely local market centres but transmitted regional products to the world beyond. These two towns have for long been well known as wool marts. William Grevel of Chipping Campden, the flower of the wool merchants of all England (*flos mercatorum lanarum totius Anglie*) and founder of a dynasty which eventually moved into the aristocracy, not only linked his native town with European markets through the Calais staple, but with the villages and

[28] R. H. Hilton in *Gloucestershire Studies* (ed. H. P. R. Finberg), p. 108.

other small towns of the region. Evidence for this necessarily survives accidentally, but we see him between 1383 and 1385 buying £133 worth of wool from the Bishop of Worcester's clip at Blockley as well as at Stratford-upon-Avon and elsewhere. The evidence for Grevel's activity comes partly from presentments against merchants who used non-standard measures, presentments which suggest a considerable scouring of small towns and villages by travelling wool merchants especially from Coventry but also from lesser places like Southam.[29] It was, no doubt the closer connections with the outside world which was reflected in Chipping Campden's greater occupational diversity and higher proportion of wage labour than Winchcombe.

The judicial records of the mid-1380s also show Tewkesbury as a market town with wide connections. It appears to have been, among other things, a centre of the grain trade, connected by river with the big Bristol market. The presentment of thirteen Tewkesbury cornmongers on charges of false measurement shows that during a three-year period they were handling in Tewkesbury market at least 3,340 quarters of malt and other grains together with 600 quarters bought up in various villages of the neighbourhood, such as Staverton, Deerhurst, Oxenton, and Haw by the Severn river crossing in Tirley. Cheltenham, too, was evidently a minor centre, seven dealers being presented during the same period for deals totalling 540 quarters. A good deal of the Severn–Avon valley grain must have gone south to Bristol, some possibly for export. The volume of the trade can hardly be calculated from the prosecutions but it does seem that it reflected to some extent the size and importance of the towns from which the merchants came. During the same period merchants in Gloucester were dealing illegally in 11,000 quarters in the town market and a further 2,000 quarters in the villages.[30]

By the fifteenth century, the big towns had each developed a

[29] WCRO, BA. 2636. 157/92007; PRO, J.I.1.977 mm. 3–6, 24. The description of Grevel is on his memorial brass in Chipping Campden Church. Eileen Power mentions him in her *Medieval English Wool Trade*, 1941, p. 50. For Blockley wool see R. H. Hilton and P. A. Rahtz, 'Upton, Gloucestershire, 1959–64', *Transactions of Bristol and Gloucestershire Archaeological Society*, lxxxv, 1966.

[30] PRO, KB9. 32. mm. 16, 20, 21.

complicated set of institutions: mayor, aldermen, recorder, chamberlains, advisory councils representing the community, various courts. The small towns still had institutional structures which in many ways resembled those of the villages: a court presided over by a bailiff or even a lord's steward, yet dominated by a jury of local notables; a primitive officialdom of constables and ale-tasters: control of the local population through the system of presentment by the heads of tithings; three-weekly meetings of the court (perhaps known as portmoot) and biennial leets for the view of frankpledge—but as in the rural manors considerable confusion between the business transacted at each. Nevertheless, even the smallest towns had a different rhythm of life from the villages, partly, as we have already suggested because the rhythm of work was necessarily different, even though the agricultural seasons must have affected supply and demand at the market.

We can see something of this difference through the records of the Pershore Abbey courts in Pershore town. Pershore, as we have seen, was a little market town like many others. By the fifteenth century it had a small manufacturing industry in glove-making and in linen and woollen textiles, though at the turn of the four-teenth century the cloth market only accounted for 6–7 per cent of the sales in the county.[31] But as the Bishop of Worcester said in a striking phrase to justify an appropriation of parish revenues to the Abbey, it was 'situated on a public street',[32] so that although the manufacturing element might have been small, the provision of services was considerable. At the beginning of the century there were up to sixty or seventy brewers and twenty taverns;[33] the butchers were numerous enough for there to be a Butchers Row,

[31] R. A. Pelham, 'The earliest aulnage accounts for Worcestershire', *Transactions of Worcestershire Archaeological Society*, xxxix, 1952. The return of 1–2 Henry IV (PRO, E.101/345/11) names 8 Pershore cloth sellers as against Evesham's 36; but only 3 are named for Kidderminster. But as Professor Carus-Wilson has shown us, we must treat aulnage returns with suspicion.

[32] *Calendar of Papal Registers; Papal Letters* v, *1396–1404*, p. 15.

[33] Mostly from the Pershore Abbey tenants, but with Westminster Abbey tenants supplying up to a third. There was, of course, a considerable overlap between the two groups. Several brewers who were presented at the Westminster portmoot of 1380 (Westminster MSS. 21976) were tenants of the Abbot of Pershore who swore fealty to him in the same year.

also known as the Shambles, with special officers to inspect the meat. Retail sellers of food, butter for example, were constantly presented for attempts to corner the market by forestalling.

Problems of urban life presented themselves with which the manorial institutions were perhaps inadequate to deal. Presentments against gaming houses in which such 'irrational' games as dice were being played began to be frequent from about 1415 and continued at a considerable level until the early 1450s. At about the same date (1415) presentments begin against the habitual reception of ill-governed men and women. More specifically, by 1429 the houses of those guilty are referred to as *bordelrys*, 'odious hostelries in which prostitutes are kept'. The presentments continue through to the beginning of the sixteenth century, their frequency clearly indicating the ineffectiveness of the measures taken against them. At the same time the jurors were issuing orders to keep the streets clean, pigs under control, food prices stable, ale drinkable, and meat eatable. They were attempting to keep order, to ensure the payment of tradesmen's debts and to apply labour legislation. On the whole, the impression is that they hardly coped. It may be that small towns like Pershore had lost the mutual solidarity of the peasant communities without yet having acquired to replace it the apparatus of social control exercised by the rulers of the bigger boroughs and cities.

There was nevertheless one institution which may have partly replaced the lost solidarity of the village, though with varying success from place to place. This was the parish fraternity or guild. As is well known, this was an institution which was common in the industrialized villages of East Anglia.[34] an area where we would certainly expect old agricultural communities to be in a state of disintegration. The evidence is rare elsewhere and this might be attributed to defects in the documentation rather than to the rarity of the institution. The fact remains that in our area the official evidences of the guild returns of 1389 and the chantry returns of 1547 coincide in suggesting that outside big towns like Bristol and Coventry, fraternities were rather few in number. We

[34] See the appendix to H. F. Westlake, *The Parish Gilds of Medieval England*, 1919.

find them for certain only in eight small towns or large villages in
Warwickshire and four in Gloucestershire. Worcestershire
references are fleeting, being retrospective from sixteenth-century
evidence for three towns. Staffordshire is a blank.[35]

There was a certain ambiguity about the fraternities. They often
begin with money given by the pious for the maintenance of
lights on one of the altars in a parish church. They could then
grow into a more ambitious fund for financing chantry priests to
say prayers for the souls of the dead and the living. When the
funding became collective, necessary, perhaps as chaplain's
stipends increased, the contributors formed themselves into a
guild or fraternity which became a permanent organization for
mutual support. It could undertake other functions, but the
original purpose remained. In fact the terms 'guild' and 'chantry'
sometimes remained interchangeable.[36]

Once established, fraternities would become formidable organs
of mutual solidarity, not necessarily of a peaceful character. Such
was an unofficial, even illegal fraternity of the Holy Trinity at
Chipping Campden whose members were indicted before the
king's justice in 1387.[37] The indictment illustrates the element of
mutual solidarity but makes no mention of pious aims. The members were said to have bound themselves together by oath to
maintain each other against other persons in pleas whether true or
false. In fact, they were accused of organizing violence against
persons in other towns such as Winchcombe and Northleach.
One amongst a number of victims, Richard Dunning, merchant
of Northleach, said that because of their threats he was unable to

[35] Westlake, op. cit., for 1389; a similar quick inspection of the gilds in 1547
may be had by examination of the PRO manuscript list of the class E.301. This, of
course, consists overwhelmingly of certificates for chantries, lamps, obits and
various services, but includes guilds.

[36] The Knowle Guild in Warwickshire began as a chantry in a chapel-of-ease
founded there at the end of the fourteenth century because of the distance from
Knowle to Hampton-in-Arden parish church. The chantry was established in 1403
shortly after the foundation of the chapel and was converted into a gild after ten
years. W. B. Bickley, *The Register of the Gild of Knowle*, 1894. There was an
institution at Deritend in Aston parish, Warwickshire which is sometimes called a
guild, but referred to as a chantry in PRO, E. 301/31, p. 15.

[37] KB.9. 32 m. 25.

trade at the fairs and markets of the region. The membership was said to include a hundred persons, not only from Chipping Campden but from the villages around. Some of the guild's members—three drapers, a merchant, a butcher, and a rich farmer from Chipping Campden—can be identified by reference to the names in the poll tax returns. If the indictment was correct, this looks like an association for extortion and trade monopoly. There were, however, more legitimate bodies, similar in form and even membership which served more stable economic and social interests.

The Stratford Holy Cross Guild whose property holdings have already been mentioned was one of those. The Guild had its pious purpose as we have mentioned, but there are three other aspects of its existence which illustrate the thesis that these fraternities provided the town with an alternative form of solidarity to that of the village community. First, it met regularly for social, perhaps even political purposes. In other words its gatherings were not purely convivial, though the accounts of purchases of food and drink for the annual feast indicate that conviviality was of some importance. The other gatherings were termed *interlocutiones*.[38] They seem to have included at least the leading men and women of the town. The collection of money for guild purposes was part of their business. New members were admitted and leases of Guild property agreed. As to what was discussed, we are left in the dark. The second point is that the Guild must have functioned as a sort of shadow government behind the official screen of the portmoot. The leading men of the guild were clearly the leading suitors of the court, whether or not the bailiff and catchpolls of the court were necessarily also aldermen of the Guild. One fragmentary record of 1386–7 seems to clinch the matter since here we have an ordinance *per totam communitatem villate Stratford* (dealing with rooting pigs and bitch dogs on heat) written down on the same page as a list of payments which are clearly part of the Guild finances.[39] Thirdly—of particular interest for the theme of this lecture—the membership of the Holy

[38] SRO, Stratford Corporation Records, Division XII, nos. 169 and 2 dorse.
[39] Ibid. No. 214.

Cross Guild represented a social, perhaps even an economic, network of interest which bound town and villages together.

During the course of the fifteenth century, in addition to members from the town itself, members were drawn from 300 villages within a twenty-five miles radius of Stratford and a further 100 places beyond this radius. Most of them, not unexpectedly, came from villages in the Avon and Stour valleys but during the course of the fifteenth century the proportions from the southern and eastern parts of the county and from the forest areas of Arden and Feckenham tended to rise. Perhaps the most interesting feature is that from the decade 1406–16, when those from outside Stratford itself amounted to about 30 per cent of the total entry into Guild membership, the proportion of outside members rose quickly so that after 1426–36 the entry of outsiders was never less than half of the total, and between 1436 and the end of the century fluctuated between 60 and 70 per cent. Was this simply a reflection of the increased prestige of the spiritual benefits of the membership of this particular Guild ? Or of the increasing popularity of guild membership when there were no comparable rival organizations within reach? Or can it also be interpreted in terms of the increasing social, even economic, contacts between town and country ?[40]

[40] J. Harvey Bloom (ed.), *The Register of the Gild of the Holy Cross, the Blessed Mary and St. John the Baptist of Stratford-on-Avon*, 1907.

# VI

# Women in the Village

IT should not be necessary to write a separate history of half the human beings in any social class. We must, however, do so, whether or not we believe that all women through history have constituted a class oppressed by all men or whether we believe that women's class position was more important than their sex. The fact is that in societies where women have few, if any, rights in other words the majority known to history, the historical records themselves either omit any reference to women (who are assumed to be represented by husbands or fathers) or push them into anonymity, as in the case of many a medieval legal or administrative record which will refer to 'Johannes Smyth et uxor ejus'. Furthermore, historians, female as well as male, are socially conditioned so that they naturally focus on the male landowners, the male heads of households, the male litigants, the male criminals, the male workers. This is to a certain extent unavoidable because of the way the records present the situation, but it is also due to their own conscious or unconscious selection for examination of those whom they consider to be playing the 'important' roles in society.

Apart from doing them historical justice, there are other reasons for inquiring into the situation of peasant women in the late Middle Ages, of which two may be mentioned. Was their status at this time, when general personal unfreedom was still widespread, such that subsequent history has seen a progressive improvement in their condition? Was their situation within their own class comparable with that of women in other classes, such as the bourgeoisie and the aristocracy, or better, or worse? I cannot answer these questions now but I have to say what on the basis of evidence from the peasant side may contribute to the discussion of the problem.

We must appreciate at this time the general atmosphere of male domination: not merely the domination of the aristocratic armed warriors over other classes but over women as well, including noble women. The flavour of this is best caught in literature, as Achille Luchaire vividly demonstrated in his book on social life at the time of Philip-Augustus of France.[1] And as has been frequently appreciated, to place women on a pedestal as in courtly romance is not so much a modification of male brutality as the other side of the same coin. All the same, there were many elements of ambivalence in male attitudes. Were women descendants of Eve the temptress, agent of the devil? Or were they sisters to the mother of God?[2] This ambivalence must have been especially strong, perhaps even painful, for the clergy who had to reconcile their devotion to Mary and to Paul. They were certainly preoccupied by the woman question to the extent that some (presumably mainly clerical) social theorists abstracted women from their social class and made them into a separate estate, alongside the nobles, the clergy and the peasants.[3] This form of classification enabled them to do what they did with the other estates—pick out their characteristic failings.

The ambivalence of which I speak is clearly demonstrated by an English writer from our period. John Hoccleve, one among a long line of civil service poets, writing at the beginning of the fifteenth century says in one place:

> 'Malice' of women, what is yt to drede?
> They sley no men destroyen no citees!
> They not oppressen folke ne over-lede,
> Betray Empires Remes ne ducheas,
> Ne men bereve hir landes ne hir mees,
> Empusone folkys ne houses set on fire,
> Ne false contractes maken for non hire.

In this poem Hoccleve contrasts women with men and blames not Eve but the devil alone for deceiving Adam. However, this

---

[1] A Luchaire, *La Société française au temps de Philippe-Auguste*, 2nd ed., 1909, p. 379.

[2] Bede Jarrett, in *Social Theories of the Middle Ages*, 1926, chap. III, 'Women', somewhat softens the sharpness of the contradictions.

[3] R. Mohl, op. cit., pp. 20–1 and passim.

verse is not Hoccleve's own. It is a translation of Cristine de Pisan's *Epistre au dieu d'amour*. What one may suppose to have been his real feelings comes out in another poem in which he denounces the Lollards, among whom women, as in the case of similar heretics throughout Europe, found more freedom than in orthodox circles:

> Some women eeke, though hir wit be thynne,
> Wele argumentes make in holy writ.
> Lewde calates! Sittith down and spynne,
> And kakele of sum what elles, for your wit
> Is al to feeble to dispute of it.
> To clerkes gret apparteneth that aart
> The knowleche of that, God hath fro yow shit;
> Stynte and leue of for right sclendre is your paart.[4]

Whatever the ambiguities in the minds of the social theorists and the poets, most upper class women seem, as Lady Stenton has emphasized, almost entirely without political or legal rights; under the perpetual guardianship of father, guardian, or husband; and with only minimal rights to dispose of even their own inherited property.[5] The 'monstrously tough' late medieval noble dowagers with their jointure, whose looming presence K. B. Macfarlane has emphasized, may have partly modified this situation, but perhaps only in the wake of the widows of peasant society.[6] It is to peasant women, then, that we must turn to see if they too were as rightless as the high-born.

When we compare peasant women to the women of higher social class, the most important feature of their life style which affected their role as a sex was that they belonged to a working class and participated in manual agricultural labour. This is the most important general feature of their existence to bear in mind. But it is not the only one. I shall therefore consider their role as

---

[4] J. Hoccleve, *Minor Poems*, ed. F. J. Furnivall, EETS E.S. 61, no. XIX, st. 48 and no. II, st. 19.

[5] D. M. Stenton, *The English Woman in History*, 1957, pp. 29–30. cf. the comment on the status of women in medieval England by F. Joüon de Longrais: 'ce droit commun (anglais) écrase la femme plus qu'aucun droit de l'occident ne le fit jamais' *Recueils de la Société Jean Bodin XII: La Femme*, II, 1962, p. 140.

[6] K. B. McFarlane, op. cit., p. 153 and *passim*.

holders of land; as workers or producers; as participants in the socio-political community; and as independent individuals making choices about their way of life.

In the tenurial system, the predominant legal and social assumption was that normally the heads of peasant households would be male. As we know, in England manorial custom tended, whether by imitating common law or because of other social pressures, to favour succession to the holding by a single male. There were, of course, important regional exceptions which this trend was unable to overcome, but in the Midlands it is usually thought to be predominant. Even here, there were exceptions, hinting at more general former practices such as ultimogeniture at Wolverley and partible inheritance at Erdington, and perhaps Halesowen.[7] This feeling in favour of shares for all children, including females, could even operate within what seems a male primogeniture system, as we have seen at Ombersley with the splitting up of a multiple holding. The same phenomenon is found too at Broadwas in the Teme Valley at the end of the fifteenth century.[8]

But in practice, even within a male primogeniture system, the manorial records often reveal that at any given time there could be a substantial number of women tenants of full customary holdings. How do we see this? Many court rolls show a significant number of issues of holdings to women, and this could include even minors. For example at Moor in 1377, Agnes the daughter of Thomas atte Lowe took up a holding which had been surrendered by a former tenant. This was a full holding of a messuage and half yardland. It was issued to her for the usual rents and services and to be held by the custom of the manor. But since she was a minor and as yet unable to keep up (*sustentare*) the holding her father provided surety that the rents and services would be performed until she came of age; while he guaranteed to put up a building on the messuage.[9] Social custom being what it was in the medieval

[7] WD & C, E.55, Thursday after St. Mark Evangelist, 13 Henry VI; Erdington, Saturday of Michaelmas, 10 Edward III and Saturday after St. Peter in Cathedra, 24 Edward III; Birmingham Reference Library 347852 and 347854; HCR, 346331, Wednesday after Michaelmas, 27 Edward III.

[8] See above p. 41; WD & C, E.85, 4 June, 10 Henry VII.

[9] WD & C, E.29, Thursday after Deposition of St. Wolfstan, 1 Richard II.

village, female tenants very quickly got married and in the eyes of the manorial administration, and no doubt of the community, the husband became head of the household and the responsible tenant of the holding. But we may note that when a holding was issued to an unmarried woman it was often recorded in the court roll that the inheritance was to descend to her *sequela*.

Although unmarried women might not last long as tenants of holdings, widows, though in principle also marriageable, seem to have been less ephemeral as a landholding group. In 1419 a list of tenants in the dozen hamlets of Ombersley manor was drawn up.[10] According to this survey one tenant in seven was a widow, and although this may have been a high proportion it was hardly abnormal. There were two factors which put widows in a strong position. The first and most obvious is that women lived longer. But to back up this longevity there were important and well-established rights.

As compared with the common law widow's free bench of one-third of the holding, the widow's right on customary tenures was normally much greater. In some cases, as at Elmley Castle, the widow could take the whole holding for the rest of her life. In others, as at Endon in Staffordshire, she may have been entitled to two-thirds of the holding. Entitlement to half the holding is more common. We find it for instance in the manor of Tarde-bigge, covering a considerable area of Feckenham Forest, and in Wolverley in northern Worcestershire.[11] These rights would override the inheritance of adult male heirs.[12] though family arrangements could be made which would in effect imply co-tenancy. The proportion of widows in control of holdings would, of course, vary according to the strength of pressures by the lord or the community to remarry. Hence the frequent cases of a

[10] WCRO, BA. 3910.24 v, Thursday after St. Valentine martyr, 6 Henry V.

[11] WCRO, 899:95, Thursday before St. Peter in Chains, 22 Edward III; SCRO, D.1490/33/m.1 (date of court illegible), 15 Richard II; WCRO, 1188.12, Friday before St. Edmund the king, 10 Edward II; WD & C, E.28, Wednesday after St. Luke Evangelist, 50 Edward III.

[12] For example, at Wolverley in 1376, William Geralt's widow, Christina, took half of the holding, her son of full age the other half; WD & C as above in note 11.

man paying fines to the lord for permission to enter the widow and the holding.

For these reasons, rentals reflecting a situation at a particular moment often underestimated the importance of landholding by unmarried women or widows. An analysis of the movement of holdings during this period shows how seriously we must take the female tenancy. This analysis is based on the records of ten estates during the period 1350–1450 for which the evidence is sufficiently abundant, and is of the movement of holdings excluding those which for lack of heirs came into the hands of the lord and were subsequently reissued outside the family.[13] Of those holdings which remained in the family above 60 per cent went to female heiresses of whom the great majority—all except 5 per cent—were widows.

There was also, as we have briefly mentioned above, a supplementary trend in the succession to customary holdings at this time which gave extra security to widows and was analogous to the freehold jointure. This was the increasing frequency of issues of leases for at least two, most often three, and sometimes four or even five lives. The lives were those of the male tenant, his wife, and one or more offspring, not necessarily male. At the death of the tenant, the next person named in the lease came to hold for life and so on. In the conditions of the land market at this period when land rather than people was abundant, this may have seemed a better option than the acceptance of a holding under more vague customary terms. Hence we find tenants actually converting their customary holdings into leases for lives. At Bishampton, for instance, in 1392 we find nine tenants-at-will converting their

[13] The sample is as follows: Worcester bishopric estate, 1–22 Richard II; Broadway (Pershore Abbey), 8–22 Richard II and 2–14 Henry VI; Halesowen, 25 Edward III to 13 Richard II and 3 Henry IV to 6 Henry V; Evesham Abbey, a consolidated list made by the cellarer, dated 1369, but covering a number of unspecified years; Bisley (Mortimer), 27 to 29 Edward III; Bishampton (Throckmorton), 15 Richard II to 5 Henry V; Shuckborough (Shuckborough), 7 Richard II to 30 Henry VI; Ombersley (Evesham Abbey), 1 Henry V to 10 Henry V; Tardebigge (Bordesley Abbey), 10 Edward II to 11 Edward IV; Elmley Castle (Beauchamp) 21 Edward III to 24 Henry VII. The runs are not all continuous chronologically and short continuous runs (e.g. Ombersley) may give more information than longer, but patchy, runs.

holdings in order to give their wives a life interest after death.[14]

To sum up: We must not picture the widow in the late medieval village as a poor cottager or small holder on the edge of the village community but as frequently the tenant of a full holding, living an active life near the centre of things. But how central to village affairs could a widow be?

It follows that women had to manage their own holdings. It will be remembered from the earlier lecture on the peasants' economy that widows, like other tenants, often had to hire contract workers for various urgent agricultural tasks such as getting in the harvest and helping with the ploughing. Furthermore women tenants, or indeed women members of peasant households, might have to do manual tasks in the holding interchangeably with men. Let us remember the famous description of the ploughman in winter in *Pierce the Ploughmans Crede*.[15] The man is the plough-holder. He guides the plough itself as the share turns over the furrow. But ploughing was done in partnership between the holder and the driver, who was responsible, goad in hand, for driving the plough-team. This man's partner holding a long goad was his wife. It might be objected that for the poet to have the wife as plough-driver with the young children lying swaddled in the furrows was another way of emphasizing the couple's poverty, already stressed by the description of the four bony plough oxen. But a case recorded in the Ombersley court rolls for 1420 suggests that this is not the necessary explanation. The report of this case shows a gang attack on a family at work on the holding. One of the gang attacked the tenant, Henry Pleydur, whilst he was cultivating his ground; meanwhile another assaulted the daughter Christina, and cut the halter of the horse which was pulling the harrow as Christina harrowed.[16] It is evident that women were not confined to traditional womanly

---

[14] PRO, SC2.210/17, Monday after St. Mark Evangelist, 15 Richard II. Tenants are said to be holding *native* at will in this court roll, but it is clear from a list of recognitions in the court of Tuesday after the Translation of St. Thomas the martyr, 3 Henry V, that tenants-at-will were holding *secundum consuetudinem manerii*.

[15] See above, p. 22.

[16] WCRO, BA.3910.24 v. m.11, Thursday after the close of Easter, 8 Henry V.

tasks such as looking after the poultry, milking the cows, and winnowing the grain.

We have seen that one of the features of the peasant economy at this period was a certain fluidity between the role of tenant and labourer. The women members of peasant families could be engaged in a wide variety of manual tasks in agriculture, and as we have seen there were also independent women labourers who seem not to have been part of their employer's household. Let us recall the significant number of women labourers paying tax in Staffordshire in 1381. Nor should we, in this context, allow our judgement to be affected by unfavourable images derived from the exploitation of female manual labour in modern industry. The question is: were peasant women paid less than men for the same work or (which amounts to the same thing) confined to traditional low-paid female occupations? J. E. Thorold Rogers tells us that women harvest workers got the same rate of pay as men in the fifteenth century, a statement which, like all remarks by Rogers, deserves at least our respect.[17] This did not necessarily hold true at all times in the Middle Ages or in all places. E. Perroy has shown that women's wages in France were much lower than men's in the post-Black Death period, but the general economic conjuncture was very different. In France, as a result of the destructive wars, population had probably fallen less than production, whereas the opposite was the case in England.[18]

I have already indicated elsewhere that on some Leicestershire estates around 1400, countrywomen were doing the same manual jobs as men, such as haymaking, weeding, mowing, carrying corn, driving plough oxen, and breaking stones for road-mending.[19] Owing to the fact that accounts give total payments, it is not always easy to tell whether they were being paid at the same rate, but it is my impression that this was usually the case. Female reapers and binders at Minchinhampton, Gloucestershire,

[17] Op. cit., i. 274, 281; ii. 495.

[18] 'Wage Labour in France in the late Middle Ages', *EcHR*, 2nd ser. viii, 1955. Rogers makes the point that women's wages improved considerably after the Plague.

[19] *Economic Development of Some Leicestershire Estates in the Fourteenth and Fifteenth Centuries*, 1947, pp. 145–7.

in 1380 certainly got the same rates, 4*d.* a day, as the men. At nearby Avening in the same year female thatcher's labourers were paid at the same daily rate as men doing the same job in Minchinhampton.[20] But this fortunate situation certainly did not apply to all forms of hired labour. Full-time manorial servants who were female usually got less than men. Dairymaids, for example, on the Bishop of Worcester's estate got less than male servants,[21] though their situation was more equitable on the Beauchamp manor of Elmley Castle. Here the dairymaid was getting in 1366–7 a cash wage of 5*s.* a year, the same as the male ploughdriver, swineherd, and oxherd, but less than the plough-holder, carters, and shepherds (6*s.*).[22] In 1455, Humphrey Stafford of Grafton's dairy maid got 10*s.* but the comparative figures for other *famuli* are not available.[23] The difference between the inequality of male and female rates paid to full-time servants and the better situation of independent female labourers is probably due to the latter's superior bargaining position. The *famuli* of either sex in the fifteenth century were still subject to seigneurial non-economic compulsion, some of them still being chosen by the reeve from among the tenantry at the lord's demand.[24]

Peasant women are sometimes found engaged in more commercialized forms of economic activity than those already described. Manorial court litigation occasionally reveals them as village money-lenders, a badly documented though probably important element in medieval village society. Juliana Wheeler

[20] PRO, SC6.856/23. The reeve at Avening paid the seven women who were collecting straw for the thatcher 3½*d.* a day each as against the two helping the thatcher at Minchinhampton, whose sex is not specified and therefore probably male. But the auditors disallowed the 3½*d.* rate in the account. This meant that the reeve would be financially liable; either the women would already have been paid the higher rate or the reeve was fiddling the books.

[21] e.g. at Blockley in 1383–4 see note on p. 89 above. The dairymaid got 7*s.* a year and a quarter of grain every 16 weeks; the lowest-paid male servant, a shepherd, got 8*s.* a year and a quarter of grain every twelve weeks. The Hampton Lucy dairymaid got 6*s.* in 1385–6. WCRO, BA. 2636. 163, 92165.

[22] WCRO, 899:95 roll 67. More equitable in comparison with male servants, though less than at Blockley twenty years later.

[23] BM, Add.Roll.47174.

[24] e.g. at Ombersley in 1414. WCRO, BA.3910.24.v, where the tithingmen nominate one person of free and one of unfree condition to serve the abbot.

of Hagley, Worcestershire, was suing Philip Brough and his sureties for a loan of three marks in 1387 in the Halesowen manor court. Agnes Hendy at Elmley Castle in 1432 was suing another villager for 6s. 8d.[25] But these are fleeting glimpses into women's part in one aspect of the village economy, not to be compared with the genuinely entrepreneurial activity of the woman brewer of ale.

Brewing is sometimes thought of as traditional women's business, one of the most famous brewstresses of the fifteenth century being that well-known mystic from King's Lynn, Margery Kempe.[26] In fact, the records of the medieval manor are by no means unequivocal on this point. Our evidence is not entirely satisfactory, since it depends on the presentments of breaches of the assize of ale. These, however, are so regular that the amercements may safely be regarded, in effect, as licence fees. The presentments do not confirm that brewing was a separate economic activity into which women were hived off, in spite of women's prominent role. The Midland material shows that the ratio between male and female brewers fluctuated considerably. In Bromsgrove, women brewers were a small minority of the total up to the 1380s when they began to predominate.[27] By the end of the fourteenth century at Broadway the two sexes were fairly well balanced. In the early fifteenth century at Ombersley there was strong numerical predominance of males. In fourteenth- and fifteenth-century Halesowen this ratio fluctuated, with a tendency for the men to predominate by the middle of the fifteenth century.

In fact, rather than specialization by sex, we have competition between brewers irrespective of sex, a competition which was not always peaceful. In 1420, for example, Juliana Bryd of Oldbury

[25] HCR, 346366 C, Wednesday after St. Valentine, 10 Richard II; WCRO. B.A.899.95, 16 May, 10 Henry VI.

[26] S. B. Meech and H. E. Allen (eds.), *The Book of Margery Kempe*, EETS. o.s. 212, 1940, p. 9, 'one of the greatest brewers in the town of Lynn'.

[27] Bromsgrove court rolls are WCRO, BA.821. At a court of Whit week 40 Edward III, for example, there were presentments of seventeen brewers, of whom five were women; and of ten retailers of ale (*traventarii*) of whom two were women. BA. 821.2.b.8793.

broke into John Skynner's house, and out of badness (*pro pravitate*) cut down his 'alestake' (the sign that ale was for sale), an act which only makes sense in the context of competition.[28] Out of this competition emerged the big village brewers of either sex, such as that John Chater of Shuckborough whom we have already mentioned and who, in the 1380s and 1390s, was presented by the ale-tasters for illegal brewing twenty to thirty times as often as the other village brewers. Around 1400 his place was taken by his wife Alice, who brewed on a lesser scale. Another prominent brewer of the period was Margery Lacy of Ombersley, one of the four prominent brewers (the other three being men) in the second decade of the fifteenth century, out of between one and two dozen lesser rivals, male and female.

As far as their place in the economy was concerned, then, there is reason to believe that peasant women enjoyed a measure of relative independence, a better situation in their own class than was enjoyed by women of the aristocracy, or the bourgeoisie, a better situation perhaps than that of the women of early modern capitalist England. A considerable body of pleadings in the manorial courts on such matters as debt and trespass seems to have been conducted by women in their own names and only rarely through attorneys. Payments for the relaxation of suit to the manorial court were made by women as well as by male tenants, which suggests, of course, that they were liable as suitors. But at the local level, as well as further afield, the socio-political predominance of the male is obvious. Women were not heads of tithings; they did not sit on local juries; nor did they fill the office of constable or reeve.

There is an interesting exception to this general rule. In the early fifteenth century, at Halesowen, women ale-tasters were several times elected.[29] This, moreover, was in a period when male brewers predominated numerically over the female. But there may have been something special about this part of the world. In

---

[28] HCR, 346394, Wednesday after Michaelmas, 8 Henry V.
[29] e.g. HCR, 346357, Wednesday after Translation of St. Augustine, 3 Richard II; 346379, Wednesday after St. Denis, 3 Henry IV; 346392 Wednesday before St. Denis, 4 Henry V.

the Romsley rebellion of 1386, when the villagers were indicted for refusing to perform their due services, and for demanding an end to bondage, a woman was picked out as the procurer and maintainer of the rebels. This was Agnes, the wife of John Sadeler. Like the others she declined to appear before the King's justice, was outlawed and disappeared, though she—or some other woman of the same name—turns up again in the court records from the Michaelmas of 1389.[30]

The structure of peasant society in England at the turn of the fourteenth century seems to have been such that women as tenants, labourers and entrepreneurs had recognized rights within their communities. There were always severe limitations to their rights as human beings. In particular the pressures of the lord and the leading elements of the village community were still powerful in a vital area of a woman's life, whether she was a young woman or a widow. It is evident that the woman fortunate or unfortunate enough to have a legal title to a holding could still be obliged to marry. On the other hand, in this period it would seem that, provided a woman did not have a holding, or provided she was prepared to renounce it, and provided she was able to pay a licence fee or prepared to leave the manor illegally, the conditions of general mobility were perhaps especially favourable to women. At any rate, the information about mobility in the late fourteenth and early fifteenth centuries indicates a high proportion of women among those leaving their villages to seek their fortune in the towns or in other villages, with—or more often without—the men of their choice.

The evidence is uneven and inconsistent. Sometimes the lists of fugitives or legal emigrants from the manor consist entirely of men, sometimes more men than women. Sometimes it is the other way round. A consolidated list of departures from the manor of Ombersley, drawn up in 1415, has forty-four names, one-third of them being women.[31] Some of the migrants retained links with the manor by paying chevage, others did not. It is interesting that fewer of the women (just over a quarter) than of the men

---

[30] See above, p. 63.
[31] WCRO, BA.3910.24.x, court of 15 April, 3 Henry V.

stayed within the county. Most of the women went quite far, and not a few of them to towns rather than villages—Oxford, Salisbury, Bromyard, Worcester. Some details from Cleeve Prior on the Cathedral Priory estate at an earlier date provide interesting extra information. This was in the 1370s when there was quite an exodus of women from various Worcester Cathedral manors. In 1374 six women left Cleeve Prior: two were known to have gone to Worcester, one to Malvern, one went off to get married, but two of them went off with men without any indication that marriage was contemplated.[32]

The departure of these women was often clandestine and at night (*noctanter*). In some cases there seems to have been an element of family organization, as when in 1412 Adam Adams and his son Richard left the Gloucester Abbey manor of Upleadon to go to work in Gloucester, while the daughters went to live in the two villages of Over and Littleton.[33] Similarly in 1423 when John Cupper, a serf in Oxhill, died, his daughter went away to marry a man in Swalcliffe, the widow went off to Brailes to marry another man, taking with her her younger son aged twelve and her younger daughter aged eight. The only member of the family who stayed in the village was the eldest son and heir.[34]

We can have little certainty about any element of freedom of choice in marriage for women, so strong was the link between marriage and the transfer or sharing of property-rights in holdings. All the same, the impression which we have of the strength of this connection is perhaps exaggerated by our use of the manorial material which is so much concerned with the business of land tenure. M. M. Sheehan's analysis of the register of the Bishop of Ely in the late fourteenth century suggests a certain lack of rigidity in the lower-class marriage pattern, ranging from couples who live together with the intention of not marrying, to clandestine marriage which consisted simply of mutual promises before witnesses without subsequent public solemnization.[35] This analysis makes

[32] WD & C, E.25, Saturday of St. Mary Magdalen, 48 Edward III.
[33] GCRO, D936a. M.4, Monday after St. Leonard, 14 Henry IV.
[34] PRO.SC2. 207/59, Friday after Discovery of Holy Cross, 1 Henry VI.
[35] 'Formation and Stability of Marriage in 14th Century England', *Medieval Studies*, xxxiii, 1971.

less surprising the examples we find in the manorial records of women who leave in the company of men without reference to marriage. Associations outside marriage within the village are naturally rarer, and references to such in the manorial records are few. But two examples may be quoted from our court rolls. One is from the village of Sedgebarrow in 1376. The lord (the Prior of Worcester) instructed John Cayn to marry a certain widow. In fact they did sleep together, but Cayn refused to marry and left the lordship with his goods. He was promised the lord's grace and returned, but left again, unwilling to accept the lord's grace, the price of which was presumably marriage with the widow.[36] The other example shows initiative by a woman tenant and suggests that behind the conventional phraseology describing men fining with the lord to acquire a wife and a holding there might be a more complicated story. Isabel Edmond, a tenant in Cleeve Prior, took a lover, Richard Wodeland (*receptat Ricardum Wodeland in amplexu concubinario*). Richard then paid a fine to marry and to hold her land. The banns were pronounced and no impediment to the marriage was found so the court pronounced that they should marry within the month or lose their holding (*messuagium et terram que tenent*—notice the plural.)[37]

The situation I have described can be taken as true for peasant women only at a particular period in the history of English rural society. It would be dangerous to extend it beyond the century after the Black Death, though comparison with the previous and succeeding periods would be illuminating. The ruling ideas of the medieval world as they affected the position of women were deeply influenced by the social and tenurial relations of a feudal society as well as by the statements about the role of women attributed to Saint Paul. These ideas worked strongly against equality between men and women, and it is against their prohibitive influence that we must see such relative gains which peasant women may have made.

If there were relatively favourable conditions for peasant

---

[36] WD & C, E.28, Thursday after Epiphany. 50 Edward III.
[37] Ibid., E.30, Wednesday before the Translation of St. Thomas, 2 Richard II.

women during this period, the uncertainties in the evidence from which we draw these conclusions are matched by uncertainties as to the reasons for this situation. It might be argued, as Lady Stenton has done, that the greater freedom of all women in the Old English period (for which the evidence is mainly from the aristocracy) continued among the lower class of English society after 1066, when the women of the aristocracy were more and more subordinated to their feudal lords and husbands. But this is to assume what is not by any means necessarily the case,[38] that before the middle of the fourteenth century peasant women were as relatively well off as they were in the period which concerns us. An alternative explanation to that which assumes the continuation of Old English freedom in the peasant class is that women benefited in the post-1350 period from the same demographic and economic conditions which permitted a temporary improvement in the conditions of all peasant tenants and all labouring men.

An illustrative footnote to this explanation may be taken from the Gloucestershire manor of Painswick in the Cotswolds.[39] In 1442, the widows of Painswick cried out against the lord of the manor, John Talbot, Earl of Shrewsbury. He had taken sixteen Painswick tenants to the war in France with him, of whom only five had returned. The women complained of losing not only their husbands but their holdings. As a result of this outcry an inquest was summoned and the women were given the right to their husbands' holdings for life—a right which, as we have seen, widows on many manors already enjoyed—as well as the freedom to choose a second husband. But in fact this settlement in favour of the widows was part of a wider settlement, one which covered a whole range of grievances concerning demesne leases, rents, and services. The upshot was entirely in the interests of the tenants; and in fact the agreement could well be seen in the context of those favourable settlements on the Worcester bishopric, Beauchamp and Syon Abbey estates to which I have already referred. Peasant women's gains went in step with the gains of the whole of

[38] D. M. Stenton, op. cit.
[39] S. Rudder, *A New History of Gloucestershire*, 1779, pp. 593–4.

their class; and as we may guess from the stories of Agnes Sadeler of Romsley and of the Painswick widows they may have occasionally been in the forefront of the agitations which, for a time at any rate, benefited all.

RELATED STUDIES

# VII

# Social Structure of
# Rural Warwickshire in the Middle Ages*

THE term social structure means, when it is applied to medieval society, exactly the same as when we apply it to the society of our own time. It means the relationship of men in society to each other. And since no society consists simply of a collection of individuals, making haphazard contact like the atoms of the early Greek philosophers, human relationships are defined according to the group or class into which individuals are born, or occasionally climb.

The class structure of medieval society was no secret to the thinkers or the practical men of the day. The philosophers and theologians in the schools and the lawyers in the courts recognized the division of their world (according to their individual stand-point), into two, three, or more main groups. The more academic thinkers pictured society as if it were the human body. Some theorists likened the head, controlling the rest of the limbs, to the king, the hands to the nobility, the feet to the toiling peasantry. There were many variations on this theme. Others, less fanciful, tersely divided society into those who fight, those who pray, and those who work in order to keep the fighters and the prayers alive. For the lawyer, the crucial division in society was between the free and the unfree. Whatever the subtleties and analogies however, there emerges always the picture, in this predominantly agrarian society, of a ruling landowning aristocracy whose members might be laymen or ecclesiastics, supported by a vast peasant population, whose surplus product, in various forms of rent, was transferred to the use of the aristocracy. It was not until the later Middle Ages that the theorists were obliged to take

* First published as an Occasional Paper of the Dugdale Society, no. 9, 1950.

notice of merchants and town artisans, and they were not altogether happy in their attempts to fit them into the picture.
Nevertheless, their picture, however schematic, was by and large
correct, as far as the main outlines are concerned. But we do not
get very far in the understanding of history if we do not go beyond
the main outlines. It is one of the major justifications for the
activities of local historians that they fill in the details and make
the modifications which are essential components of the historical
truth, to which we seek to approximate, even if in the nature of
things it is something that we can never achieve.

In writing about the social structure of medieval Warwickshire,
I am obliged both by the limitations of my own knowledge, and
the space at my disposal, to confine myself to a comparatively
restricted period of time. Most of my remarks will refer to the
second half of the thirteenth century. The reason why I have
chosen to concentrate on this period is that there is in existence a
remarkable document of the year 1279 which illustrates the theme
of my paper. This document is a contemporary transcript of the
Hundred Rolls of that year for the hundreds of Stoneleigh and
Kineton. It is a book of 113 folios and is kept in the Public Record
Office.[1] Unlike the majority of the extant hundred rolls for this
year[2] it has not been printed. Like the printed rolls it embodies a
very full description of the obligations and privileges of all classes
of rural society—even, I may say, of one urban society, for it
contains a complete list of all the burgage holders of the town of
Warwick. The great majority of the hamlets and villages of the two
hundreds are described in full, and the only limitation to a complete record is that the writing on some of the folios is now illegible.

With such a full record, even if for only part of the county, I
thought it suitable to concentrate my examination of other evidences illustrating the social structure of the county, in the main,
to the same period. I shall, however, illustrate some of the arguments in my paper with materials of the two succeeding centuries,
indicating where necessary any limitations on conclusions drawn
from sources of different date.

[1] Exchequer KR Misc. Bks., no. 15.
[2] *Rotuli Hundredorum*, Record Commission, 1818, vol. ii.

I shall begin my description of Warwickshire's social structure with some consideration of the lay and ecclesiastical nobility. In modern times, social attitudes differ in a region where large-scale industry and monopoly conditions of ownership predominate, as compared with regions where industry is small-scale and where ownership is divided among many entrepreneurs. Making allowances for the great differences between an agrarian and an industrial society, we can say that similar considerations are important in the Middle Ages. A region which is dominated by a few big and powerful landowners will differ in many respects from one in which landownership is on a smaller scale, in which there is a comparatively large number of medium-sized estates, and in which, consequently, there are no great concentrations of political and economic power.

It should be noted that, as in all societies, political and economic power go hand in hand. But there are important modifications that must be made to too simple an equation of the political and economic power of a feudal baron in any given region. The most influential lord in any area of the medieval world will tend of course to be he who owns in that area many manors whose daily activities are controlled by his own officials. If we read the inquisition *post mortem*[3] of any medieval tenant-in-chief we find that the jurors summoned by the king's escheator to assess the dead man's estate will describe in great detail those manors which he held in demesne as of fee.[4] They will describe the annual value of his manor house, his gardens, his orchards, his dovecot, his land, meadow, or pasture, as well as the rents owed by his free and villein tenants. The demesne manors were those of which the great man was the immediate lord. They represented the main source of his income. In addition, it was in them that he was in the closest contact with all classes of the country population. From time to time he would come to stay in the manor house. His bailiff and his steward would be even more constantly in the fore-

[3] These are summarized in the *Calendar of Inquisitions*, published by H. M. Stationery Office, 1904–52. The details of the manorial extents contained in inquisitions *post mortem* are not given in the Calendars, but the existence of such extents is always indicated.

[4] That is, kept in his own hands and descending to his heirs, lineal and collateral.

front of the peasant's life, as collectors of rent and as the enforcer of labour discipline.

It is well known, however, that a medieval honour or barony did not only consist of those manors which the lord held in demesne, that is in immediate ownership and control. William the Conqueror and his immediate successors granted huge estates to the Norman, French, Breton, and Flemish nobles who had shared the enterprise of the conquest. A large number of the manors and other lands on those estates were then enfeoffed to military followers who in return made up the quota, or part of the quota, of armed knights owed by the tenant-in-chief to the crown. So in any given county a mighty baron would hold some of his manors in demesne. Others—probably a greater number—would be held by military tenants as knight's fees, that is in return for military service. The effective lord, as far as the peasantry was concerned, of the enfeoffed manor, was not the great lord, but his military tenant. Through the military tenants, the great lord would of course wield great social and political influence, particularly among the upper strata of feudal society. But by the period with which we are most concerned, the end of the thirteenth century, the close bond between baron and military tenant had been much loosened as a result of the collapse of the original organization of the feudal host. Knight's fees had been subdivided through inheritance, and various forms of alienation, so that the tie between holders of knight's fees and their lord was largely financial.[5] As far as local influence was concerned, the immediate control of manors held in demesne, with the social and political control of persons through the manorial and franchise courts, was much more important than lordship over a larger number of fragmented knight's fees.

The three biggest estates in Warwickshire at the time of Domesday Book (1086) were those of the Abbey of Coventry, of the Count of Meulan, and of Turchil of Warwick.[6] The two

[5] The writings on this subject have recently been summed up by Mr. Sidney Painter in his *Studies in the History of the English Feudal Barony*, 1943.

[6] *The Victoria County History of Warwickshire*, vol. i, 1904 contains a translation of the Warwickshire section of Domesday Book with an introduction by J. H. Round.

great lay estates, those of the Count and of Turchil, were soon to be united to form the estate of the first Earl of Warwick. These lay estates are an interesting contrast to that of the Abbey. The Abbey had 18 manors in demesne, that is under its direct control, and only one held by a tenant. The Count of Meulan held 24 manors in demesne, and 43 were enfeoffed to tenants. Turchil held only 6 in demesne, while 63 were enfeoffed. It is probable that in the history of Warwickshire it was the smaller, but more permanent and more closely knit estate of the Abbot (later Prior) of Coventry that exercised the greater influence on the lower ranks of Warwickshire rural society.[7] The contrast is even more pointed when we consider the structure of the estate of the early fourteenth-century successor of Turchil and the Count of Meulan, Guy de Beauchamp, Earl of Warwick, who died in 1315.[8] At his death, Guy had 10 manors in demesne in Warwickshire. In addition, 58 military tenants, some great, some quite insignificant, were holding from him 97 separate knight's fees, scattered over 110 Warwickshire villages and hamlets. Only 28 of these fees were full knight's fees. The rest were fractions, many less than half a fee, one even a forty-second of a fee. We must realize that whatever influence the Earl of Warwick had over these feudal tenants his effective power over the humbler members of the Warwickshire community was mainly exercised in the ten manors held in demesne. Here he was the arbiter of the most vital issues of medieval rural life—the exaction of rent, of labour service, and of the incidents of villeinage. This is not to forget of course his influence as a great and wealthy magnate in the county and hundred courts, or over the assizes and the many administrative and judicial commissions which ran through this much-governed country. This concerned principally the freeholders—certainly an important class in Warwickshire as I shall show.

If the immediate economic interests of so great a man as the Earl of Warwick affected only the communities of ten manors in the county, it should not surprise us to find that other working

---

[7] The best evidence for this is in the as yet unpublished Coventry Priory Cartulary, PRO, Exchequer KR Misc. Bks., no. 21.

[8] *Calendar of Inquisitions*, v, no. 615.

estates were of more modest dimensions. It is possible to give some figures illustrating this point. Let us consider the tenants-in-chief of the Crown in Warwickshire in the reigns of Henry III and Edward I. This is admittedly a somewhat arbitrarily chosen class. A tenant-in-chief could be a humble holder in serjeanty with a mere yardland or two to his name, whereas an under-tenant holding all his land mediately and not directly from the Crown could be of baronial status socially. However, by the end of the thirteenth century the royal escheators tended to investigate the landed possessions of all men of consequence who died in their bailiwick, so that in practice an analysis of the inquisitions *post mortem* for a county gives a good guide, if not a complete answer, to the problem of the size of the holdings of the county nobility.[9]

Fifty-eight inquisitions into Warwickshire estates have survived from the reigns of Henry III and Edward I, representing information about 46 estates,[10] and of these 46 estates just under half (21 to be precise) represent the whole, or the greater part of the owners' landed property in England. These men, in other words, were real Warwickshire gentry with no, or few, interests outside the county. Yet none of them was a great magnate *within* the county. Most of them held only three complete manors, or less, in demesne with scattered lands and rents in perhaps one or two other villages. Only one held as many as five manors, and this was John de Montfort, grandson of the Peter who was killed at Evesham fighting for his more famous namesake, Simon. These Montforts, like the Ardens, the Oddingsels, and the Wavers, were important people in the Warwickshire of the period, but they were not great magnates such as one finds in some other English counties.

The other twenty-five Warwickshire estates described in the inquisitions *post mortem* belonged to lords who held the greater part of their landed property outside the county. The majority

[9] I have used for the purposes of the following analysis vols. i–iv of the *Calendar of Inquisitions.*

[10] The information about estates the heirs to which also died in the period covered is of course duplicated. There are, for example, three inquisitions on earls of Warwick during the period—John de Plessetis, 47 Henry III; William Mauduit, 52 Henry III; William Beauchamp, 26 Edward I. *Cal. Inqu.* i, 558, 679; iii, 477.

of these, too, were holders of only four manors or less in Warwickshire, and consequently cannot be imagined to have had a
dominating influence on the economic and social life of the
county. Some of them, like the Marmions and the Langleys,
were important Midland figures, but in no position to determine
the social or economic life of Warwickshire.

Many important Warwickshire families of the late thirteenth
century do not appear in the inquisitions *post mortem*.[11] This limits
the value of figures derived from this class of evidence. But in
fact the indication in the inquisitions as to the general character of
the Warwickshire nobility is borne out in further investigations
of evidence about this class. A careful collation of the information
compiled by Sir William Dugdale, an unrivalled genealogist, who
had access to much evidence now lost, confirms our conclusions
about the modest to middling status of these landowners.[12] The
thirty-odd members of the Warwickshire nobility and gentry who
suffered royal disapproval because of their support for Simon de
Montfort provide more supplementary evidence.[13] In 1265 their
estates were surveyed and valued by royal command, and in no
case do we find a man holding more than two or three manors,
with perhaps a few scattered rents, in the county. The wealthiest
of them, Henry of Hastings, was undoubtedly of baronial status,[14]
but in Warwickshire, at any rate, he only had two manors and
lands in three or four villages. It may of course be objected that
evidence of the landed holdings of the rebels of 1265 is invalid for
the point I am making, since Simon de Montfort had by the
Battle of Evesham lost much of his support from the magnates. It

---

[11] This may only be partly due to the fact that some of the families did not hold
in chief. There are other reasons for the non-survival of inquisitions, apart from
the fact that escheators did not always take an inquisition where necessary.

[12] *The Antiquities of Warwickshire*, 1730 edn. (two volumes). I have discovered no
evidence here to contradict that which I present from other sources. The manner
in which Dugdale presents family history does not, however, permit the construction of statistics covering a limited range of years such as I have derived from the
inquisitions *post mortem*.

[13] *Calendar of Inquisitions, Miscellaneous*, 1916, i, 927–31.

[14] He was a grandson of the Earl of Huntingdon and father of a claimant to the
Scottish crown. See Sir Maurice Powicke's account of his career in *King Henry III
and the Lord Edward*, 1947.

may therefore be argued that the rebels of 1265 are not representative of the county nobility. The evidence can, however, be used to the contrary effect. Is it not significant that a leader who in his last months was appealing so much to the support of the middle and lower strata of the nobility should have received so much support in Warwickshire, in which, as I have indicated from other evidence, this very element was numerically so important?

From the point of view of the estates in their immediate possession the ecclesiastical corporations were undoubtedly the most important Warwickshire landowners. The pre-Conquest Benedictine house of Coventry was the wealthiest of these and apart from scattered lands, rents, and appropriate churches, possessed between fifteen and twenty manors in the county. The Augustinian canonry of Kenilworth was second in importance, and nearly twice as wealthy as the next, the Cistercian Abbey of Combe.[15] I do not propose to discuss in any detail the landed estates of the religious houses, but an important point must be made, for it relates to the general subject of our discussions. We are interested in the extent to which large-scale landed property affected the social structure of the county. Two special factors are relevant here. The first is the age of any large and well-organized estate. Lay estates tended to be split up among heirs, or to be alienated piecemeal. This instability applied less to the estates of undying corporations. Consequently, old-established monastic estates influenced greatly the social structure of their region, especially as regards the enserfment of the peasantry. This is strikingly illustrated by the records of manorial life in East Anglia, the Severn valley, and the south of England, which were strongholds of the great wealthy monastic establishments, some dating back to the tenth century and beyond. But Coventry (founded 1043) was the only comparable establishment in Warwickshire and it was in the second rank of the older-established Benedictine

[15] The materials I use for a quick estimate of the relative wealth of the religious houses are the *Taxatio Ecclesiastica*, 1291, and the *Valor Ecclesiasticus*, iii (Record Commission 1802 and 1817), together with the somewhat unsatisfactory summaries of the histories of the religious houses in *V.C.H.*, *Warwickshire*, ii, 1908.

houses.[16] The date of foundation of the majority of Warwickshire monasteries was round about the middle of the twelfth
century when the social structure of feudal England had become
fixed in its main outlines.

It should also be noted that the type of property of the majority
of the religious houses was such as not to affect existing social
relations drastically. It is true that the Priory of Coventry and the
Abbey of Kenilworth, earliest in foundation, were manorial lords
whose decisions as to how the manorial economy was to be
organized would affect the lives of many village communities.
But the Cistercian and Augustinian houses, with the exception
of Stoneleigh, whose impact on the upper Avon valley was more
positive,[17] tended to build up their estates piecemeal from small
parcels of land and from the glebes of appropriated parsonages.
They fitted themselves into the existing social structure rather than
dominated it.

From this general survey of the economic and social position
of the Warwickshire nobility, lay and ecclesiastical, we may draw
some conclusions not only about the nobility but about the lower
ranks of society as well. At the end of the thirteenth century we
have seen that no great lay or ecclesiastical lords were in a position
of sufficient economic pre-eminence to mould the social structure
of the county, or even of part of it. Furthermore, it would seem
that in earlier centuries too, the most stable class of landowners,
the ecclesiastical corporations, did not have the large estates under
their control which similar organizations had elsewhere. This
means that seigneurial pressure on the peasantry, both in the early
period before the conquest when the landed aristocracy was
forming itself, and during the thirteenth-century agricultural
boom, would be divided rather than concentrated. Even before

[16] Its gross general income on the eve of the Dissolution was £753. Compare
this with Worcester Priory (£1,445); Evesham (£1,313); St. Peter's, Gloucester
(£1,744); Ramsay (£1,849); Canterbury Priory (£1,762); Glastonbury (£3,642);
Abingdon (£1,876); St. Albans (£2,909). A Savine, *English Monasteries on the
Eve of the Dissolution*, 1909, Appendix.

[17] It appears that the transfer of the Cistercians of Radmore to Stoneleigh
resulted in some evictions of freeholders 'to the end that these Monks should
have Stoneley intire'. W. Dugdale, op. cit., 256. Dugdale quotes the Stoneleigh
Leger Book. f. 11a.

examining the actual evidence concerning peasant obligations, we might guess that these conditions would be favourable to a comparative degree of economic freedom and to a comparatively low level of rents, whether in labour, money, or kind.

There is a further factor in the development of medieval Warwickshire which must have been influential in determining the county's social structure. It is well known that as late as the sixteenth century the Arden country north of the River Avon was different geographically and socially from the southern part of the county, known to the topographers as the Felden.[18] The south was more populous. The typical settlement was the nucleated village, and the field system was the regular two- or three-field system characteristic of the greater part of midland and southern England. In the Arden country there was still much of the ancient woodland untouched. Settlements tended to be more scattered, in isolated homesteads or small hamlets. Although there was some open-field cultivation, enclosures were much more common than in the south of the county.

These differences were undoubtedly due to the uneven development of the original settlement. Whilst place-names reveal that there were a few early Anglian settlements in the north of the county coming from the Trent valley, they also show that the most intensive early settlement was in the south, resulting from a double penetration from the Severn valley and from the east. Early settlement in considerable numbers resulted in early clearance of the forest. Furthermore, early settlement tended to be communal in character and resulted in the sort of village community where collective outweighed individual farming—as in the typical open-field village. Another consequence of early intensive settlement was that in those areas where it took place, social differentiation between the aristocratic landowner and the working peasant established itself most firmly. We must expect to find therefore that the normal characteristics of manorial life

[18] John Leland was the first to make this distinction familiar in his *Itinerary in England* (ed. L. Toulmin Smith, 1906, ii, p. 47), though not using the term 'Felden'. The subject is discussed in the introduction to *The Place Names of Warwickshire*, ed. Gover, Mawer, and Stenton, 1936.

will be more common in south Warwickshire than in the Arden country.

Judging by the evidence of place-names and of charters record-ing land transfers, the penetration of the Arden forest did not take place on any scale until the twelfth century. The twelfth-century monastic foundations were of course an important part of this economic movement. By this time the clearance of the woodland was not so much the work of peasant communities as of indi-viduals of varying social status. Because the clearance was indi-vidual rather than collective, enclosure was more common than open cultivation. And the movement seems to have had social as well as economic consequences. The twelfth century was a period of rising population.[19] Younger sons were leaving the old-established agricultural settlements because there was no room on the family holding, and no more virgin soil available for colonization within the township boundary. When these younger sons came to an uncolonized area such as the Arden country, they would not reveal that they were of villein status at home. And perhaps the local lords, particularly the newly founded monastic houses, were not anxious to insist on a knowledge of their new tenants' status, being concerned rather to obtain willing hands to fell the trees and open up new areas of cultivation. Here then would be another factor making for comparative freedom in the legal status of the peasant population.

So far most of my statements about the condition of the peasan-try have been inferences from what can be said with some cer-tainty about the economic and social status of the nobility and about the development of settlement. It is now time to test these inferences against direct documentary evidence of peasant status. The Hundred Rolls of 1279 are the best possible evidence at our disposal for this purpose, not only for the end of the thirteenth century, but perhaps for the whole medieval period. The reason for this is that the Hundred Rolls describe all the landholders of

---

[19] This was a European phenomenon, commented on by such historians of economic and social development as Professors Henri Pirenne (*Economic and Social History of Medieval Europe*, 1936) and Marc Bloch (*Caractères originaux de l'histoire rurale française*, 1927).

the village, whereas the vast majority of documents illustrative of local history describe the landholders of the manor. The manor, as is well known, was not necessarily coincident with the village. One village might contain several manors. On the other hand one manor might include the whole, or parts of several villages. Furthermore, the average manorial rental or survey is only concerned with those tenants holding directly of the lord of the manor. It is not concerned with the many sub-tenants who were in some, though not in all villages, quite a numerous and important section of the population. It is perhaps the greatest value of the Hundred Rolls, drawn up from the evidence of local juries under the supervision of royal officials, that they give us a unique glimpse under the surface of the official village community.[20]

The division of the evidence in the Hundred Rolls as between the Stoneleigh and Kineton Hundreds does not necessarily coincide with the geographical division between the Arden and the Felden country. There is now, in fact, no generally accepted dividing line between the two areas. Modern geographers appear not to agree with the topographers of the sixteenth and seventeenth centuries for whom the River Avon marked the frontier. According to one opinion, the physical southern limit of the Arden forest coincides with the Lower Lias escarpment several miles south of the Avon. According to another, the whole of the Avon valley shares the characteristics of the Felden country. It is not, however, the soil alone which determines the pattern of settlement. Man does not merely fit into nature's pattern, he also imposes his own pattern upon her. Most important, therefore, as far as the character of the settlement is concerned, is its date, and consequently the form of the settlers' social organization. To lay down a rigid frontier between two areas differentiated as much by the tempos of reclamation and settlement as by varieties of soil is impossible.

Yet Kineton Hundred for the most part can certainly be identified topographically with the Felden, and the northern half

---

[20] There is a valuable discussion of the Hundred Rolls as historical evidence by Professor E. A. Kosminsky, in his *Studies in the Agrarian History of England in the Thirteenth Century*, 1956.

at least of Stoneleigh Hundred with the Arden country. A comparison of the two hundreds will therefore usefully illustrate both differences and similarities between the two regions, especially if the curious tongue of the Stoneleigh Hundred, extending south of the River Leam, is allowed for. We have also to bear in mind that the real heart of the Arden country was north of the hundred of Stoneleigh, and consequently I shall use later evidence from the Arden country proper to reinforce any conclusions drawn from the evidence of the Hundred Rolls.[21]

I propose first to offer some statistics from the Hundred Rolls as to the relative proportions of the different classes in the villages, leaving out the manorial lords. I divide them for the sake of effective comparison into free tenants, villein or servile tenants, and small holders. There are minuter sub-divisions within these classes which I propose to ignore for the purposes of this paper. The free tenants were those members of the village community, who though not normally *economically* superior to the unfree villagers, enjoyed a superiority of legal status. They could leave the village if they wished to do so. They could buy, sell, and otherwise alienate their land. They were entitled to the legal protection of the royal courts. Their rent was usually low or even nominal. They did not normally owe more than a few token seasonal labour services to their lord, and most often none at all. They could not be arbitrarily tallaged, and were not subject to the many irritating and financially onerous incidents of villeinage. On the other hand, their legal freedom did not free them from poverty and starvation. If they had not much land, and crops failed they were subject to the same disadvantages as the villein.

The villein tenants were those members of the community whose status I have described by implication in listing those bur-

---

[21] The percentage figures of social classes in the two hundreds are given below (pp. 126, 127). The figures in brackets show the relative proportions when the villages in that part of the Stoneleigh Hundred south of the Leam (Offchurch, Whitnash, Radford Semele, Harbury, and Bishop's Itchington) have been subtracted from Stoneleigh and added to Kineton Hundred. Two different views on the Arden Forest southern boundary will be found in 'The Early Historical Geography of the Forest of Arden' by Miss P. A. Nicklin, in *Transactions of the Birmingham and Midland Archaeological Society* lvi, 1932, and in Professor R. H. Kinvig's contribution to the *British Association Handbook*, 1950.

dens to which the free tenant was not subject. The obligation to perform labour services, to pay tallage, and to submit to the many degrading forms of control exercised by the lord over the unfree were the main features of their condition. But as we shall see there were many variations in their condition, and some were not only wealthier than the free tenants but subject to hardly more exacting forms of exploitation. The small holders were a class whose name describes their place in village society. Most often they were officially named *cottagers*, but to the cottagers I have added those not so named who only held one or two acres of land. What is important about them is that they had not enough land to keep themselves and their families alive, and therefore had to supplement their income from their holdings by working as craftsmen or as agricultural labourers. The fact that many of them were of 'free' status could hardly have alleviated the wretchedness of their conditions.

In Stoneleigh Hundred, 50 per cent (52 per cent) of the landholding population were free tenants, 27 per cent (23 per cent) were villeins or serfs, and 23 per cent (25 per cent) were small holders. These figures are very revealing, especially for a midland county west of the Danelaw boundary. It is possible that I have exaggerated the number of free tenants. The reason for this is that the free tenants are a very complex class, many of whom hold from other free tenants. Consequently, there is a great risk of counting one tenant holding, let us say, three separate lots of land, three times.[22] But even allowing for possibilities of error, the proportion of free tenants is very high and confirms the inferences I have made about the effects of the twelfth-century expansion into the forest on the one hand, and the comparatively light yoke of the landowning nobility on the other. It suggests that racial influence, sometimes used as the principal reason for the large number of free tenants in the Danish settled east of England, is of secondary importance to economic and environmental factors.

The other remarkable feature shown by these figures is the large number of small holders. We must picture the core of the

[22] The total of free tenants also includes money-rent paying tenants who, while not designated 'liberi tenentes', are certainly not serfs or villeins.

village or hamlet community as being composed of a group of free or villein tenants holding from between a third to a whole yardland, say 10 to 30 acres of arable with meadow, pasture, and common rights appurtenant. Leaving aside for a moment the occasional richer free tenant—or even villein—with 50 or more arable acres, the rest of the community would consist of cottagers, squatters on the waste, or acre-holders, some of free and some of villein status. This is an economically very important class, especially for the future. From it came the wage labour employed by manorial lords, and also by the wealthier peasants who were only just beginning to be a socially significant group in rural England. It is also possible, though this requires proof, that the poor small holders of the forests of north Warwickshire, east Worcestershire, and south Staffordshire were the first recruits to the as yet embryo midland metal industry.[23]

The figures for the various classes in Kineton Hundred provide an interesting comparison. These figures are not as comprehensive as those for Stoneleigh Hundred, for some pages of the volume are illegible. It is unlikely, however, that those missing would drastically affect the figures if they were legible. The free tenants were 30 per cent (21 per cent) of the population, the villeins or serfs were 46 per cent (47 per cent), and the small holders of various categories were 24 per cent (22 per cent). I have already mentioned that the conditions which produced earlier settlement in the south of the county would also result in more complete manorialization, meaning a more complete reduction of the peasant population to serfdom in the interests of demesne farming by the lords. This is known by the fact that there were 20 per cent more serfs or villeins in Kineton than in the Stoneleigh Hundred. I shall show in a moment that there were greater demands in the south for labour services from the villeins than in the Stoneleigh Hundred. But before we come to this, it should be noticed that in spite of the higher proportion of servile tenants in Kineton

[23] Worcestershire inquisitions post mortem and Warwickshire and Worcestershire feet of fines are types of evidence which reveal to us, in the later Middle Ages, the sort of specialization in iron-smelting and working which we would expect in a forest area where fuel was abundant.

Hundred, the proportion of free tenants was still quite high. Generally speaking, we can say that for the whole of this area peasant conditions were much freer than in many parts of the country. This conclusion is reinforced by another calculation made by the Soviet historian, Professor Kosminsky.[24] He calculates, for both hundreds, the relative value of peasant rents in labour and kind, and peasant rents in money. He finds that 70 per cent of rent was paid in money. This is a remarkable figure when we remember that at this time over England as a whole, the demand for servile labour was at its height.

We now come to consider the sort of labour services which peasants were obliged to perform on the lord's demesne (home farm) as part of their rent, the weight of which was held to indicate the degree of their servility. This is not an easy matter to illustrate satisfactorily and briefly in figures. When I say that in a certain village heavy labour services were performed, this may conceal the fact that some of the inhabitants of that village did not owe those heavy services. At the real risk of concealment of this sort, I nevertheless propose to mention figures of villages, and the sort of labour rents or otherwise that peasants in them were liable to pay. I divide the labour services into three general categories. First, light services, which were often owed by freemen as well as by villeins. Examples are the day and a half mowing and haymaking services annually owed by the villeins of the Templars at Cubbington. Second are seasonal services. These were often quite heavy services which lords demanded of their villeins at peak periods of the agricultural year, especially in August, and September. They are described in the Hundred Rolls in great detail, and include ploughing, harrowing, hoeing, reaping, haymaking, carrying, and other services. These services might amount to twenty or thirty days a year performed by the tenant, or someone in his place. Thirdly, there was week-work. This was the heaviest sort of labour service and was often considered by lawyers to be the true hallmark of servility. The tenant was obliged to work himself, or provide labour, for a fixed number of

[24] Op. cit. His very full statistical analysis of the evidence of the Hundred Rolls confirms the figures given in this paper.

days per week throughout the year, apart from other specified services. Tenants at Tysoe holding half a yardland from the Baron Stafford owed 10 labour-days a week from Michaelmas to 24 June; 12 labour-days a week from 24 June to 1 August; and 10 labour-days a week from 1 August to Michaelmas.

Out of 45 villages and hamlets in Stoneleigh Hundred, no labour services at all were owed in 18; only light services were performed in 12; seasonal works in 13; and week-work in only 2. Clearly in this area, whatever might have been the incidence of money rent and other money exactions, demands for servile labour were remarkably moderate. The picture is, as we should expect, somewhat different in Kineton Hundred. Out of 48 villages and hamlets in this area, no labour services were owed in 10; light services were performed in 8; seasonal works in 22; and week-work in 8. There is a distinctly heavier demand for labour services in the south of the county. Nevertheless, compared with other parts of the country, such as parts of Gloucestershire controlled by St. Peter's Abbey, the amount of rent demanded in the form of forced, unpaid labour, was not great.

I have already mentioned that other forms of evidence of the fourteenth and fifteenth centuries reinforce some of the conclusions to which a study of the Hundred Rolls brings us, both as regards the prevalence of free tenure and the lightness of labour services. The inquisition *post mortem* of Guy Beauchamp who died in 1315[25] gives us information about the proportionate value of free and servile rents on Guy's demesne manors. It is noteworthy that on the manors of Brailes and Lighthorne in the south, and Sherbourne in the Avon valley, servile rents predominated over free in ratios varying from 2:1 to 15:1. On the other hand, on the mainly Arden manors of Tanworth, Haseley, Beausale, Claverdon, and Sutton Coldfield free rents predominated over servile in ratios varying from 2:1 to 4:1. Similarly, while the serfs of Brailes owed much of their rent in the form of weekly labour, in Haseley and Beausale no labour services were owed, and in the other Arden manors the serfs paid between 50 per cent and 80 per cent of their rent in money.

[25] PRO, Chancery Inquisitions Post Mortem, Ed. II, file 49.

A mid-fifteenth-century rental of the manor of Tanworth confirms this impression.[26] Out of a total of 69 tenants, 53 were freeholders. A rental of about the same date describing the agricultural tenures of 35 tenants of the Catesbys in Henley-in-Arden shows that they were all freeholders.[27] A rental of the manor of Erdington of 1463[28] describes 75 tenements, 28 of which are specifically described as freehold. Of the rest only one is stated to be held by customary, that is originally villein, tenure, and the majority were probably freehold. I believe that further investigations into medieval conditions of tenure in north Warwickshire would show the same predominance of freehold. This phenomenon has already been noticed by Professor Gill in north Warwickshire towns and villages in the sixteenth and seventeenth centuries.[29] The reasons for it, I suggest, are to be sought in the conditions of four to eight centuries earlier.

I do not propose, in this paper, to describe the technical peculiarities of the north Warwickshire field systems.[30] These local departures from the general system of open-field agriculture are not unconnected with the social conditions of the peasant population, for both derive from the same special causes. In conclusion, I shall return for a few moments to the Hundred Rolls of 1279 in order to show how extremely complex the legal and social structure of many medieval villages was.

One aspect of this complexity results from the high proportion of free tenements in Warwickshire. Since free tenants had (except in certain special cases) the right of the free alienation of their land, many sub-tenancies in free land tended to be created. This was an inevitable consequence not only of the potential freedom of movement of free land, but of economic incentives. In the late thirteenth century there was a brisk market in agricultural produce. This produced a brisk market in land. So we find on the one hand an accumulation of large free tenancies, and on the other

---

[26] In the repository of archives at Shakespeare's Birthplace, Stratford-on-Avon, not yet catalogued.
[27] W. Cooper, *Henley in Arden*, 1946, pp. 170–2.
[28] Birmingham Reference Library, MS. 347913.
[29] C. Gill, *Studies in Midland History*, 1930, pp. 131, 185.
[30] See Appendix.

the reletting of sub-tenancies by these large freeholders. An example of the complicated situation which resulted, and which the Government attempted to remedy by the statute of *Quia Emptores Terrarum*[31] is found at Halford on the Stour. Margery de Cantilupe was lady of this village, holding it of the Earl of Warwick as a knight's fee. There was no manorial demesne, but there were a large number of tenants and sub-tenants. No fewer than sixteen persons were interposed as lords between the lady of the manor and a large number of sub-tenants. In addition many of these small lords were also themselves sub-tenants. Nicholas of Halford is a good example. He held two-thirds of a virgate of the Hospital of Grafton, two cottages of William Dasset, and a virgate of a certain Master Guy. But Nicholas had six tenants holding each a cottage of him and another tenant holding 3 acres of him. One of the cottagers was none other than the William Dasset from whom Nicholas already held two cottages.

The complexities arising from sub-tenancy are not explained in the majority of accounts of medieval village life. This is partly because the popular historical descriptions of the medieval village are based on manorial documents. These, as I have mentioned, concern themselves with only those tenants holding immediately of the lord. It can happen of course that the manorial documents give a broadly correct picture. In Kineton Hundred, for instance, there appears to have been no subletting in twenty-eight out of forty-eight villages. This applied especially where there was a majority of villein tenants. Villeins could not sublet legally. What they did was to sublet illegally, usually for short periods. Even the Hundred Rolls will not tell us about this illegal land-market. We can only learn about it by studying the lists of convictions in the records of the manorial courts.[32]

Another aspect of village life which tends to remain concealed

[31] Sir Maurice Powicke, in his illuminating paper 'Observations concerning the English Freeholder in the 13th Century', shows how landlords were privately anticipating *Quia Emptores* before the passing of the statute, *Wirtschaft und Kultur*, (Festschrift for Alfons Dopsch), 1939; also in French in Recueils de la Société Jean Bodin, *La Tenure*, t. iii, 1938.)

[32] See my article, 'Peasant Movements in England before 1381', *EcHR*, 2nd Series, 11. 2, 1949.

if one studies only the manorial documents is the multiplication of manors and manorial lords in a single village. Here again we must not go to the opposite extreme in assuming that village and manor never coincided. Fifty out of ninety-five villages and hamlets in the two hundreds of Stoneleigh and Kineton were ruled by only one lord. But in the rest we find between two and seven manorial lords sharing one village between them. These lords often possessed manors composed of both demesne and tenant land. Almost as often their manors consisted only of a group of tenants, bound to them through the obligation of attendance at a court, by the payment of rent, and by ties of homage and fealty. In the Stoneleigh Hundred there were 32 manors consisting of tenants alone as compared with 50 composed of both tenants and a manorial demesne. The proportion of manors composed only of tenants was higher in Kineton Hundred, being 47, as against 49 manors which also contained demesne land.

The large village of Tysoe[33] is an interesting example of complex organization in 1279. In it there were five manorial organizations consisting of a number of tenants grouped around a manorial demesne. First, there was the manor of Nicholas, Baron Stafford, who held the village in chief of the king as 1 knight's fee pertaining to his barony of Stafford. He had 2 ploughlands of demesne land served by 13 serfs who owed all their rent in the form of week-work. In addition, he had 9 free tenants of varying status, some of whom were subletting. He also had 5 cottages. Secondly, there was the sub-manor of Robert of Stafford, Baron Nicholas's son. Robert held this manor of his father's gift for the rendering of homage. It consisted of a ploughland of demesne land, 6 serfs, and 8 free tenants. The 6 serfs did the same services on Robert's demesne as their fellow serfs did for the baron. Thirdly, the Priory of Stone which was the appropriator of the parish church had a manor. This consisted of 3 yardlands in demesne, 10 serfs, 3 cottagers, and 4 free tenants. The serfs owed a fairly heavy money rent and correspondingly light labour services. Two of the free tenants had 3 sub-tenants holding from them. Fourthly, the Priory of Arbury had a manor which it had received as a gift in

---

[33] Now Upper, Middle, and Lower Tysoe.

free and perpetual alms from the ancestors of Baron Stafford. It consisted of 2 ploughlands of demesne and 3 serfs, who paid heavy money rents and did light services. Fifthly, the Templars of Balsall held a manor also in free and perpetual alms as a gift of the baron's ancestors. There was a ploughland of demesne and 16 servile tenants. The tenants owed a small money rent and heavy seasonal works.

Four of these five manorial organizations were quite independent judicially, as well as economically, in the sense that the tenants attended different courts. The exception was that the tenants of Robert of Stafford probably went to the manorial court of the baron. In addition to these five manors with demesnes there was a separate organization of a manorial type for the serfs of the Prior of Kenilworth of whom there were five. Finally, a wealthy freeholder of south Warwickshire named Thomas of Stok had a group of six freeholders holding of him.

Not far from Tysoe was the small village of Winderton. The social organization of this village was utterly different from that of Tysoe. There was only one lord in the village, so that here village and manor were identical. Roger de Clifford held the manor of the Earl of Warwick as half a knight's fee. There was a manorial demesne of one ploughland, nineteen villein tenants, seven cottagers, and one large free tenant. There was no subletting. We cannot say that either form of rural organization was typical, for there were other large and complex organizations like Tysoe, and other smaller and simpler organizations like Winderton. It remains true that in both types of village, the essential fact of the subordination of the peasant to the lord was the underlying and most important element in the social structure. But the examples which I have quoted show what an immensely rich variety of social relationships went to make up the county community of our forebears.

# APPENDIX

## The North Warwickshire Field System

It has been shown above that the tenurial arrangements of north Warwickshire were of a special kind. It seems clear that these special features had their origin in economic and geographical circumstances associated with settlement in the medieval forest. These circumstances are not peculiar to Warwickshire. The Arden should be compared with the Weald of Kent and the forest areas of Essex if the general significance of its history is to be appreciated. In fact we find that the field system of the Arden country was, in the late Middle Ages, unlike the traditional 'Midland System' which characterized much of south Warwickshire and most of the surrounding counties. This was recognized by H. L. Gray in his book on *English Field Systems*, though he did not investigate the Arden country in any detail, or the northward extension of the forest area into Staffordshire.[1] However, he did recognize what were the two principal peculiarities of these forest areas, namely, the multiplicity of fields and the frequency of enclosure.

The rentals and accounts of the fifteenth century are very rich in field names, and from them it is possible to see how unlike the 'normal' open-field system were the systems of the Arden villages, even if the exact nature of the agricultural system remains unclear. It is normally quite impossible to pick out those two or three main fields which were in many cases the real, in others the ideal basis of the traditional rotation system. A detailed sergeant's account of the Westminster Abbey manor of Knowle[2] for the year 1408 names, under various headings, something over seventy fields. Whilst these, as units of cultivation, are virtually identical with the 'shots' in the main fields of the traditional two- or three-field system, no main fields are mentioned. In fact twenty-two of the names embody the word 'field', such as 'Milnefield', 'Middlefeld', 'Parkefeld', 'Bernefeld', 'Westfeld', 'Tounshamfeld', 'Shepenfelde', &c. One of these 'fields', called Marleputfeld, is also described as a croft. There are, in addition, ten other pieces of land whose names do not embody the English word 'field' but which are described as 'campus'. Clearly it is not possible to envisage the even distribution of spring crops, winter crops, and fallow over these fields. In fact the grange account of this manor gives us

[1] Op. cit., pp. 86–7.
[2] PRO Min. Accts. 1040/1. I owe my thanks to Mrs. D. Styles for permission to use her transcript of this document.

the names of the fields on which the lord's grain was sown. In the year 1408–9 23 acres were sown in Parkefeld, consisting of 12 a. wheat, 3 a. rye, 5 a. peas, and 2 a. drage. In addition 11 a. were sown with oats in Windmellefeld. The next year the same fields were sown, together with one other, called Salvercroft. There were 9 a. sown with wheat in Wyndmellefeld and Salvercroft, 8 acres of peas and 5 of drage in Parkefeld, and 12 a. of oats in Parkefeld and Wyndmellefeld. It would appear that what little demesne arable there was, was concentrated in one or two small areas, and this may very well have been the case with the tenants' land.

A study of field names in other Arden villages reinforces the impression that there was no organized grouping of the shots or furlongs into 2 or 3 main field areas. In the Erdington rental of 1463 there are 87 separately named pieces of land. Eight of these names embody the word 'field'. But there is no indication that these 8 fields contain within their boundaries the whole of the arable land of Erdington: in fact there were only 10 tenancies in these 8 fields, out of a total of 75 tenancies in the whole manor. The 1446 Rental of Henley-in-Arden, incomplete as it is as a survey of the whole village, shows that the holdings were scattered over 29 separate lots of land, eleven of which were called 'fields'. One tenant holds some strips which are fairly regularly distributed over 3 fields, the Wooton Field, the Henley Field, and the Whitley Field. This tenement at first sight seems to suggest at any rate a regular 3-field core to the Henley-in-Arden arable. But if we look at the next tenement we find the strips distributed between only two of the above-mentioned 3 fields, in the very irregular ratio of 13:4. Any illusions one may have entertained are shattered when the next tenements composed of open-field strips are examined. Here we find the strips distributed in several quite different fields. One tenement appears to consist of 46 strips all lying in the same field, called Hemfeld. In any case the majority of the land-holders in the Catesby rental do not appear to have holdings in the common intermixed arable at all.

Evidence for other Arden villages of later date, that is of the sixteenth century and later, shows substantially the same situation. The 1538 Rental of Handsworth (then in Staffordshire, now in Birmingham) does not identify the location of as many tenements as do the fifteenth-century rentals, but mentions some twenty-five to thirty names of pieces of land. From this rental, and from later (pre-enclosure) evidence, it appears that six pieces of land were actually called 'fields'. A reconstruction of a map of pre-industrial Handsworth[3] shows these fields scattered oddly over a wide area, dispersed about the waste, and

[3] Gill., op. cit., p. 166.

usually adjacent to small clusters of homesteads which lay, hamlet like, in various parts of the parish area. In other words, there is no resemblance to the open fields around a nucleated village. At Wooton Wawen, according to a pre-enclosure map made in 1736, there were 10 fields, 6 of which were known by the name 'field', but there is no indication of an organized 'system'. Of 46 fields of the same parish mentioned in the *Place Names of Warwickshire*,[4] none of a later than seventeenth-century origin, 7 were named 'fields'. One of them demonstrated by a change of name how unlike the traditional 'common fields' these fields were. It is 'Sondy croft' in a rental of 1475, but by 1572 has become 'Sondy field'. Birmingham's field evolution had gone far by the mid-sixteenth century, for of 72 of the ancient freeholdings, 36 were several pastures, and of 36 possibly arable holdings only 8 or 10 were described in such a way as would admit the possibility of their containing intermixed arable strips.[5]

This feature of Birmingham's earliest full rental (1553) brings me to the second feature of the Arden forest area noticed cursorily by H. L. Gray, namely the prevalence of holdings in severalty and of enclosure. This is usually found to be one of the natural consequences of assarting, and that H. L. Gray's suggestion is correct is proved, I think, by the fifteenth-century evidence which I have already quoted in other connections. The way in which many of the fields are described in the Knowle account of 1408 shows that they must have been held in severalty. Under the heading 'New Rents' are payments for 6 'parcels from the lord's waste' which must have been assarts held in severalty. Individuals are taking on lease as 'farms' 22 complete fields in addition to 'parcels' which are apparently only *parts* of fields. At Tanworth in the middle of the fifteenth century, out of 75 holdings, both free and customary, 51 are so described as to imply severalty rather than distribution in strips in the common fields: the descriptions that I take to imply severalty being 'a croft', 'a tenement with land adjacent', 'a field'. In the Erdington rental of 1463, out of 87 tenures, 39 are described as 'tofts' or 'crofts' (which I take generally to indicate severalty) 20 imply severalty without doubt; 7 tenements are *in* fields and may well have been in strips, though one tenant is said to hold a 'whole field' (*campo integro*); 10 probably are distributed as strips—in fact one tenancy is described as being in sellions in a croft—a warning that crofts are not always held in severalty; 19 holdings are described so vaguely (e.g. as 'certain lands') that it is not possible to decide whether they were in severalty or not.

That severalty led to enclosure is a natural supposition, since protection against foraging animals by ditch or by fence, was an immediate

[4] p. 372.    [5] Gill., loc. cit.

need. Many of the field names indicate such enclosure, as for instance, 'Newclosfeld' (Knowle), or are stated to be such, as for instance, 'Ladyland, a close' (Erdington). The maintenance of enclosures was in fact a condition of tenure. An account roll of the manor of Erdington for the year 1439 speaks of a field called Pipefelde, leased for a term of twenty years. The only obligation besides the payment of rent which is mentioned is that the tenant should keep up the enclosure of the field during the period of the lease.[6]

In considering the problem of the north Warwickshire field system, it is essential to be cautious about one point. In spite of the weight of evidence showing the tendency for the cultivated land, during the long process of improvement of the waste, to be appropriated in severalty, the old open-field system, and its natural accompaniment of rights of common on the waste, are not entirely eliminated. There were still open fields and common rights for the eighteenth-century enclosers to attack. And earlier, as the Henley-in-Arden rental shows, there did exist old free tenements whose arable lay in scattered strips. This ancient core of common cultivation had its own peculiarities as we have seen. Its routine was not that of the other villages of the midlands, and in any case it would inevitably become of less and less importance as the individually assarted area grew bigger.

There is one feature of Leland's time which might well be mentioned as a conclusion of this rough sketch. In 1549 a third enclosure commission toured Warwickshire, among other counties, and added to the evidence that had been collected by other royal commissioners in 1517 and 1519. The enclosure which they were instructed to investigate was the deliberate enclosure of ancient open-field arable for pasture, or of common woodland pasture for making large parks for the gentry. This sort of enclosure, attacked as early as the 1480s by John Rous, the Warwick chantry priest, was different in kind from the piecemeal enclosure of assarts in the Arden country. Its extent may have been exaggerated, and in Warwickshire certainly it was not so much the work of large capitalists from the cities enclosing by the 100 acres, as the activity of smaller local men, gentry and rich peasants, enclosing 20 or 30 acres at a time. The bailiff of Brailes in 1480[7] was accounting for small payments made in the manor court by such men for the lord's licence to enclose.

However, whoever did it, the geographical distribution of this new type of enclosure gives point to what has been said about the Arden country. The majority of these new enclosures, from Rous's time onwards, were in the Felden, while the greater part of the enclosures that

[6] Birmingham Reference, Library, MS. 347930.

[7] PRO, Min. Accts. DL/29/642/10421; *Ministers' Accounts of the Warwickshire Estates of the Duke of Clarence 1479–80*, Dugdale Society, 1952, pp. 71–72.

did take place in the Arden region, were of forest land for parks. The point was of course that there was little arable left in the Arden country which was not enclosed by the beginning of the sixteenth century.[8]

[8] This appendix is adapted from a paper which I read in Cambridge in 1948. Mr. M. W. Beresford has since written about late medieval enclosures as agents of depopulation in Warwickshire, *Transactions of the Birmingham and Midland Archaeological Society*, lxvi, 1950, with maps.

# VIII

# Gloucester Abbey Leases of the Late Thirteenth Century*

It is now generally accepted that the development of money rent at the expense of labour rent in England in the later Middle Ages was a very uneven process. On the whole the feudal estates of south-eastern England maintained the labour rent system after it had been abandoned in the north and west. But even within the zone where labour rent seemed to predominate there were considerable variations, largely due to the great differences in structure between the estates of big feudal lords (especially ecclesiastics) and of the lesser nobility. E. A. Kosminsky has shown what a great quantitative predominance there was of money rent over labour rent at the period of demesne farming *par excellence*, using a long-accessible source, the *Rotuli Hundredorum* of 1279.[1] His survey, more comprehensive than any hitherto made, nevertheless, underlines the fact that there are very considerable gaps in our knowledge. The Hundred Rolls cover only a few Midland and Eastern counties. There is still an enormous area with which we have only a superficial acquaintance, and this includes the west and south-west Midlands. In this article I propose to deal with some materials from the records of St. Peter's Abbey, Gloucester, principally (though not entirely)) from its Cotswold property.

We know extraordinarily little about the medieval agrarian conditions of the Cotswolds. The international connections of this region through its production of wool for the European cloth trade have made it famous enough. But its special product has concentrated all attention. Little work has been devoted to questions of manorial structure, trends of rent payments, and the other well-known problems of agrarian history.

* Reprinted from the *University of Birmingham Historical Journal*, iv, 1953, 1–17.
[1] *Studies in the Agrarian History of England in the Thirteenth Century*, 1956.

The printed Cartulary of Gloucester Abbey[2] has for a long time been famous because of the mid-thirteenth-century manorial extents which it contains. These extents at first glance show a great preoccupation with the minute definition of the labour services of customary tenants. The same cartulary also contains a set of instructions to manorial officials (the *Scriptum Quoddam*) which seem to confirm the impression of an old-established ecclesiastical estate mainly composed of manors of 'typical' structure, worked by forced labour. Of course, the Gloucester Abbey estate also contained a number of properties which did not conform to the typical manorial structure. The character of some of these properties can be discerned from the unprinted register of obedientary property in Gloucester Cathedral Library.[3] It is clear, for instance, that the various endowments of the Almonry of Standish, mostly in the wooded valleys and slopes of the south-western edge of the wolds, were not of the normal manorial type. However, none of the big medieval English estates was completely homogeneous in character and one need not be surprised that Gloucester Abbey, too, had small manors and scattered possessions of a non-manorial type in its estate.

But was the Gloucester Abbey estate typical of the Cotswold region? Such evidence as exists suggests that the south-western edge where the cloth industry was to develop was not manorialized in the traditional sense. The printed Minchinhampton Custumal presents a picture at the end of the thirteenth century[4] of scattered settlements, of holdings consisting to a large extent of assarts won from the wood, of a considerable pastoral and industrial (woollen textile) element in the economy, and of rents and services where forced labour plays only a secondary part. Early-fourteenth-century surveys of the Berkeley manors of Wotton-under-Edge and Cam show a vast predominance of money rent and a considerable numerical inferiority of customary tenants of the traditional type. For the most part tenants are free

---

[2] *Historia et Cartularium Monasterii Gloucestriae* (Rolls Series), 1863–7.

[3] Frocester Register B (1393).

[4] *Trans. Bristol and Glouc. Arch. Soc.* ii, 1877–8, liv, 1932. The editor of the Minchinhampton custumal gives this date, but the MS. is in a late-fourteenth-century hand and some of the reasons given for the earlier date are mistaken.

and there are many smallholders.[5] This impression of the importance of freeholds in the area seems to be confirmed from Smyth's *History of the Hundred of Berkeley*,[6] although one should naturally be cautious in reading tenurial conditions back from the early seventeenth century.

But what was the situation on the main Cotswold plateau? There is very little evidence. Cirencester Abbey was disputing about their status with its Cirencester tenants, both burgess and villein, from the twelfth to the fifteenth century. As a by-product of this dispute there is a good deal of evidence concerning Cirencester tenants.[7] From this it seems clear that the Abbey at no time succeeded in imposing on its tenants here a uniform system of labour services. From the middle of the twelfth century until the early fifteenth century all the surveys emphasize money rent and light labour services. This was so in spite of the fact that in Cirencester the Abbey had a demesne of twelve ploughlands.[8] But Cirencester Abbey was a comparatively late foundation (Augustinian),[9] and it is well known that the estates which had the most complete system of labour services had started on the enserfment of their peasants by the tenth century, if not earlier.

The estates of the Knights Templars in the Cotswolds, at Guiting and Kineton, were the gift of Gilbert de Laci and probably reflect conditions on lay estates. When they were surveyed in 1185[10] there was a system of quite heavy labour services. But the extent to which it was actually operated is doubtful. The services owed from the virgate *qui operari debeant* are listed. But the list of tenants, of holdings and of money rents show all peasant virgates paying 4s. to 5s. a year. This payment does not preclude the performance of some labour services, but it is unlikely that week works were demanded as well as the money.

[5] PRO, SC12. 36/11.

[6] *Berkeley MSS.*, iii, ed. MacLean (1885).

[7] E. A. Fuller in *Trans. Bristol and Glouc. Arch. Soc.* ii, 1877–8. Documents quoted by Fuller can be studied in *The Cartulary of Cirencester Abbey*, ed. C. D. Ross, 1964.        [8] PRO, SC12. 18/22.

[9] If it was a re-foundation, the estates of the pre-Conquest collegiate church were insignificant.

[10] B. A. Lees, *Records of the Templars in England in the Twelfth Century*, British Academy, 1935, pp. 47 ff.

On the other hand the Gloucestershire estates of the Bishop and the Cathedral Priory of Worcester can be strictly compared with that of Gloucester Abbey, in that they had a pre-Conquest origin. It is clear that on the Bishop's manors of Blockley, Paxford, Withington, and Bibury, and on the Priorys' manors of Cutsdean and Iccomb the foundations of an economy based on peasant labour services had been laid. The services due on all these manors are described in detail in the Priory Register and in the Bishop's Red Book.[11] But at Iccomb and Cutsdean the labour service regime had disappeared by 1249 (the approximate date of the Register) since the demesne had been leased to the tenants. It seems to have been in force in the Bishop's manors in 1182, despite evidence of some commutation of services. By 1299, the date of the elaborate survey of Bishop Giffard, the situation is not clear. Although labour services assessed on the peasant holding have been increased, it is by no means certain that these increased services were in practice demanded, for the survey gives the alternatives of money rent and light services on one hand, and full labour services with smaller monetary contributions on the other. What was actually demanded would depend on the will of the lord, and this would in turn depend on more general economic and social conditions.[12]

Now this contrast between peasant holdings at money rent and holdings *ad operationem* or *ad opera* is quite common and also applied on the estates of the Abbey of Winchcombe, another important Cotswold landowner. As I have pointed out elsewhere,[13] there is no evidence for details of the labour services that were originally demanded from Winchcombe Abbey tenants but a reference to a holding in the manor of Sherborne as being once *ad opera* is to be found in a court roll of 1340, by which date

[11] *Register of Worcester Priory*, Camden Society, 1865. *Red Book of Worcester*, iv, Worcester Historical Society, 1950.

[12] Miss Hollings, the editor of the *Red Book of Worcester*, argues in her introduction to vol. iv that in fact by 1299 labour services were mostly commuted. Generalizations from one vacancy account, 1302–3 (printed in vol. iv, pp. 498–547) are risky, and later manorial evidence does not support this view.

[13] 'Winchcombe Abbey and the Manor of Sherborne', *University of Birmingham Historical Journal*, ii, 1, 1949, p. 45; reprinted in *Gloucestershire Studies*, ed. H. P. R. Finberg, 1957.

money rent seems almost completely to have replaced labour rent. But labour services as heavy as those on the Gloucester Abbey estates may have been in force at the time when the Gloucester Abbey extents were compiled. And at the period when the tenants of the Bishop of Worcester might either pay money rent or hold *ad operationem*, Winchcombe Abbey tenants may have been in the same position; the decision to abandon labour rents being taken some time before 1340.

This evidence (scanty though it is) seems to imply that for special reasons some parts of the Cotswolds had not developed a manorial regime based on the cultivation of demesnes by peasant labour services; and that elsewhere, on some of the bigger estates where such a regime was evidently once well established, the payment of money rent had made considerable inroads by the end of the thirteenth century. Such a conclusion is by no means revolutionary, though it may distinguish the chronology of agrarian development in the west from that in the south-east which has been most closely studied. But corroborative evidence from the estates of St. Peter's, Gloucester, would be desirable before even tentative conclusions are reached.

The dated extents of Gloucester Abbey manors were apparently made between 1265 and 1267. Those that are undated seem to bear so strong a resemblance to the others that it may be presumed that they were made at the same period. There can be no escaping the conclusion that in the purely rural manors of the estate[14] labour rent overwhelmingly predominates, at any rate as far as the evidence of the rentals shows. It has been argued that the fact that works are carefully valued means that they are normally sold.[15] But the most that, I think, may be assumed is that in estates where there was careful annual accounting (as on most big

[14] In Hampshire, Littleton and Linkenholt; in Gloucestershire, Clifford Chambers, Hinton, Buckland, Hartpury, Frocester, Boxwell, Highnam, Buckholt, Upleadon, Churcham, Brookethorpe, Ridge, Abload, Maisemore, Aldsworth, Eastleach, Duntisbourne, Coln St. Aldwyn, Coln Rogers, Amney and Coberley. The semi-urban economies of King's and Abbot's Barton and to a lesser extent Northleach are a slightly different case.

[15] e.g. by Miss Hollings, op. cit. It should be remembered that the double entry in estate documents of the rents and services from holdings when *ad censum* and when *ad opera* is not only found in the late 13th century. The reference in the 12th-

estates in the thirteenth century) works would have to be valued in anticipation of partial and temporary commutation, the fluctuating *venditio operum*. The *Scriptum Quoddam* makes it clear that Gloucester Abbey estates must have been administered as rigorously as any. On the great majority of manors most of the tenant land was held by customary tenure, and this land was almost invariably held for labour rent. There are a few exceptions. On the Hampshire manors of Littleton and Linkenholt the main customary tenements were held for a *firma* in money combined with labour rent, comparable to those tenements held partially for money rent on the Bishop of Worcester's manor in 1299.[16] At Boxwell, a manor at the head of one of the valleys of the south-west edge of the Cotswolds, a majority of the customary tenants held partly by money and partly by labour rent, but these are small holders of two acres or fardell-holders of 12 acres. The full virgate-holders (48 acres) owe labour rent only. Customary tenants elsewhere on the estate, according to the extents at any rate, owed money to their lord only for aid, pannage, and similar dues. The rent due from the tenement was in labour and was valued for the most part at about £1 a virgate, sometimes more, since virgate areas varied.[17] Of course these straightforward symptoms of natural economy arrangements might in practice be modified not only by annual sales of works for money, paid to the lord, but also by subletting for money among the tenants themselves. However, we can but consider the evidence that we have, and this emphasises labour rent, not only from the larger holdings which were the normal mainstay of the manorial labour rent system, but from a large number of quarter virgates and small holdings as well.

century records of the Templars (above p. 141) implies as much. The distinction is also fully made in the 12th-century cartulary of Evesham Abbey (British Museum, Cotton MSS., Vespasian B. XXIV).

[16] Littleton virgates paid a 5s. money rent and works (not week-work) valued at 12s. 2½d. At Linkenholt the corresponding figures were 5s. and 8s. 1½d.

[17] e.g. 36s. at Buckholt; 40s. 5d. at Abload (virgate of 48 acres). Since the virgate was a holding including other elements than its arable land apparent variations in rent per acre can mean little, e.g. Buckland and Clifford Chambers virgates contained 36 acres of arable and were liable to works worth 20s. and 22s. 7d. respectively. Highnam half virgates (24 acres) owed works valued at 21s. 1½d.

But although the customary tenements owing labour rent predominate in the extents, there are a number of tenements which seem to herald already the erosion of the old system by non-customary tenures. The principal features of the non-customary holdings are money rent and terminability. It seems to have been the payment of money rent which to the compilers of the extents—that is local jurors[18]—was the main differentiating feature of the non-customary holdings. In most of the extents the list of customary tenants is preceded by a list including not only the normal type of free tenants, holding in fee, but also tenants at will and for life. There is no reason to assume that all or even most of these holdings at will or for life were regarded as free holdings. In many cases the tenants were burdened with characteristically servile obligations. At Upleadon, for instance, tenants at will whose rent was entirely in money, except for one reaping service, owed brewing toll, pannage, merchet, heriot, and a licence fee for the sale of stock—marks of servitude.[19] The Highnam extent emphasizes that while these tenants had certain features in common, they were not to be confused; the money total of rents is, we are told, from holdings *libere tenentium et eorum qui tenent ad voluntatem domini ad terminum vitae per certum servitium.*[20] In other places also the phrase *summa certi redditus* stresses the importance of this feature of all types of non-customary holding.[21] They are always distinct from the normal customary tenements assessed at labour rent alone.[22]

The number of small holdings of one or two acres owing works

[18] e.g. *Cart. Glouc.* iii. 35, 61, 67. However, guidance from above on the categories to be adopted may in most cases be assumed.

[19] Ibid., pp. 126–7. These for short are often referred to as *consuetudines non taxatas*, cf. p. 91. A pair at Frocester held *quamdam terram servilem* for money rent, boon workings and *consuetudines non taxatas* (p. 90). The holdings at will included in a list of free tenants on p. 109 were not burdened with servile customs. Terminable holdings could clearly be either 'free' or 'villein'.

[20] Ibid., p. 115. cf. the phrase in the Churcham extent, *Summa utriusque redditus tam liberorum quam tenentium ad voluntatem*, p. 137.

[21] e.g. at Hinton, p. 61; Buckholt, p. 123; Churcham, p. 134.

[22] These are always grouped together, and easily identified, even when the rubric *consuetudinarii* is omitted. e.g. Colne Rogers, p. 205. Perhaps it is a little odd that only money rent was thought of as fixed. The lists of works give as definite an impression of permanence—and in fact probably were more permanent.

but no money is striking, especially on the Cotswold manors. Such small holders in other parts of England are usually found paying money rent. However, there are plenty of these, too, in the Gloucester extents. Squatters on the waste who paid money rent need not be regarded as being inconsistent with the maintenance of a labour-rent system, but as its necessary complement, providing extra hired hands both for the demesne and for the larger peasant holdings.[23] But it is not this sort of holding with which we are primarily concerned, important though the role of small holders was in agrarian structures which were not typically manorial. On the contrary our concern here is those larger holdings at will or for life which may represent the beginnings of the direct transformation of the main body of customary labour rent tenements into terminable holdings at money rent. This was a transformation primarily of the economic features of the holdings rather than of status. Examples of persons *redempti a servitute domini abbatis*[24] are infrequent, and though paying money rent, are a negligible factor in the general development of money rent tenure.

The list of tenants paying money rent, *certi redditus*, in the extents is the immediately apparent sign of the beginnings of non-customary tenures in the Gloucester Abbey manors. Although the number of money-rent holdings is about equal to that of customary holdings in the large semi-urban manor of Abbots Barton, it is greatly inferior in most manors.[25] Some are quite clearly old free holdings owing a money rent which bears no relation to area, with suit of court, and perhaps some personal service of an honourable character. These are often large holdings whose internal structure was probably quasi-manorial.[26] Others are average sized peasant holdings—say half a virgate—owing money rent and suit of court but without much indication

---

[23] We see them in process of absorption at Highnam, *memorandum de novis bordellis sine licencia levatis quae de novo ponuntur ad annuum redditum qui quidem redditus debet inseri in istam extentam* (p. 61).

[24] e.g. at Frocester, p. 90; Eastleach, p. 190.

[25] e.g. at Hartpury, pp. 16 and 108; Frocester, pp. 11 and 44; Eastleach, pp. 13 and 23; Duntisbourne, pp. 5 and 20.

[26] See the extent of Walter de Bause's tenement at Randwick, p. 44.

as to their age and origin. They might have originated in piece-meal acquisitions or newly cultivated land or have been special enfeoffments. Those which are described as at will or for life are a minority. The holdings at will usually owe *consuetudines non taxatas* as well as their money rent. One may surmise that some of these holdings too may have been assarts, but leased by the Abbey on terms more profitable to it than were enfeoffments in free tenure. Others may have been ordinary customary holdings, lapsed into the lord's hand, and re-leased in such a way that the rent could be increased without the tenant or his heir being able to appeal to custom.[27]

Tenants at will, of course, had no certain title to their land. Tenants for life or lives were secure, though their heirs were not. There are not many of these over the estate as a whole according to the evidence of the extents, and they are unevenly distributed. On some manors there are none, in other places they are quite a significant minority of the money rent tenants.[28] But although they were not numerous at the end of Henry III's reign, there are indications that they were becoming more numerous and that these life agreements may have played a big part in the turn away from the labour rent system. Fourteenth-century evidence for the Gloucester Abbey estates is lacking, but there are indications that tenure for life was common in some parts of the Cots-wold area. For example, the court rolls of the Kingswood Abbey (Cistercian) manor of Kingscote during the last two decades of the fourteenth and the first half of the fifteenth centuries show that the great majority of holdings taken up in the manor court were granted for life or lives.[29]

Now besides those referred to in the extents there are recorded

[27] A life lease at Buckland says that the land had been in the lord's hand, ii. 201. The extents refer to customary holdings in *manibus domini* at Eastleach, Duntisbourne, Coln Rogers.

[28] e.g. at Boxwell, Highnam, Eastleach.

[29] Gloucester County Record Office, D. 471. On Winchcombe Abbey's manor of Sherborne, after 1340, leases for lives or years of customary holdings occur, though customary tenements were more often let at money rent, without a term being stated. It may be mentioned that W. Marshall noticed that a peculiarity of Cotswold townships was tenancies for 3 lives under renewable leases. *The Rural Economy of Gloucestershire*, 2nd edition (1796), ii. 10.

in the Gloucester Abbey cartulary quite a number of agreements with tenants, usually in the form of a chirograph, by which holdings for the life of the tenant and his wife, and often for one son are granted. It is not clear exactly why those that are in the cartulary were enrolled. It is, however, certain that many were not, for there are a considerable number of originals in the Cathedral Library at Gloucester which were not copied into the cartulary.[30] Some of these life agreements (both those printed and those in manuscript) were made before the compilation of the extents. The *Constitutio quaedam*, a list of rules concerning the financial administration of the abbey which is sandwiched among the extents, and may be of the same period, refers to the need for the careful custody of *cartae ad terminum vitae concessae*,[31] so their existence was taken for granted. But there was a spate of life agreements during the abbacy of Abbot Reginald (1263–84), and this may be the crucial period of a turnover from labour to money rent. Out of 49 leases examined 26 were granted by Abbot Reginald, 9 of them after 1284, and only 12 can with certainty be dated before 1263. Compared with the total number of tenements on the whole estate, these 49 leases may seem quite insignificant, and so they are, quantitatively. The point is, however, that they obviously represent a tendency which is developing and which achieves significance in the light of the other indications of change at this time. The fact that Abbot Reginald had to face an abbey debt of 1,500 marks on his accession[32] should not be regarded as the fortuitous occasion of these leases in view of the general trend apparent on the other West Midland estates we have mentioned. The debt itself may indeed have been a symptom of an economic problem common to many large landowners, the response to which was the search for the security of a *rentier*.

We have implied that these leases for life become significant only if they were created out of tenures that had hitherto been

[30] Mounted in ten volumes entitled 'Deeds and Seals'. There is a typewritten calendar. I must thank the Reverend Canon Fendick, Cathedral Librarian, for his great help to me when using the Cathedral muniments.

[31] *Cart. Glouc.*, iii. 106.

[32] Ibid. i. 31.

burdened mainly with labour rent and villein customs. The discussions of the legal historians have hitherto been based on the assumption that life leases were creations from land held in fee, and hence it has been assumed that life tenures were almost equivalent to free holdings.[33] Naturally, the Abbey of Gloucester was holding most of its estate either for free alms or by knight service so that any new tenure created by it could be interpreted in a legal sense as a conversion from land held in fee. The issue here, of course, is the creation by a lord of life tenures out of land that had previously been held from the lord by customary tenure. In any case we must not dwell too long on legal niceties. It is the economic and social implications of the Gloucester Abbey life leases which are most important. For here we find a development of money rent tenures which, though by no means so adjustable by the lord to his needs as tenures at will, were better from that point of view than free holdings.

Of the leases known to us from the cartulary or still preserved in manuscript the majority were of land which can be presumed to have been villein land. In most of these cases some villein customs were still to be rendered by the life tenants. This distinction between 'free' and 'villein' life holdings needs some clarification as it does not come into the concepts of this tenure elaborated by the lawyers. A clear example of a life lease of land previously held in villeinage and whose tenant was to continue to render villein customs is from Maisemore (1263–84). The lessee took on all the servile land and appurtenances, with 2 acres of meadow which a named tenant had held before him. He was to hold for his life and his wife after him, so long as she remained chaste. A money rent was to be paid, and all the customs, suits, and services as done by the previous tenant were to be rendered. The lessee took the customary oath of fealty, promised to pay the rent at the due terms, to do nothing which would harm the abbey's interests, and not to alienate the land without the abbey's permission. At the expiration of the term, the land was to revert to the abbey with all improvements. Now, the 'customs, suits, and services'

[33] Pollock and Maitland, *History of English Law*, ii, 1898, pp. 7–10, 38, 110. Holdsworth, *History of English Law*, iii, 1909, pp. 120–5.

are not described in the lease, but they are to be found in the Maisemore extent. The previous tenant (named in the lease) figures in the extent with the same holding (12 acres with a messuage and curtilage) and was already paying the same money rent (7s.) as the life lessee was to pay. In the extent the other customs and services are enumerated and they are characteristically servile, namely pannage, brewing toll, toll on the sale of stock, merchet, and heriot.[34]

An even clearer case of the continuing servile status of these life lessees, despite the new terms of tenure, is seen in a lease from Coln Rogers, of 1289. The abbey grants to William, its reeve of Coln Rogers, and his wife, for their lives, two-thirds of a virgate which may have been free and half a virgate of land stated to be servile, for money rents of 10s. and 8s. respectively. They were to be responsible for pannage, brewing toll, the toll on the sale of stock and other small customs as done by other *nativi*. They were not to do ploughing, harrowing, carrying, reaping or mowing or manual works. Their condition was in no way to change, but they and their heirs were to remain of servile condition.[35] This lease is unusually specific as regards the personal condition of the lessee and the limitations of the tenure. Others, however, clearly imply, though at less length, that the category of life tenants, if to be distinguished from that of customers burdened with labour service, had its origin there. These lessees for life, therefore, retain the birthmarks of their origin. A *nativus*, a carter from Preston, takes 20 acres of arable for two lives for 8s. and villein customs; another man takes on a servile tenement in Abbots Barton for a money rent and the same customs as the previous tenant; a *nativus* of Stanbald is allowed to hold as a life tenant land which he himself had bought—probably illegally (*quas predictus W. emit cum bonis nostris*, an expression of the doctrine that the serf could own no money of his own); a man and wife at Upton take half

---

[34] *Cart. Glouc.* ii. 88; iii. 171. See also Appendix for a mid-14th century lease which enumerates the various customs and services.

[35] 'Ita tamen quod sanguis eorum nullatenus immutetur sed ipsi et eorum successio nostri servi et servilis condicionis existunt.' 'Deeds and Seals', vi, fol. 18. See Appendix.

a virgate which had been in villeinage for 15*s*. and all previous services.[36]

Other leases are less detailed even than these and lead to guess-work. I have assumed that where a lease states that the land leased is held freely, or that the suit of court is with the free tenants of the manor, the tenure is a 'free' life estate possibly created out of an estate in fee.[37] There are cases also of 'free' life tenancies being created out of tenancies at will. For example, a man and wife at Hope Mansell, Herefordshire, who had held 24 acres at will from demesne now took it on a life lease for 13*s*. 4*d*. and suit of court with other free tenants.[38] But there are also many leases which cannot be presumed to have been made of land previously in free tenure, or on conditions which presume the free character of the life tenure. Indications of a dubious status tending towards servility are the continued payment, in addition to money rent, of such dues as heriot and aid, with unspecified customs previously due from the tenement.[39]

There can be no doubt that these life leases were considered by the peasants who took them to be worth having, for they paid money to have them. Not all the leases tell us that the lessee paid a sum down for his lease. In cases where there is no information it cannot be assumed that a payment was not made. Undoubtedly the lord would profit from leases in all possible cases. But even where we know about payment we cannot expect to find a regular scale of payment. Land alienation was not sufficiently commercialized as yet, and many non-commercial considerations may have played their part in fixing the sum paid, not the least of which was the social and political power which the lord had over

[36] *Cart. Glouc.*, ii. 87; i. 219, and iii. 152; 'Deeds and Seals', i, fol. 27; *Cart. Glouc.*, ii. 295 and iii. 152. Stanbald is unidentified.

[37] e.g. Churcham, ibid. i. 249, and Aldsworth, ibid. i. 161–2.

[38] Ibid. i. 339. A lease which remits all servile customs once owed may be considered to have created a free tenure. But the suit of court is not with the free tenants. 'Deeds and Seals', x, fol. 12 (see Appendix).

[39] For example William Murie's tenement in Abbots Barton, quoted above, is not entered in the Abbots Barton extent amongst the customary tenements, appearing simply as a money rent-paying tenement owing, in addition to the rent an aid of 2*s*. a year, and the usual customs (pannage, etc.). In the lease to his successor the land is described as servile.

his tenants. Sometimes the purchase price was not even a lump sum down. A free tenant at Frampton got a life lease of two virgates for a rent of two pounds of pepper a year. In return he remitted a payment of 10s. a year for life which the abbot owed him.[40] At ten years purchase this would be equivalent to a lump sum payment of £5.

Some premiums paid for life leases were as great as or greater than one would expect the price of freehold land to be. A holding at Over consisting of a messuage, 3 acres of arable, and one acre of meadow was leased in 1252 to a tenant for three lives. The lessee paid 25 marks for his lease. Admittedly the buildings on the messuage were valued at 10 marks, but the rent was not inconsiderable (2s. 6d.)[41] Once again taking 10 years' purchase as determining the price of land in the thirteenth century, the 25 marks might have been expected to buy a free tenement with an annual net income of £1 13s. 4d. Other large sums can be quoted, though not all equivalent to the price paid for free land. In 1258 the same lessee bought a lease for three lives at Over for a messuage, four acres of arable, and adjacent meadow. He paid a premium of 6 marks. Now it happens that this lessee was a Gloucester burgess, but large premiums were not only paid by townsmen. A man in Barnwood bought the reversion for two lives of a mill for 10 marks, the rent being 21s. a year with an aid of 22d. and a tithe of 4s. Premiums paid elsewhere for half virgates amounted to 5 marks, and for virgates, 10 marks. In Upleadon premiums of £5 were paid for leases for two lives of half virgates whose rent was 13s. 4d. These, it happens, were 'free' life leases. But a payment at Upton of a 12 mark premium for a lease for two lives of villein land, for 15s. a year and all services, shows that the status of the land need not affect the premium paid.[42]

The high premiums paid for life leases could only have been found by peasants who had been able to accumulate considerable sums. They would be tenants already of fair-sized holdings (whether free or customary) and would probably have acquired

---

[40] *Cart. Glouc.*, i. 295.        [41] Ibid., ii. 67.

[42] Ibid., ii. 273, 205; i. 385; ii. 292, 295. The leases for which dates are not given were issued during the abbacy of Reginald de Homme (1263–84).

their accumulation by selling their produce on the market, or by usury. There must have been many who were actually buying and selling land on their own account. The man quoted above who, as a serf, had to regularize his land purchases by taking them on lease from his lord is only symptomatic of commercial activity which must have been general among the richer peasants. Their wealth and eminent status receives indirect recognition in the way in which they negotiate with their lord. The chirograph as the written form of these life leases is a type of document which presumes the equivalent status of the two parties. By the end of the thirteenth century Gloucester Abbey chirograph leases had been so much in use that their form was stereotyped as far as the clauses of warranty and the record of the terms of the oath sworn by the lessee were concerned. The selling clause was more elaborate in early leases than in later. A Wotton lease of about 1230 has the following rather lengthy clause: '... In cuius rei testimonium presens scriptum diviso inter nos cyrographo confecimus cuius unam partem sigillo ecclesie nostre munitam ei tradimus alteram vero partem sigillo ipsius roboratam penes nos retinuimus.' By 1312 a Barton lease says more laconically, '... in cuius rei testimonium huic scripto indentato sigilla nostra mutuo sunt appensa.'[43]

Both of the leases just quoted concern land which had clearly not been in free tenure. The lease of 1230 was of half a virgate, whose lessee was to perform ploughings and bederips in addition to a money rent of 10*s*. and an aid of 2*s*. The lease of 1312 was of that traditional customary tenement, a Mondayland, with another six acres added. The lessees were, as likely as not, villeins. But as the sealing clause shows, they had seals and made a contract with their lord. Since the half of the chirograph which the Abbey kept was that part bearing the lessee's seal, we have in some cases the very seal with which Gloucester Abbey villeins were authenticating their documents. The 1230 Wotton lease has a seal attached to it of the simplest character, though somewhat defaced. The name of the lessee, a widow named Emma, can be discerned on the outside edge of the seal and the central device is a cross.

---

[43] 'Deeds and Seals', vii, fol. 12; v, fol. 19.

The leases printed in the Gloucester Cartulary are chirographs, and can be presumed to have involved the use by villein lessees of seals.[44] Extant chirographs in the possession of the Dean and Chapter of Gloucester prove the point. The villein already mentioned whose land purchases had to be transformed into a life tenure sealed the portion of the chirograph retained by the abbot, with a seal whose device is unfortunately not visible, which may have been his or provided for him by someone else.[45] But the clearest villein seal in the collection comes from Coln Rogers.[46] It is attached to the appropriate portion of the chirograph by which the abbey in about 1274 leased a mill in Coln Rogers, with the messuage and land appurtenant, to Walter of Coln Rogers, their *nativus*. The seal, which is perfect, is small, white, and round, about the size of a penny. The central device is a simple floral pattern and the inscription round the edge reads: + S. WALTERI DE COLNA ROG'. No evidence either of the legal recognition of a villein's right to enter into contractual relations with his lord or of his right to a legal personality expressed through a seal could be clearer.

Walter's floral seal was not unique, and is all the more interesting for that. Other Coln Roger deeds with an almost identical seal (except for the name of the sealer) have survived. A Coln Roger lease of about 1268 by which all servile dues from the land are remitted bears a similar floral seal. Another lease of the same period from Coln St. Aldwyn, probably of a one-time villein virgate, has a seal with the same device. There have also survived similar seals purporting to be from burgesses of Gloucester, from a chaplain in Bristol and from a peasant of Malle in Standish manor, this last having been drawn up and sealed, not at Standish, but as the chirograph informs us, at Gloucester.[47] The chirographs were

---

[44] e.g. the lease to Gilbert, carter of Preston, a *nativus*. *Cart. Glouc.*, ii. 87. Cf. i. 160; ii. 201.

[45] 'Deeds and Seals', i, fol. 27.

[46] Ibid. vii, fol. 23.

[47] Ibid. x, fol. 12; vi, fol. 6; vii, fol. 7. There are several of these burgess seals in vols. VIII and IX. The Bristol chaplain was a donor of land (in Churcham and Morton), to the abbey, and the deed to which the seal is attached is an ordinary charter. Its date is 1330.

probably all drawn up and sealed at the Abbey in Gloucester, so the floral device may have been a favourite one of an abbey or town matrix-engraver.[48] Villeins or other peasants could have seals with other devices, of course, or perhaps borrowed some other person's seal. The Coln Rogers indenture (1289) by which the abbey leased land to their reeve and by which he was forbidden to escape from his villein condition was sealed with a seal bearing a bird device. The lettering is illegible but seems not to bear the reeve's name. Another Coln Rogers lease of 1310, again appearing to involve unfree tenants, was sealed with a seal bearing a device looking like a squirrel. A lease at La Hyde of a half virgate bears two seals, one with the name of the lessee and what appears to be a boar's head, as a device, the other (perhaps belonging to the lessee's wife) bearing a shield with a bird. A much later lease (1339) of Coln St. Aldwyn of a messuage, curtilage, and four acres, for life or 60 years, carries a comparatively large seal, which, though broken, has the remains of a rather elaborate device.[49]

The original deeds and seals are not abundant and their evidence is fragmentary. But at any rate they reinforce that impression of the increasing scope of the economic activity of the richer peasants in the second half of the thirteenth century, which the development of life leases and the substitution of money for labour rent would also imply.

[48] The device is not unlike that of the seal on the extreme top left of the collection of seals of the men of Frieston and Butterwick, Lincs., reproduced with Sir Hilary Jenkinson's article, 'The Study of English Seals', *Journal of the British Archaeological Association*, 3rd Series, i, 1937.

[49] 'Deeds and Seals', vi, fols. 18, 11; fol. 15; vi, fol. 18. La Hyde is possibly Monkhide, Heref.

# APPENDIX

Transcripts of some Gloucester Abbey Leases

Deeds and Seals, x, fol. 12
Chirograph

Sciant presentes et futuri quod nos Reginaldus dei gracia Abbas Sancti Petri Glouc' et eiusdem loc conventus con / cessimus et tradidimus Ricardo de Webbeleya et Alicie uxori sue quandam dimidiam virgatam terre cum pertinentiis / suis et unum mesuagium in villa de Culna Rogeri Que quidem terram et mesuagium cum pertinenciis suis Lucia de / Fraxino aliquando de nobis tenuit in eadem villa. Habendo [sic] et tenendam dictam terram cum mesuagio et omnibus / pertinenciis suis eidem Ricardo et uxori sue prenominate ad vitam illorum tantum videlicet si virum suum supervixerit et dum / continens fuerit bene quiete et in pace Reddendo inde annuatim nobis et successoribus nostris dimidiam marcam / argenti ad quatuor anni terminos videlicet ad festum annunciacionis dominice viginti denarios Ad festum beati / Johannis Baptiste viginti denarios ad festum sancti Michelis viginti denarios et ad festum beati Andree Apostoli / viginti denarios Pro quo quidem redditu omnes consuetudines serviles de dicto tenemento debitas nobis / remisimus eisdem et omnes alias demandas de dicta terra ad nos pertinentes salva nobis secta curie / nostre de Culna Rogeri cum aliis hominibus quociens eam teneri contigerit. Iidem vero Ricardus et Alicia iuram / entum nobis prostiterunt quod fideles erunt ecclesie nostre et maxime de reddendo redditu nostro plenarie ad terminos sta / tutas et quod nec artem nec ingenuum exquirent unde domus nostra per tenuram suam dampnum incurr / et Et quod prefatum terram seu eius aliquam partem necque vendent necque excambient necque in vadimonium ponent / nec alicui sub aliqualis forma convencionis tradent sine assensu et voluntate nostra. Prefati eciam Ricardus et Alicia / tam certa inter nos convencione facta quam tenore huius scripti se obligarunt quod si dictam terram vel aliquam eius partem / alicui ad firmam tradere vendere seu invadiare voluerint nos omnibus aliis erimus propinquiores Dum tamen tan / tum eis pro dicta terra racionabiliter dare voluerimus quantum et alii dare voluerint Post decessum antedictorum / Ricardi et Alicie tota terra prenominata cum suis omnibus pertinentiis et cum omni melioratione superposita ad nos seu / ad successores nostros plenarie et integraliter revertetur absque alicuius impedimento clamio seu contradictione. In cuius rei / testimonium presens scriptum in modum cyrographi inter nos confectum est cuius

unam partem sigillo ecclesie nostre sig / natam prefatis dicto Ricardo et
Alicie tradidimus alteram vero partem sigillo ipsius Ricardi roboratam
penes nos / retinuimus Hiis testibus Willelmo Jorge Johanne Masseys
Johanne filio / Hugonis de Feyreford Johanne de Frax / ino Waltero
Gylwy Johanne de Bristoll clerico et multis aliis.
  Seal: Flower device.
  Richard's inscription.


Deeds and Seals, vii, fol. 23
Chirograph (in parts defective)

  [*Sciant presentes*] et futuri quod [*nos N. Dei*]⁵⁰ gratia Abbas Sancti
Petri Glouc' et eiusdem loci conventus concessimus et tradidimus
Waltero de Culna nativo nostra / [*molendin*] um nostrum de Culna
Rogeri cum mesuagio et terra ad dictum molendinum pertinente que
quidem Willelmus Sleyt de nobis tenuit in eadem villa Tenenda / et
[*habenda*] de nobis et successoribus nostris ad vitam ipsius tantum et ad
vitam prime uxoris sui si eum supervixeret et continens fuerit Reddendo inde annuatim nobis et successoribus nostris / viginti tres solidos ad
quatuor anni terminos usuales et duodecim denarios annuatim ad
auxilium in festo Sancti Michelis pro omni servicio et seculari demanda
ad / . . . inde pertinente salva nobis secta curie nostre apud Culna
Rogeri cum aliis hominibus nostris Idem vero Walterus iuramentum
nobis prestitit quod fidelis erit ecclesie⁵¹ nostre et maxime de reddendo
redditu nostro plenarie terminis statutis et quod artem nec ingenium
exquiret unde domus nostrum per tenuram suam dampnum incurrat /
Et quod prefatum molendinum seu terram neque vendet neque
excambiet neque in vadimonium ponet neque alicui sub aliqualis forma
convencionis tradet nec ad alium locum / religionis transferet sine
assense et voluntate nostra molendinum et prefatum et cetera edificia in
adeo bono statu vel meliori sustinebit sicut a nobis ea recepit / Que
tempore huius concessionis et tradicionis appresiata triginta solidos
sterlingorum per veram valebant estimacionem Quod ut liquido
observetur concessit idem Walterus quod balivus [sic] / et prepositus
loci prefati assumptis secum decem vel duodecim hominibus nostris
iuratis de eadem villa molendinum antedictum et cetera edificia bis vel
ter singulis annis vide / rint Inquisitionibus⁵² si aliquis invenerint
deterioracionem Walterum prefatum incuntanter facient premuniri et
quod infra mensem post visum huiusmodi perpetratum que deteriorata
re / [*peranda*] faciat reperari Et si infra terminum prefixum non emendaverit que fuerunt emendenda tam certa convencione quam tenore

⁵⁰ Probably Reginald de Homme, 1263–84.  ⁵¹ MS. *e / defic'*.
⁵² *Sic*; the abbreviation is *Inqbz*. The sense of this sentence is difficult, though the
general drift is clear.

huius scripti nobis licebit dictum Walterum / ... em distringere quousque emendaverit plenarie que correctione indiguerint Eandem securitatem nobis faciet prima uxor eius si eum supervixerit et continens fu / [erit Post decessum] vero predictorum [*Walteri et ux*] oris sue sepedictum molendinum et terra cum suis omnibus pertinentiis [*et*] cum melioratione superposita ad nos seu ad / [*successores*] nostros plenarie et integraliter [*revertentur absque*] alicuius sue successione contradictione In premissorum omnium robur et testimonium presens scriptum in / [*modum*] cyrographi inter nos confectum est cuius unam partem sigillo ecclesie nostre signata prefato Waltero tradidimus alteram [*vero par*] tem sigillo ipsius Walteri roboratam / penes nos retinuimus Hiis testibus Johanne Marcys Johanne Clerebaut Johanne de la Hascle Willelmo de Lynceholte Waltero ... et multis aliis.

Seal: Walter of Coln Roger—flower.

Deeds and Seals, vi, fol. 18
Chirograph

Notum sit omnibus Christi fidelibus ad quos presens scriptum pervenerit quod nos J.[53] permissione divina Abbas Sancti Petri Glouc' et eiusdem loci conventus / concessimus et tradidimus Willelmo preposito nostro de Culna Rogeri et Agneti uxori sue Duas partes unius virgate terre quam quondam tenuit Robertus de Aula et unam / dimidiam virgatam terre servilem in Culna Rogeri predicta Habendas et tenendas dictis Willelmo et Agneti ad vitam eorom tantum vel alteri eorum qui alium / supervixerit ad eius vitam tantum salvo iure cuiuslibet ulterius vel aliorum si quod ius habeant in premissis Reddendo annuatim nobis et successoribus nostris pro Duabus / partibus dicte virgate terre Decem solidos sterlingorum et pro dimidia virgata terre Octo solidos ad terminos ipsius manerii consuetos Et faciendo similiter in / pannagio porcorum tolneto cervisii et equorum et aliis huiusmodi minutis consuetudinibus secundum quod faciunt alii nostri Nativi ibidem. Hoc dumtaxat excepto / quod arare herciare cariare metere et falcare vel alias operaciones manuales facere non tenentur. Et quod post mortem eorum dicta terra cum omni melioratione / superposita ad nos et successores nostros absque reclamacione quorumcunque heredum suorum integraliter revertatur Ita tamen quod sanguis eorum nullatenus immutetur sed / ipsi et eorum successores nostri servi et servilis condicionis existant. In cuius rei testimonium huic scripto inter nos cyrographato sigilla nostra mutuo sunt appensa / Dat' in capitulo Gloucestr' die beati Eadmundi Regis et martiris Anno Regni Regis Edwardi Octavodecimo.

[53] John de Gamages, abbot 1284–1306.

Seal: device—an eagle standing with spread wings holding a palm
leaf? in its left claw; inscription, illegible, but certainly not
William of Coln Rogers.
At top of seal separating lettering is star and crescent.

Deeds and Seals, x, fol. 10
Chirograph

Die Jovis post festum Annunciacionis dominice Anno regno Regis
Edwardi tercij post conquestum quartodecimo Inter religiosos viros
Abbatem et convencionem sancti Petri Glouc' ex parte una / et Henri-
cum Dun et Mathildam uxorem eius quam habuit die confeccionis
presentis ex altera ita convenit videlicet quod dicti Religiosi tradiderunt
et dimiserunt dictis Henrico et Mathilda illud mesuagium / et molendinum cum terra et prato adiacentibus quod Robertus Dun quondam
tenuit in Culna sancti Aylwyni cum dimidia secta villanorum eorundem de eadem eciam de Aldesworth que quidem sec / ta dicto molendino fieri consuerat tempore Roberti Dun patris eiusdem Habendum
et tenendum predictum mesuagium cum molendino terra et prato de
predictis religiosis et eorum successoribus predictis Henrico / et
Mathilda ad terminum sexaginta annorum si tantum vixerint Reddendo inde et faciendo annuatim dicti Henricus et Mathilda et eorum alter
qui alium supervixerit / dictis religiosis et eorum successoribus viginti
solidos et quatuor denarios argenti ad quatuor anni terminos in villa
predicta usuales per equales porciones et auxilium singulis annis / in
festo Sancti Michelis sicut predictus Robertus reddere consuevit
Invenient eciam dicti Henricus et Mathilda et eorum alter qui alium
supervixerit duos homines ad metendum bladum / dictorum religiosorum per quinque dies in autumpno et unum hominem ad falcandum in
prato eorundem Religiosorum per duos / dies Et unum hominem ad
faciendum mulones feni per unum diem. Et unum hominem ad faciendum tassum in grangia ipsorum Religiosorum per unum diem. Et si
braciaverint / ad vendendum dabunt quatuor lagenas cervisie vel
precium Et si vendiderint equum vel bovem infra manerium antedictum dabunt unum denarium ad theoloneum Dabunt / et pannagium
pro porcis suis scilicet pro porco superannato unum denarium et pro
porco minoris etatis obolum si habilis fuerit ad separandum ffacient
etiam prefati Henricus / et Mathilda vel eorum alter qui supervixerit
sectam ad curiam dictorum Religiosorum de Culna Sancti Aylwyni
quociens eam teneri contigerit Habebunt eciam dicti Religioso / libera
moltura bladi et brasii pro se et famulis suis de Culna predicta ad dictum
molendinum sine Theloneo Dabunt et decimam molendini sicut
predictus Robertus Dun / facere consuevit et herietum cum successive
decesserint ijdem vero Henricus et Mathilda sustentabunt idem molen-

dinum cum reliquis edificiis superposita in adeo bono/statu vel meliori quo fuerunt in tempore confeccionis huius scripti que fuerunt appreciata ad valentiam decem librorum Nec licebat eisdem vastum facere in / arboribus accrescentibus nec earum aliquas prosternere nisi ad dicti edificii sustentacionem quod si contra presentem articulum per visum celerarij nostri et tenencium / nostorum dicti manerii quos ad se vocare voluerit pro visu faciendo quociens sibi placuerit reperti fuerint transgressores amerciabuntur iuxta quantitatem / delicti per consideracionem Sectatorum Curie antedicte Dictum vero tenementum post decessum dictorum Henricus et Mathilda cum omni melioracione superposita / ad dictos Religiosos plenarie revertetur In cuius rei testimonium sigilla partium predictarum scripto indentato mutuo sunt apposita Data in capitulo dictorum / Religiosorum Glouc' die et anno supradictis

Two seals.

# IX

# A Study in the Pre-history of English Enclosure in the Fifteenth Century*

## INTRODUCTION

Perhaps there is no darker century in the history of English rural society than the fifteenth. The important controversies between the exponents of two theories, that of universal economic stagnation during this period, and that of economic progress within the framework of a collapsed seigneurial economy, have not progressed as yet beyond generalities.[1] One aspect of the agrarian development of the period has, however, been examined in some detail by several generations of historians. I refer to the dispersal of communities of arable farmers as a result of a number of economic and social developments, of which the most publicized (in the fifteenth and sixteenth centuries as well as in the twentieth) was the conversion of open-field arable into pasture land for sheep. This dispersal was placed in the general perspective of the development of English capitalism by one of the great masters of economic history as early as 1867,[2] and has since been discussed from different angles by other economic historians.[3] Interest in the

---

* Reprinted from *Studi in honore di Armando Sapori*, 1957, pp. 674–85.

[1] M. M. Postan, 'The Fifteenth Century', *EcHR*, ix, 1939, and 'Some Economic Evidence for Declining Population in the Later Middle Ages', 2nd ser. ii ibid., 1950, both reprinted in *Essays in Medieval Agriculture and General Problems of Medieval Economy*, 1973. E. A. Kosminsky, 'Feudal Rent in England', *Past and Present*, no. 7, 1955. [Since this introductory sentence was written, the debate has been carried forward. For more recent statements see M. M. Postan, *The Medieval Economy and Society*, 1972 and A. R. Bridbury, *Economic Growth: England in the Later Middle Ages*, 1962.]

[2] The date of publication of the first volume (in German) of K. Marx's, *Capital*, where this problem is discussed in Chapter XXIV on 'Primary Accumulation'.

[3] The outstanding names are those of I. Leadam and E. F. Gay, who discussed the returns of the Enclosure Commission of 1517, edited by I. Leadam for the

subject has been revived by more recent work, whose weakness, perhaps, is a tendency to dramatize the subject.[4] Its attention, however, to the history of individual villages is a useful correction to the earlier general statistical approach based on the returns of the 1517 commission of inquiry.

The concentration of the attentions of historians on the grazier as the villain of the piece, responsible for the destruction of villages, seems to have had the effect of discouraging research into other important elements in the situation. These include the question of whether there was alternative and possibly more attractive employment in rural and urban industry. Even more important is the question of the disintegration of the medieval village or hamlet community as a coherent organism.[5] I will try to illustrate these points in the following notes on three rural settlements in Warwickshire, based on rather scanty and scattered documents from a family collection of archives.[6]

Warwickshire in the fifteenth century was a typical county of the English lowland zone in that it contained a varying physical landscape and many different types of rural settlement. Contrasting with the recently assarted country of the Forest of Arden in the north of the county, where scattered settlements and small hedged or ditched enclosures were already common, was the more anciently settled southern region. Here woodland had early given place to big communities of arable peasant farmers, and here the manorial regime was more firmly established. Even so, south Warwickshire as early as 1279 had a surprisingly high pro-

Royal Historical Society (*The Domesday of Enclosures*, 1897) and R. H. Tawney, *The Agrarian Problem of the Sixteenth Century*, London, 1912.

[4] W. G. Hoskins, *Essays in Leicestershire History*, 1951; M. Beresford, *The Lost Villages of England*, 1954, and 'The Deserted Villages of Warwickshire', *Transactions of the Birmingham and Midland Archaeological Society*, lxvi, 1950.

[5] I do not suggest that such matters have not been discussed. Geographers have made illuminating comments in discussion of the general problems of agglomeration and dispersal of rural settlements; e.g. M. A. Perpillou in his Sorbonne lectures, *L'Habitat rural*, 1953, M. Sorre, *Les Fondements de la géographie humaine*, Paris, 1943–52, iii; H. Thorpe, *The influence of Inclosure on the Form and Pattern of Rural Settlement in Denmark*, Institute of British Geographers, Publication No. 17.

[6] The Willoughby de Broke MSS. at Shakespeare's Birthplace, Stratford-upon-Avon.

portion of small manors and a comparatively large number of peasants unburdened by domanial labour services.[7] By the end of the fourteenth century peasants in the Avon valley south of Coventry held land hardly subject at all to customary terms of tenure.[8] The estate economy of the typical south Warwickshire gentry family, the Catesbys, at about the same period was based on a village where an arable demesne was worked almost entirely by wage labour (Ladbrooke), and an adjacent village (Radbourn) where a domanial flock of some 400 sheep was kept.[9] The evidence, such as it is, indicates a region where the predominance of money rents and the prominence of wage labour must suggest a considerable amount of production for the market. Coventry, Warwickshire's biggest town, was a well-known textile centre, and though the country cloth industry of the Midlands was not as prominent as that of Yorkshire, East Anglia, and the West Country, its existence caused some anxieties in established urban cloth centres in the fifteenth and early sixteenth centuries.[10] In other words, in town and country there was probably a substantial demand by non-producers of agricultural produce for wool and meat as well as cereals.

The three villages to which these notes are devoted were Compton Verney, Chesterton Magna, and Kingston (sometimes called Chesterton Parva, being in Chesterton parish). Situated within four or five miles of each other, they lie as many miles south-east of the Avon valley within easy reach of the market towns of Stratford-upon-Avon, and Warwick, and no great distance from Coventry and Banbury. They were all mentioned

[7] See E. A. Kosminsky. *Studies in the Agrarian History of England in the Thirteenth Century* (English edition 1956), and R. H. Hilton, *Social Structure of Rural Warwickshire in the Middle Ages*, 1950.

[8] The *Stoneleigh Leger Book*, ed. R. H. Hilton, Dugdale Society, 1960, contains a very detailed rental of this period.

[9] PRO, Ministers' Accounts, 1041/10 and 13.

[10] Cf. *Worcester City Ordinances 1467*, in 'English Gilds', ed. T. Smith, EETS o.s. 40, 1870; *Worcester Liber Legum 1497*, printed as an Appendix to V. Green, *History of Worcester*, 1796; *Coventry Leet Book*, ed. M. Dormer Harris, EETS 1907–13, pp. 661, 723, 789, 791; *Act for the Protection of Worcester, Evesham, Droitwich, Kidderminster and Bromsgrove, 1534*, in R. H. Tawney and E. Power, *Tudor Economic Documents*, 1924, i. 173–5.

by the Warwickshire man John Rous, writing about or before 1490, as being partially or completely depopulated. He was right in suggesting that two centuries earlier they had been much more populous than in his days, although he may have exaggerated the extent of depopulation.[11] Compton Verney, or Compton Murdak as it was then called, was in 1279 a village of perhaps forty families, of whom half were mere smallholders. The tax return of 1332 suggests little change.[12] Chesterton parish in the late thirteenth and early fourteenth centuries seems to have contained about as many families, distributed over three nuclei of settlement, that is Kingston, Chesterton Church End, and Chesterton Green.[13] By the middle of Henry VIII's reign there were only eight tax-payers beside the lord of the manor (John Peyto) and six of these were assessed as wage earners, not as property owners. The hamlet of Kingston simply does not appear in the tax returns, and un-fortunately the returns for Compton Murdak (or Verney) are defective.[14] There have clearly been big changes in these villages in the two centuries and more which separate the evidence pro-vided by royal administrative and fiscal inquiries. The private documents of the late fourteenth and fifteenth centuries suggest how these changes happened. They indicate clearly that before

[11] J. Rous, *Historia Regum Anglie*, ed. T. Hearne, 1745, pp. 121 ff. Rous quotes the Warwickshire Hundred Rolls of 1279 as evidence of village depopula-tion at that date. Although not entirely accurate, he is clearly not imagining the changes about which he speaks. A critical examination of his evidence is desirable. Hitherto historians have been either too sceptical or too trusting.

[12] PRO, Exchequer KR Misc. Books, no. 15, lxxxi b. and *Lay Subsidy Roll for Warwickshire, 1332*, ed. W. F. Carter, Dugdale Society, 1926, p. 22.

[13] *Lay Subsidy Roll*, p. 22. Willoughby de Broke MSS. 222 and 266 mention 'Church End' suggesting that the present division of the village into two portions is ancient (early fourteenth century) rather than the result of depopulation, as Mr. Beresford's thinks, art. cit., p. 89. Chesterton's two portions were usually referred to as one and had not the same lord as Kingston. A single bailiff's account roll of 1354–5 accounts jointly for (apparently) two manors of Chesterton, one of William de Peyto, the other of John de Peyto. See W. Dugdale, *Antiquities of Warwickshire*, 1730, i. 477, for a sub-manor in Chesterton, bought up by William Peyto in 1352.

[14] PRO, E/179/192/122. The returns of 35 Henry VIII for Chesterton show symptoms of depopulation. There are four members of the Peyto family sepa-rately assessed on land, three other taxpayers assessed on goods as between £3 and £6, four assessed at 40s. and three at 20s. PRO, E/179/192/153.

there was any dramatic depopulating enclosure, the ancient communities of arable farmers were breaking up as the old tenemental system disintegrated, as some tenants left the manor and others concentrated their holdings, and as significant changes in the use of the land by the peasants themselves made their appearance.

## THE PEASANTS AND THEIR HOLDINGS ON THE VERNEY MANORS

Apart from charters, the first documents that tell anything about the social and economic structure of Kingston are two bailiff's accounts for the years 1393–5.[15] Symptoms of economic change are only just appearing. Most of the lettings of tenements are customary, though for money rent. However, there are also a number of ten-year leases, both of regular tenements as well as of odd tofts. Concentration of holdings in few hands has not gone far, and there are seven or eight holdings *in manibus domini*. All these phenomena are found in many manorial documents of the period, and the most interesting symptoms of change at this time are to be found, as we shall see below, in changing land use rather than (as yet) in changing social structure. By 1430, however, it is clear that important social changes have come about. A rental of this date[16] shows a fall in the number of tenants of nearly a half, but rather less land *in manibus domini*. One tenant has acquired a holding of considerable size, consisting of five yardlands (say 120 to 150 acres) of which three were from the demesne.

Contemporary evidence from Compton Verney suggests that lapses of holdings into the lord's hands were not simply due to the failure of the population to replace itself naturally. Court rolls between 1397 and 1401[17] show a number of surrenders of holdings by tenants still living, there being eight to ten such withdrawals to one surrender through the death of a tenant. Since in the same rolls there are a number of presentments of villeins for living outside the manor without licence, we might conclude that surrender

[15] Willoughby de Broke MSS. 438 and 439.

[16] Ibid. 465. A court roll of the same year shows which tenants had done fealty for various tenements but gives an incomplete picture. Ibid. 463[a].

[17] Ibid. 63, 64[a], and 67.

of land at Compton and the considerable fall in the number of tenants at Kingston were aspects of a drift away from these villages to other centres. The reasons for the surrender of holdings are not given. We cannot conclude therefore that these were simply old men no longer able to maintain their holdings, for there is no sign of sons taking over. One man was so poor that he could not pay a heriot. Poverty therefore—not lack of land but lack of equipment and money reserves[18]—may have been a factor, not incompatible with a drift to towns or to country industry.

As at Kingston and in many other English villages at this period, the departure of poor men from holdings in Compton was accompanied by the accumulation of land by the more fortunate few. A rental of 1406[19] shows that small portions of holdings once in other men's hands (the previous tenants often being named) were being accumulated, some tenants paying three or four times as much rent for different portions of land taken by the acre or by the ridge as for their basic yardland or half yardland. As at Kingston and elsewhere, the number of terminal leases, mostly of eight to ten years, was increasing in proportion to customary lettings.[20] Another significant feature of peasant holdings in Compton at this period is the tendency to the illegal appropriation of portions of lapsed holdings. The court rolls already quoted contain a number of cases where tenants are accused of sowing portions of tenements *in manibus domini* without obtaining the land officially on lease in the manor court. If this practice were widespread the quotation of holdings *in manibus domini* in manorial documents does not necessarily imply the falling out of cultivation of such land.[21]

[18] In one case the lord may have provided the tenant with equipment, for on surrender the tenant not only paid a heriot but left behind *certa principalia* viz. an iron bound cart, a plough with share and coulter and harness, a cauldron, a pan, a vat, and a kneading trough (*knedtrowh*). The holding had been two messuages, a yardland and three acres, held at will. Willoughby de Broke MSS. 63.

[19] Ibid., 31ª.

[20] The rather fragmentary evidence quoted by authors of articles on social and economic history in the volumes of the *Victoria County History* suggests an increase in leases of this length of term at the end of the fourteenth and beginning of the fifteenth centuries.

[21] In 1400 John Compton, for example, is presented for sowing the following land without permission: three sellions with drage on land of one lapsed holding; two sellions of another holding, also with drage; nine sellions with wheat and

LAND USE

The documents of Compton and Kingston already quoted contain indications that there was a trend among peasants towards a greater specialization in pastoral farming. The Kingston account roll of 1393–4 immediately invites this conclusion. More than a half of the manorial receipts (excluding arrears) are derived from various aspects of the pasturing of tenant beasts.[22] Income entered *venditio pasture et herbagii* brings in as much as the total rent from holdings. It consists of payments by tenants for the pasture or herbage of a variety of pieces of meadow, uncultivated land, heath, pasture, enclosures, headland, and even «sellions» (a term normally used for open-field arable ridges). The use of previously arable strips as pasture is confirmed by an entry under rents of holdings, where we find a tenant for life holding, *inter alia*, ten sellions of pasture at the 'Waterforewes'. The place-name might imply no more than the existence of drainage ditches, but deliberate irrigation need not be ruled out.[23]

The Compton rental of 1406, as mentioned, contains details of piece-meal leases, mostly by the acre and by the ridge. These include a good number of cases of sellions leased as pasture, which are described either as *seliones terre tenentium*, or located more precisely in named open-field furlongs. It will be remembered that there is also court roll evidence from Compton. Here we have a number of presentments of trespasses by peasant beasts in the lord's meadows and separate pastures. These include, on three occasions, trespass by complete sheep flocks from the adjacent hamlet of Combrook.

SEIGNEURIAL POLICY

Social and technical changes may have presented difficult problems to the traditional manorial administration at this period. In

seven sellions with peas on land of the first holding; one sellion of peas on demesne land. He also occupied and fallowed six sellions of the first holding. Willoughby de Broke MSS. 64ᵃ.

[22] There would appear to be no arable demesne worked. One of the lord's servants, however, is described as 'warden of the beasts'.

[23] At Boarstall, Oxon., there was a 'Waterfurowfurlong' in Arngrove field in 1453. *Boarstall Cartulary*, ed. H. Salter, Oxford Historical Society, 1930, p. 221. For drainage ditches in Chesterton see below, note 37.

1394 the lord of Kingston had to pardon the heavy arrears both of the current bailiff and of his three predecessors. The arrears, we are told, were in part due to the inability of the bailiffs to collect rents. The 1406 rental of Compton shows a curiously frank recognition of the same problem. It is a rental for the Michaelmas term only, and for each tenant we are given the figure of his arrears (sometimes going back several years), his liability for current rent, the amount paid off and the amount still owed. The rent collector's entries are not always clear, and are very untidy, but the conclusion is nevertheless clear. All tenants seem to have been complacent debtors. The apparent incompetence of management may have been due to local and temporary conditions. It may have been a symptom of the dislocation which probably occurred as lords who had exploited their demesnes became *rentiers*. It seems likely, however, that the drop in the number of tenants, the tendency to the accumulation of holdings and the turn towards pasture farming also destroyed the cohesion of the medieval rural community. Given such conditions a vigorous landlord could carry these tendencies to their logical conclusion and become himself the final accumulator of all holdings, which he could then turn to pasture.[24]

Such a landlord family appears in Compton and Kingston. The Murdaks of Compton and the Leighs of Kingston (or their representatives) disappear at the beginning of the fifteenth century,[25] and although the situation is confused, the Verney family was in possession by 1430. The origins of this family are obscure. William Dugdale was unable to trace them back with certainty beyond the beginning of the fifteenth century, in spite of his unrivalled knowledge of Warwickshire family history.[26] His suggestion that

[24] For another example of heavy rent arrears see my article on Kibworth Harcourt in *Studies in Leicestershire Agrarian History*, ed., W. G. Hoskins, 1949; and above, p. 65.

[25] *Victoria History of the County of Warwick*, v, 44 and 59, where the acquisition of the manors by the Verneys is dated too late (in the 1440s). In the documents, Kingston is referred to as Kingston Verney by 1430 and Compton Murdak was held by John Verney in 1432 or before. Willoughby de Broke MSS. 89ᵃ and 465. Mr. Beresford, art. cit., who quotes from this collection, nevertheless follows the dating of the *VCH*.

[26] *Antiquities of Warwickshire*, p. 565.

they originated in Staffordshire is, however, very plausible, for the man who seems to have founded their later fortunes, John Verney, rector of Bredon and archdeacon of Worcester, was also Dean of Lichfield Cathedral. These ecclesiastical honours did not make him a person of influence, but were themselves probably the consequence of the fact that he already was a person of influence in the entourage of Richard Beauchamp, Earl of Warwick. From about 1430 he was Receiver and Supervisor of the Beauchamp estates and deeds of the period show him as the familiar of such gentry as the Throckmortons of Coughton and the Lucys of Charlecote, and of such Beauchamp officials as Rody, Baysham, and others.[27] A number of enfeoffments in the Wiloughby de Broke manuscripts at this period make for some doubt as to who was, in law, the actual lord of Compton manor,[28] but there is no doubt that the use of the property was in the hands of the Verney family and that in fact this meant Richard Verney, John's brother.

## ENCLOSURE

The first document revealing the economic policy of the Verneys concerns the manor of Kingston. It is a lease indenture, dated February 1437, between Richard Verney and John Lichfelde of Coventry, grazier, by which Verney leases the manor to Lichfelde for ten years for forty marks a year and the right to take forty cartloads of hay a year. This transaction has several interesting features. The lessee was a prominent Coventry citizen who usually appears in the city records as a butcher,[29] and who therefore may have wanted to graze beasts for meat rather than sheep for wool. The manner in which the land leased is described makes it clear that it was already enclosed and that it must have com-

---

[27] See the introduction to my edition of *The Ministers' Accounts of the War-wickshire Estates of the Duke of Clarence*, Dugdale Society, 1952, and *The Estates and Finances of Richard Beauchamp, Earl of Warwick*, by C.D. Ross, Dugdale Society, 1956.

[28] e.g. nos. 89s, 97, 115ᵃ etc. Attached to 89a (1432) is a well-preserved seal of John Verney, bearing his shield of arms, crested, with the inscription *Sigillum armorii Johannis Verney*.

[29] *Coventry Leet Book, passim* (see index).

prised a great part of not the whole of the land in the manor.[30] The rent due from the lessee (40 marks or £26 23s. 4d.) was more than the gross receipt, less arrears, of the whole manor in 1395 (£17) and very much more than amount of cash handed over by the bailiff that year to the lord (£11 11s.), an amount which we may take roughly as the net value. In other words, an enclosed manor was worth much more, even when the lord leased it, than a manor run on the old lines.

Although the terms of the lease of Kingston show that a considerable portion if not all, of the manor was enclosed as pasture by 1437, there is no record of the process of enclosure. Nor is there such record at Compton Verney. Compton Verney, however, had largely been transformed by 1461. In that year a «renewed rental» was made of the domains and lands of Sir Richard Verney in Warwickshire and Northamptonshire.[31] In both Kingston and Compton a farm or rent in round figures is given for each field, so that even if we did not know, in the case of Kingston, that enclosure had already taken place, we should have been reasonably sure from the evidence of the rental alone, since open fields with intermixed arable holdings are not valued in this way. At Kingston, three fields are mentioned (East Field, South Field and Middle Field), farmed at £14 13s. 4d., £14 6s. 8d. and £13 6s. 8d. respectively, with an extra farm of £5 from the herbage of the three fields.[32] At Compton there were six fields

---

[30] Lichefelde has the manor (house?) of Kingston *cum omnibus suis pertinenciis infra cepes et fossata campi de Kingston dicto manerio adiacentibus*; distraint for rent is to be *infra cepes et fossata campi predicti;* the lessor's hay is to be collected *ubicumque infra pratum campi predicti.* Willoughby de Broke MSS. 473. This phraseology is used in a conveyance of the manor a fortnight later from Richard to John Verney. The reason for this conveyance within the family is obscure. It need not have affected Lichfelde's terminal lease. Ibid., p. 474.

[31] Willoughby de Broke MSS. 504a. Kingston and Compton are the only complete manors in this rental. The other income consists of rents from other south Warwickshire villages and from Northampton town, making a total rental of £130 11s. 4d.

[32] Professor Beresford, quoting this document, thinks that because three fields are mentioned they must have been open fields. The Kingston account roll of 1395 however contains a phrase under the rent heading, *vi acris terre divisim in duobus campis de Kyngestone,* which suggests a two field village in pre-enclosure days. Willoughby de Broke MSS. 439.

(Ladyes Field, West Field, East Field, Middle Field, Northfield and Stafford Field) and here we are given the values of the farm rents of the *pasture* of the fields. Another field called Court Field is assessed at a farm rent but without specifying pasture, and here is a meadow called Northslade meadow also assessed at a farm rent. There seems little room for doubt that the two villages had ceased to exist as communities of arable farmers long before 1461, but whether at that date there were any villagers left is unknown. The rent and farm of Kingston village was assessed at £2 13s. 4d. and of Compton at £4, so there may still have been a few payers of rent living there.

## GREAT CHESTERTON

The history of Great Chesterton, the village adjacent to Kingston, has not yet been mentioned. We have no documents which enable us to see erosive forces at work prior to final enclosure as at Kingston and Compton. Judging by a bailiff's account of 1354–5, it not only had an unusually large arable demesne (354 acres under crop), but the livestock included a flock of nearly 800 sheep.[33] A series of fourteenth- and fifteenth-century deeds, in which the lands transferred are described in detail, suggest that until the second half of the fifteenth century the village fields were arable and open.[34] But some time before 1484 the lord of the manor, John Peyto, had adopted the enclosure policy of his neighbours. A fragmentary and almost illegible document, which seems to record a plea in the court of King's Bench in that year, contains sufficient legible matter to point to the existence of such a policy. The plaintiffs were two tenants of the manor, seised of arable holdings of thirty acres and forty acres respectively. They claimed, on their own behalf and for other tenants of the manor, common pasture at a rate of one beast and five sheep for one and a half arable acres. Their complaint was that Peyto, as lord, had turned

---

[33] Willoughby de Broke MSS. 393b.
[34] An analysis of twenty of these deeds shows about 180 separate furlong names in the open fields.

the arable into pasture, to their own loss, presumably by enclosure —the record is obscure.[35]

An agreement of 1520 confirms that some enclosure had happened some time previously. It contains a lease by the rectors of the parish (the vicars choral of Lichfield Cathedral). In it they lease to John Peyto, Esq., lord of Chesterton, 66 acres of arable land in his demesnes, being every tenth acre after nine had been counted for the lord. The phraseology suggests that when the demesne was in arable ridges the rectors had one-tenth of the land in place of a tithe of the produce, for the 66 acres are described in the agreement as being 'in three several pastures within the lord's demesnes', their names being 'the Grett Felde otherwise called the Conyngrefeld', 'the Moore', and 'a pasture called the Owe field'.[36] To legalize the enclosure of the rectors' land he had to take it on lease from them. And yet, although many of the fields referred to in this agreement are described as pastures, there still remained some open field arable in the village. In the same agreement there is another lease by the rectors of twelve acres of arable land in a field called 'the grett towene fylde'. The location of these acres, lying 'by various parcels' is described in terms of adjacent parcels held by other tenants, and by the terms of the lease, if Peyto could not get a tenant for the twelve acres, the rectors were to have it back, to relet it as they wished.[37] This field, with its divided occupancy, could only have been open arable.

Although the evidence for Chesterton is late, it is likely that the history of its conversion to a comparatively sparsely populated

[35] The following words can be read, namely that Peyto 'totam terram arabilem ibidem iacere permittit recenter et incolumen sine cultura et subversione carucarum et ad depascendum animalium et pecorum totam terram ibidem pos . . . tenens ibidem habere(?) . . . t plura animalia et pecora quam prius unquam habere solebant si terra illa arat subu'e et cult' fuerit [sic].' Willoughby de Broke MSS. 527.

[36] Ibid., 551.

[37] This part of the lease seems to cast doubt on the theory that a field called 'Town Field' betrays the site of a disappeared village. The 'considerable signs of former buildings', west of Chesterton Green have been tested with soil augurs by a party under the direction of Professor H. Thorpe of the Department of Geography of the University of Birmingham. It seems likely that the regular lines thought to be building foundations were in reality drainage ditches, 'water furrows' perhaps. Cf. M. Beresford, art. cit., p. 89.

village, where pastoral farming predominated was similar to that of its neighbours. The late fourteenth- and early fifteenth-century evidence from Kingston and Compton is at least as significant as that from the end of the fifteenth century, which merely confirms what we already know about seigneurial enclosures and evictions. English peasant communities in the thirteenth and fourteenth centuries had been capable of great resistance, even successful resistance, to attacks on their conditions by the landlords. If they allowed themselves to be evicted in the fifteenth and sixteenth centuries it was because economic and social changes had destroyed the cohesion that had been their strength in the past.

# X

# Rent and Capital Formation in Feudal Society*

MANY different aspects of the economic history of the Middle Ages could be examined within the framework of this discussion. Those aspects on which one historian can touch are necessarily limited by his own knowledge and appreciation of the subject-matter. I take for convenience a modern definition of capital formation, a definition particularly related to underdeveloped societies which are primarily agrarian in economy. Mr. R. Nurkse writes: 'The meaning of capital formation is that society does not apply the whole of its current productive activity to the needs and desires of immediate consumption, but directs a part of it to the making of capital goods: tools and instruments, machines and transport facilities, plant and equipment—all the various forms of real capital that can so greatly increase the efficacy of productive effort.'[1] The contribution made to capital formation in this sense from trading profits, from profits derived from financial operations, or directly from the profits made from productive activity, should in theory be excluded in this paper. In practice, however, as will be seen, it is not easy to separate the sources of income from which the formation of capital proceeds. In particular it is almost impossible, in the sources which best illustrate capital formation, to separate income in the form of rent and income derived from production.

The relations between rent and capital formation may perhaps be examined under two headings: I. The formation of capital from

* Reprinted from the proceedings of the *Second International Conference of Economic History 1962*, 1965, pp. 33–68.
[1] R. Nurkse, *Problems of Capital Formation in Under-developed Countries*, 1953; repr. 1966.

income in the form of rents paid to landowners, who reinvest part of that income. II. The limitation of capital formation by tenants as a result of the diversion of income in rent payments to land-owners. In both categories, attention will be directed to the primary source of rent in feudal society, that paid by tenants of agricultural land to landowners. Rents paid from urban land must also be considered, but these are not only less important quantita-tively, but less well documented. The constituents of capital for the purposes of this study must be clearly defined. They include the tools and equipment of landlord and peasant economies; buildings; other permanent improvements such as enclosures, drainage, roads, bridges, and waterways; industrial premises and equipment such as water mills for grinding corn, fulling cloth, or processing metal; mines and forges. I also consider the building up of herds of cattle, sheep, and other animals to be one of the most important ways of capital formation in feudal society.[2] On the other hand, investment in land must be excluded, for even though such investment might increase the total income of the purchaser, it does not in itself contribute to capital formation.[3] It is, however, true that land purchase or exchange made with the object of consolidating scattered holdings, thereby economizing on labour, can be considered as important elements in capital formation.

Many medieval historians, writing economic or social or techni-cal history, have given valuable examples of the type of capital formation we have described. The growth of medieval archae-ology will add further and more concrete evidence. What has not been done, and what is extremely difficult to do, is to show not only how capital formation was financed but what was the pro-portion of available resources which were diverted at different periods precisely for these purposes. To go further, and to show

---

[2] 'Parmi les formes de la propriété, celle du bétail était l'une des plus précieuses', W. P. de St. Jacob, 'Mutations économiques et sociales dans les campagnes bour-guignonnes à la fin du xvie siècle', *Études rurales*, i, 1937, 37.

[3] Professor J. A. Raftis in his interesting work, *The Estates of Ramsey Abbey*, 1964, p. 103, refers to 'capital investment in land'. This seems to be a wrong use of terms which might lead to errors in analysis. However, Professor Raftis's book is notable, compared with other studies, for its attention to questions of capital investment.

what proportion of available resources came from rent, makes the task no less significant but much more difficult. The most satisfactory type of source for these investigations will of course consist of continuous financial records of rent income and of capital expenditure. Estate and manorial accounts from England are, as it happens, the most abundant, hence one or two soundings from the English evidence seem the best way to pose the questions on the subject.

The English evidence has many defects, but the two most important limitations seem to be these: (i) Those estate records which have the best detail about expenditure on capital items are inevitably those where the landlord's income was not only from rent but from agricultural production. It is not difficult to separate these two sources of income entered on the receipt side of the accounts, but it is extremely difficult to say from which source of income expenditure was derived. (ii) The evidence about capital expenditure is that made by landlords, primarily on demesnes in hand. Capital formation within the peasant economy is not documented and can only be inferred. In spite of these limitations, the evidence from the manorial economy is of the greatest importance, not least because it is sometimes possible to estimate the annual average expenditure over periods of ten years or more. Annual expenditure on capital items whose usefulness might last for many years necessarily fluctuated considerably. Hence, although accounts for single years, or for a few years, need not be ignored, it is preferable to take average annual expenditure over a number of years.[4] It is surprising that in the many valuable studies which have been made of the economic development of particular estates, calculations about capital expenditure in relation to income, or to profits, have hardly ever been made.

Capital formation may be restricted by the smallness of the available surplus from production above basic subsistence needs. Other factors, such as the diversion of the surplus product to other requirements, must have been considerably affected by the prevailing mental attitude of those social classes who had available surpluses at their disposal. No doubt this attitude was a social

---

[4] Cf. the remarks about the measurement of capital formation on modern estates by D. R. Denman, *Estate Capital*, 1957, p. 44.

product, largely determined by the economic and social circumstances of the formative period of European feudalism. But in the thirteenth century (when our evidence is best), as at other times, mental attitudes were not simply the by-product of social and economic circumstances. They themselves had a positive influence on economic policy.

Many medieval landowners, it is well known, tended to spend up to the hilt on personal display, on extravagant living, on the maintenance of a numerous retinue, and on war. This expenditure was necessary to them for the support of their social status, for the reinforcement of their political influence and for the acquisition, through violence, legal process, or marriage, of landed property. These were the 'wasters' of the mid-fourteenth-century allegorical poem *A Good Short Debate between Winner and Waster*.[5] They were the military element among the ruling class ('stout men of arms, bold squires of blood'), who are contrasted in this poem with the clergy, lawyers, and merchants (the 'winners'). According to Winner, the allegorical spokesman for this group, Waster's lands are untilled and his equipment sold off to support his hunting and his military expeditions. Overeating, drinking, and other pleasures are paid for by ancestral lands sold off and woods cut down. Capital formation on Waster's estates would clearly be nil. Now Winner, Waster's severe critic, is represented in this poem as speaking for a substantial element in medieval landowning society. Were these winners savers and investors? Was their mental outlook one which would promote capital formation? According to Waster, (Winner's opponent), hardly so, for Winner's carefully gathered wealth was simply hoarded.

> What should wax of that wealth, if no waste were to come?
> Some would rot, some would rust, some rats would feed.
> Let be the cramming of thy coffers for Christ's love of Heaven,
> Let the people and the poor have part in thy silver.
> . . .
> When Christ's people have part, it pleaseth him better
> Than if it be huddled and hidden and hoarded in coffers,
> That no sun may it see through seven winters once!

[5] *Select Early English Poems*, ed. Sir Israel Gollancz, iii, 1920. The editor's modern English translation is used here.

Another expression of Winner's mentality is contained in those didactic treatises on estate management which proliferated in thirteenth- and fourteenth-century England.[6] Here, if anywhere, we should be able to see to what extent the medieval landowner or estate manager was mentally prepared to divert part of his income to capital formation. On the whole the treatises confirm Waster's criticism of Winner. An attitude favourable to investment in improvement would lay stress on the expenditure of profits from rents and production in new buildings, drainage, fertilizers, and livestock with the object of increasing yields. Instead, all of the treatises are pervaded by an atmosphere of careful parsimony. A fixed ceiling of production is assumed, and all advice is directed towards the elaboration of administrative means by which managers can be prevented from allowing production to fall too far below this ceiling. It is assumed that accounting officials intend to cheat, so the whole of the elaborate apparatus of control aims at defeating dishonesty rather than at promoting the expansion of production. The object of stock husbandry is to keep numbers steady rather than to promote increase. Should there be a surplus from production, it is not to be reinvested but either put aside for a rainy day or used for the comfort of the household.

In practice the ceiling is represented by the extent. The Bishop of Lincoln's first advice to the Countess of Lincoln is to make sworn surveys of all her lands and rights. This is the steward's first duty in the anonymous *Seneschaucie*. Walter of Henley's fictitious father says to his son 'Order your life according as your lands are valued yearly by the extent and nothing beyond that.' He adds 'If you can approve (*aprower*) your lands by tillage or cattle or other means beyond the extent, put the surplus in reserve (*en estu*) for if corn fail or cattle die or fire befall you, or other mishap, then what you have saved will help you.' This is echoed in *Fleta* (Bk. II, ch. 71). The Countess of Lincoln is to arrange her

---

[6] *Walter of Henley's Husbandry, together with an Anonymous Husbandry, Seneschaucie and Robert Grosseteste's Rules*, ed. E. Lamond, 1890; *Fleta*, ed. H. G. Richardson and G. O. Sayles (Selden Society), 1955, cf. D. Oschinsky, 'Medieval Treatises on Estate Management', *Ec.H.R*, 2nd series, viii, 1956.

economy so that as far as possible her household, her manorial servants, and her almsmen are victualled direct from the produce of the estate. Profits beyond this, to be derived from the yield of wool from sheep and cheese from cows may be turned into cash— to be spent on wine, robes, wax, and the wardrobe.

The treatises were written when an elaborate system of accounting, dating from the twelfth century at least, was well understood and almost universally applied. It was based in general on the checking, often twice a year, of the accounts of reeves, bailiffs, and other agents by auditors, against the extent. Within this system of account and audit, all sales and purchases had to be vouched for by tallies. Such a system would by no means be incompatible with an expanding economy. But in our treatises the checking of accounting officials is the dominant concern, and clearly limits any initiative which local managers might use. 'View of account', writes Walter of Henley 'was made to know the state of things . . . and for raising money. If there be any, let it be raised and taken from the hands of servants.' According to the thirteenth century *Scriptum Quoddam* of St. Peter's Abbey, Gloucester,[7] no new buildings or ditches could be begun without superior authority. These rules from St. Peter's show, throughout, the parsimony and excessive regulation of the treatises applied to one particular estate. But it was clearly a general tendency. A form of account of the fifteenth century states that bailiffs are not to sell stock without authorization, a regulation already to be found in the *Seneschaucie*. The author cautions them always to obtain warrants for any sales or purchases, disposal of dairy produce, employment of cash receipts from rents. The key word, in fact, in a long paragraph of advice to bailiffs is 'Caveas'.[8]

The attitude to livestock, that Achilles heel of the medieval agrarian economy, typifies the limitations of the economic attitude of the careful managers of the era. Walter of Henley's advice is directed to the maintenance, not an increase in numbers. The anonymous *Husbandry* aims to impart the conception of a fixed maximum. The *Seneschaucie* likewise concentrates on the

---

[7] *Historia et Cartularium Monasterii Gloucestriae*, iii, 1867, pp. 213–21.
[8] PRO, E. 163/24/34.

elimination of weaklings rather than the building up of herds. The reason is implied—pastures must not be overcharged. The Bishop of Lincoln also lists normal pasture stints. It should be emphasized of course that the agricultural writers had good reason for this attitude. A ceiling on the amount of stock which could be maintained was undoubtedly imposed by the shortage of hay and pasture, particularly in the thirteenth and early fourteenth centuries. To some extent then, objective limitations in the economy were responsible for the subjective attitude of economical operation within strictly fixed limits.

Another source for economic attitudes is the writings of those monastic chroniclers who concentrate primarily on the history of the estate. These are particularly relevant for our theme in view of panegyrics written by some modern historians about the administration of monastic estates at the end of the thirteenth and beginning of the fourteenth centuries.[9] It must be admitted that here we get a distinct impression that investment was favourably regarded, that is the outlay of cash in tangible, permanent, and material acquisitions. But a credit balance at the end of an abbacy was also regarded in the same light. Debtor abbots, however borrowed money might have been spent, were ill regarded. The acquisition of land, rights, and privileges bulks largest in chroniclers' accounts of the accumulation of income yielding resources. But there is clearly a favourable attitude as well, to those administrators who invested in building and in the stocking up (with live- or deadstock) of manors. Admittedly there is no attempt to discriminate as forms of investment between the building of churches and the building of barns, but this would be unlikely in view of the writers' profession.

Professor Knowles has quoted some of the most interesting of the chroniclers who comment on the economic activities of abbots and priors in the thirteenth and early fourteenth centuries.[10] One of the most notable examples is the chronicle of the Cistercian abbey of Meaux in Yorkshire. That part of the Meaux chronicle which was written in the abbey itself is almost entirely

[9] e.g. in D. Knowles, *The Religious Orders in England*, 1948, chaps. iv–vii.
[10] Op. cit., pp. 45–7, 72–4.

devoted to economic affairs. Most of it is occupied with records of acquisitions of, or disputes about land, but much too is devoted to recording the building of barns and mills, and especially to the construction of dykes. All agriculturalists and pastoralists great and small, in Holderness, had to build dykes for drainage in order to exist, though they used them also for fishing and for water transport. This was indeed an effort of capital formation, but it is clear from the chronicle that the barons and free tenants of the district contributed as much to building and dyking as did the monks.[11] But it must not be imagined that it was only in the twelfth and thirteenth centuries that monastic chroniclers praised investing abbots. The description *De bonis operibus* in the life of Roger Yatton, abbot of Evesham (1379–1418) shows as great—or as little—a spirit of investment as if he were living in the days of so-called high farming.[12] More laconic, but analogous, is the Gloucester monk's description of the good works of abbot Walter Frocester (1381–1412). This abbot *in temporalibus quam in spiritualibus multipliciter acquisivit.*[13] If we are looking for evidence of an investing mentality, we must not assume that the monastic chroniclers reflect it. It is the piling up of acquisitions which impresses them, and whether it was land, buildings, livestock, jewels, books, or church vestments seems to have mattered little.

Evidence about capital formation before the fourteenth century is rarely reducible to statistical form. However many examples we have, either from written sources or from the archaeological record, of the building of mills, the draining of marshes, the making of roads, etc., we do not usually know what proportion of the total effort of capital formation this constitutes. Nor can we know, before we have accounts, what proportion of income was put into capital formation. Perhaps the only useful comprehensive figure before the thirteenth century comes from Domesday Book. This tells us that in those parts of England which were

---

[11] *Chronica Monasterii de Melsa* (Rolls Series), 3 vols, 1866–8.
[12] *Chronicon Abbatiae de Evesham* (ibid., 1863), pp. 303–5.
[13] *Historia et Cartularium Monasterii Gloucestriae* (ibid., 1863), i. 55.

surveyed, there were something like 6,000 mills.[14] If we say that this represents a mill for every 46 or so households over the country as a whole, we shall be concealing great regional variations. In one respect the figures, however complete, would be significant only in so far as they can be compared with total figures of mills at other dates and in other countries. In another respect, however, they do show that already there must have been a diversion of resources for capital formation, perhaps fairly recent. How recent was this?[15] We can hardly know in view of the nature of the evidence. Was this particular effort of capital formation sustained? It is possible that it was not. Historians think that most mills were built by lords because they were the only class with the resources to make them and with the political and military power to enforce the monopoly of milling which would guarantee a return on the investment.

The possibility that mills were built by peasants, individually or in partnership, should not be ignored. Who built the mills that were attacked by seigneurial monopolists? In the twelfth century it may be that lords were strengthening this monopoly rather than building new mills. A Worcester charter of the twelfth century shows the endowment of a strong man, hired by the Cathedral Priory, to pull down a rural mill, who was to stay in the village to prevent its re-erection.[16] As far as the English feudal landowners were concerned (particularly the ecclesiastical landowners) the impression given by the cartularies is that the major expenditure in the twelfth and early thirteenth centuries was on land rather

[14] Figures given in R. Bennett and J. Elton's *History of Corn Milling*, 1899, ii. 131–80. The difficulties of interpreting the figures are explained by Reginald Lennard, *Rural England, 1066–1135*, 1959, p. 278.

[15] Documentary evidence for water mills in England is scanty and uncertain before the tenth century. (I owe this information to Professor P. H. Sawyer.) But a 'large and sophisticated mill with three verticle water wheels working in parallel' has been excavated at Old Windsor. But although a ninth-century date has been suggested, this is based on provisional pottery dating. *Medieval Archaeology*, ii, 1958, 184; iii, 1959, 21. An eighth-century mill has been excavated at Tamworth, Staffs., possibly associated with the Mercian royal palace. Philip Rahtz and Kim Sheridan, 'A Saxon watermill in Bolebridge Street', *Transactions of the South Staffs. Archaeological and Historical Society*, 1971–2.

[16] R. R. Darlington (ed.) *Cartulary of Worcester Cathedral Priory*, 1968, p. 21.

than on capital resources. Since for every buyer of land there was a seller, this thought should be elaborated a little further. A sustained expenditure of money on land purchase seems to have been undertaken mainly by the big ecclesiastical landowners, to a less extent by certain lay landowners.[17] The sellers were smaller lay landowners. But this does not mean that while the church landowners were diverting their cash revenues from a possible investment in capital resources, the sellers were on the other hand accumulating funds with which they could contribute to capital formation. The sellers were selling because they were financially embarrassed by rising prices and expenditure of a non-capital-forming kind. Very often the buyer got the land by paying the seller's debts to the Jews. The financial difficulties of the Northern barons in the time of King John, poignantly described by Professor Holt, and reflected in such local records as the chronicle of the Cistercian Abbey of Meaux, are found in other parts of the country.[18] Investment of estate profits, then, possibly tended in the twelfth and early thirteenth centuries to be directed more to land purchase than to capital formation. If this was indeed a period of the contraction of the direct cultivation of the demesne, this diversion of expenditure is understandable. The tendency would therefore be either for capital formation to slacken, or for it to be undertaken rather by farmers and other tenants than by landowners.[19] During this phase, then, since most land acquired added to rent rather than to production income, increases in rent income may have been in inverse ratio to expenditure on capital

---

[17] The emphasis on the church landowners is partly due to the better survival of monastic documents.

[18] J. O. Holt, *The Northerners*, 1961, esp., chap. v; *Chronica Monasterii de Melsa*, i, 1866, pp. 115, 172–4, 367, 375; ii, 1867, pp. 12, 25, 109, 115, 116. These are only examples. Small lay owners seem to have been bought up in the same way during the same period (say 1150–1250) by Worcester Cathedral Priory; *The Cartulary of Worcester Cathedral Priory (Register I)*, ed. R. R. Darlington, 1968. Examples could be multiplied. See H. G. Richardson, *The English Jewry under the Angevin Kings*, 1960, chap. v; R. H. Hilton, *A Medieval Society*, 1966, pp. 57–2.

[19] Capital formation by peasants in this earlier period is not well documented. But it was mainly peasant tenants who were responsible for Fen drainage, and this may have been the case in the Kentish marshes. Cf. H. E. Hallam, *The New Lands of Elloe* 1954; N. Neilson, *The Bilsington Cartulary*, 1928, introd., pp. 44–5.

resources. But this is guess-work, and figures from the later period of demesne leasing do not altogether confirm this conclusion.

The prevailing assumption among historians is that the extension of demesne cultivation on the big estates in the thirteenth century was one of many aspects of an economic 'boom' which lasted until the early years of the next century. Another aspect of this 'boom' is supposed to have been the investment of estate profits in permanent improvement. It is true that the most recent studies, some yet unpublished, are modifying this over-optimistic picture. Expenditure on reclamation from forest and marsh may, for instance, have been a sign of decline rather than of progress. It might have been essential to take in new lands, because of the falling yields of the old, just as an extra effort in marling and manuring may not have been a sign of improved farming but of a desperate attempt to keep yields up to a previous level.[20] This is rather a crucial change in emphasis. It so happens that this period (say from 1250 onwards) is about the best documented of all periods in the agrarian history of medieval and early modern England. The documents give fairly complete evidence about capital expenditure as well as about income. Hence we may perhaps be able to put varying views about this period to the test. If the answers are not satisfactory, at any rate one method of solving the problem can be discarded.

The question is, was the big estate in the thirteenth century, monastic or lay, such a great contributor to capital formation as has been assumed? Our previous remarks have been largely impressionistic, but now impressions must be discarded, since we have figures. But even figures can mislead, or rather can still contribute to impressions rather than to precise indications. For example, Professor Knowles quotes a figure of an average annual investment of £100 by an Abbot of Peterborough, saying: 'It was a very large sum to put back into the land, year in, year out and one which speaks eloquently not only of the profits and expectations of commercial farming on the grand scale, but of the firm resolution of the monks to give all their surplus wealth to the

[20] J. Z. Titow, *English Rural Society, 1200–1350*, 1969, pp. 52–3. Cf. E. Miller, *The Abbey and Bishopric of Ely*, 1951, p. 100.

## TABLE I. Earldom of Cornwall 1296

| Bailiwick | Rent* Income £ | Ratio to total receipt per cent | Production income £ s. | Ratio to total receipt per cent | Total† receipt £ s. | Capital Expenditure £ s. | Cash Liveries | Capital Expenditure as ratio of total receipt per cent | Capital Expenditure as ratio of cash livery per cent | Total Expenditure not including cash liveries £ s. |
|---|---|---|---|---|---|---|---|---|---|---|
| Berkhamstead | 270 | 48 | 181 | 32 | 571 | 20 | 326 | 3·5 | 6 | 164 |
| Mere (Wilts.) | 126 | 60 | 68 | 28 | 306 | 5. 7 | 243 | 1·8 | 2 | 91 |
| Wallingford | 267 | 66 | 60 | 15 | 408 | 14 | 296 | 3·5 | 4·7 | 33 |
| Honour of St. Valery | 240 | 85 | 5. 10 | 2 | 278 | 2. 14 | 258 | 1 | 1 | 17 |
| Honour of Eye | 17 | 85 | nil | nil | 22. 10 | 5 | 71 | 1 | 0·35 | 12 |
| Oakham | 284 | 60 | 14 | 3 | 470 | 10 | 496 | 2 | 2 | 33 |
| Knaresborough | 353 | 66 | 53 | 10 | 535 | 24 | 640 | 4·5 | } 4·6 | 41 |
| Howden | 275 | 65 | 97 | 24 | 392 | 5. 16 | | 1·4 | | 12 |
| Devon | 170 | 76 | 9. 13 | 6 | 223 | 9. 7 | 178 | 4 | 5 | 23 |

\* Less decay of rent.
† Work on Ashridge and Hodenhall Castle (83) is not considered as a part of capital formation.

development of their land, as a great industrialist of today puts back his profits into his spreading works and the sources of supply.'[21]

Whatever the total income from the Peterborough estates was at the beginning of the fourteenth century, it was unlikely to have been less than the gross income on the eve of the dissolution of the monasteries—nearly £2,000.[22] On this assumption, the annual average investment was therefore not more than 5 per cent of income. Another figure quoted by Professor Knowles to reinforce his views about 'high farming' and the 'lavish ploughing in' of profits by monastic landowners comes from the priorate of Henry of Eastry of Canterbury Cathedral. Professor Knowles prints a summary made at Canterbury of Eastry's economic activities 1285–1322, a period of thirty-seven years.[23] During this period £3,739 was spent on new building and repairs of mills and other structures; £111 on marling; and £360 on land reclamation. Another £1,343 was spent on buying land, but we will omit this total as not contributing to capital formation. The annual average investment therefore was £114. According to R. A. L. Smith, the annual average income of the monastery in the 1320s was £2,540. Investment as a proportion of this was 4·4 per cent. We must bear these figures in mind, since we can only understand the investment effort of an estate owner at such a remote epoch by comparing figures from a number of estates of varying size and structure.[24]

The figures in the following tables have been worked out from annual estate or manorial accounts. Although accounts were fairly standardized by the second half of the thirteenth century, items which for our purposes should be kept apart cannot always be separated. I have attempted to calculate (where possible) four sets of figures: *income from rent, income from production, total income* and *expenditure on capital formation. Rent income* includes assize rents and farm rents from land. It also includes payments for the use of

[21] Op. cit., p. 46, quoting Robert Swapham's *Continuatio Historiae Coenobii Burgensis* in *Historiae Anglicanae Scriptores*, ed. J. Sparke, 1723.

[22] A. Savine, *English monasteries on the eve of the Dissolution*, 1909, p. 279.

[23] Op. cit., Appendix II.

[24] *Canterbury Cathedral Priory*, 1943, p. 13.

meadow and pasture where this was obviously a rent for the use of land even when in the account it might be described as a *sale* of herbage or pasture. *Income from production* includes sales of all types of produce and (where appropriate) the values of produce sent from the manor for the estate owner's consumption. There are some difficulties, as will be appreciated, in separating these different elements of income. The difficulties in calculating *capital expenditure* are greater. Where possible, current expenditure on farming operations (for example on seed) is excluded. But it is impossible to separate replacements of deadstock from new elements of capital formation. Therefore I include all expenditure on equipment and buildings. All expenditure on ditching and fencing is included. But as far as possible military and ecclesiastical building expenses are excluded, even some seigneurial building expenses, where these do not seem to contribute to capital formation.

Comprehensive as estate and manorial accounts may be, it is in fact impossible to determine what items of income were spent on capital formation. The choice to be made is not simply as between rent income and production income. Profits of jurisdiction also make their contribution. These are not separately calculated in the figures which follow, though the income remaining after the subtraction of rent and production income from total income in fact largely consists of the profits of jurisdiction.

The first figures are intended to illustrate the situation on a very big lay estate. They are calculated from the accounts of one year (1296–7) of the lands of the Earldom of Cornwall, the estate of Edward I's cousin Edmund.[25] Ideally, the figures should be calculated as an average over a period of say ten years. This cannot be done here, but over such a huge estate some averaging out as between manors in different regions necessarily happens.[26]

The reason for calculating capital expenditure as a proportion

---

[25] *Accounts of the Earldom of Cornwall*, ed. L. M. Midgeley, Camden Society, 2 vols., 1942 and 1945.

[26] The object of making an average of several years is because of the great variations of capital expenditure from year to year. In the (probable) absence of estate policy, there would be similar variations from manor to manor which average out within the bailiwick or at any rate within the estate.

of liveries is that, short of making elaborate and perhaps unreliable calculations of profit, the liveries in cash and/or kind give a rough and ready indication of the profitability to the lord of the estate. These liveries are entered on the expenses side of the cash account, being usually payments to the lord's receiver by the manorial bailiff. They might also be payments to other officials or debtors. The liveries in kind (not found on the Earldom of Cornwall estate) are entered in the grange and stock account, and could of course, constitute a substantial part of the yield of a manor. They are found mostly on the manors of monastic estates, the monastery being largely victualled direct from the manors.[27]

It is to be noticed that on the Cornwall estate the income from production never exceeds one-third of total receipt, so that rents and profits of jurisdiction made up the bulk of income. Whether considered as a proportion of income or of profits (i.e. of liveries) the amounts contributing to capital formation are not impressive. What is impressive is the size of the cash liveries.[28] Wealth was going from the manors, and very little was being put back. Investment as a percentage of income was low compared with the figures quoted from Peterborough and Canterbury.

This impression of an economic exploitation which takes much but puts little back could easily be tested from the accounts of innumerable manors and estates during this period of abundant documentation. There are weaknesses, of course, in the way in which I have related capital formation to income or to profit. In an economy where some of the replacement of old, or the manufacture of new equipment was achieved by the use of local materials without purchase, such a contribution to capital formation would not be recorded. To balance this, however, it should be stressed that some of the expenditure recorded must have been replacement of old rather than creation of new elements of capital. Again, a comparison between medieval and modern expenditures on capital formation would be meaningless in view of the rela-

---

[27] However liveries in kind to the Cathedral Priory (Benedictine) of Worcester, which were originally used for direct victualling were, by the end of the thirteenth century, sold on Worcester market, the Priory being victualled by purchases.

[28] There were no liveries in kind.

tively low cost, at any rate of equipment, if not of livestock or buildings.

I will quote two more sets of figures from the so-called era of 'high farming'. The first set is from a Northamptonshire manor of the prosperous Fenland Abbey of Crowland, for many years well known from the writings of two English economic historians.[29] Miss Page praises the economic organization of Crowland precisely because a manor such as Wellingborough provided such a flow of cash, grain, and wool to the monastic centre. Ten years' accounts[30] show the following *cash* averages.

TABLE 2.    *Wellingborough 1203–1303*

|  | Rent income | Production income | Total receipt | Capital expenditure | Cash Liveries | Total expenditure |
|---|---|---|---|---|---|---|
| Average of ten years | £51 | £15 | £110 | £8 | £77 | £114 |

But these figures from the cash side of the account misrepresent the situation very gravely. In the first four years of the ten there was an average export of perhaps £90 worth of grain from Wellingborough to Crowland Abbey. The appearance of tithe grain on the receipt side of the grange account from 1292 falsifies the picture of grain export from the demesne after that, and it would seem that there was probably a slackening. There were, however, transfers of stock from the manor, in addition to sheep (which were partly subject to inter-manorial management).[31] At any rate if we add the values of the fluctuating deliveries to Crowland or elsewhere of pigs and poultry for the larder to the grain exports, we should have to quadruple or more the production income, double the total receipt and more than double

[29] *The Wellingborough Manorial Accounts, 1258–1323*, Northants, Record Society, viii, ed. F. M. Page. See her *The Estates of Crowland Abbey*, 1934. Also, M. Wretts-Smith, 'The Organization of Farming at Crowland Abbey, 1257–1321', *Journal of Economic and Business History*, 1931.

[30] Not consecutive years, but some for which complete evidence survives, viz. 1283, 1285, 1289, 1290, 1292, 1296, 1297, 1298, 1299, 1302.

[31] Cf. F. M. Page, 'Bidentes Hoylandie', *Economic History*, i, 1929.

the liveries out. As a proportion of total receipts, expenditure on equipment, buildings etc. would fall to less than 4 per cent.

Another convenient series of manorial accounts of about the same period is susceptible to the same sort of analysis. These are the accounts of the Wiltshire manor of Sevenhampton, a principal property of Edward I's notorious and rapacious official, Adam de Stratton.[32] I have made calculations from the accounts of eleven successive years (1272–83).

TABLE 3.   *Sevenhampton 1272–1283*

|  | Rent income | Production income | Total receipt | Capital expenditure | Liveries (cash) |
|---|---|---|---|---|---|
| Annual average | £51 | £115 | £212 | £12 | £177 |

It will be noticed that average annual income from productive activity on this manor was more than double that from rent income. This emphasizes the difficulty of estimating in isolation the role of rent income in contributing to capital formation at this crucial period. The amount taken from the manorial economy in cash liveries is very great. Only 6·5 per cent of the amount paid out in liveries was spent on buildings, equipment, stock or other elements in capital formation. It was only 5·6 per cent of the total receipt. It is interesting that this absentee layman, notorious for his greed, probably put back into the economy of this manor a greater proportion of what he took out than did the Abbot of Crowland.

The fourteenth and fifteenth centuries are reputedly a period of economic stagnation during which capital formation slackened off from a presumed high level. Further investigation may show that the level of the supposed period of boom was not all that high, as the figures quoted would suggest. A few later figures are of considerable comparative interest. It should of course be remembered that these figures are derived from a period when the amount of

[32] *Accounts and Surveys of the Wiltshire lands of Adam de Stratton*, ed. M. W. Farr, Wiltshire Record Society, 1959.

demesne land under cultivation was contracting. The direct cultivation of the soil by landowners through the agency of bailiffs was declining and agricultural production was falling almost entirely into the hands of tenants of the peasant class. One would therefore expect the landlord's contribution to capital formation to dwindle in so far as their expenditure on agricultural equipment would naturally fall. This does not mean of course that their role in capital formation was disappearing. In the first place demesne cultivation by landlords did not entirely cease. In the second place landlords still contributed to what has been called 'estate capital', that is buildings, fencing, drainage, etc.

Some figures taken from eight surviving accounts of the Bishop of Worcester's manor of Hampton Lucy in Warwickshire show what at first sight seems an interesting contrast with those already quoted. The Hampton Lucy accounts begin in 1377. The eight accounts chosen include two made up after the final leasing of the whole demesne, an event which took place some time between 1387 and 1393. Expenditure on equipment, buildings and enclosures amounted to about 10 per cent of the total manorial income and about 17 per cent of the cash and grain liveries paid out from the manor. On the Warwickshire manor of Lighthorne, owned by the Beauchamp Earls of Warwick, although the equipment and building expenditure in the account for ten years between 1390 and 1436 was only 4 per cent of the total cash receipt, it was a high figure compared with what was taken out of the manor in cash liveries, being about 15 per cent. When the estates of the earldom of Warwick were in the hands of the crown in 1480, expenditure in the rural properties in Warwickshire contributing to capital formation was 9 per cent of total receipt and 12 per cent of cash liveries. If the figures for building investment in Warwick town are added to the figures from the rural manors, the proportions would be 4 per cent and 25 per cent.[33]

There are indications in the accounts from parts of the Beau-

[33] Hampton Lucy Accounts, Worcester County Record Office, Church Commission, MSS., 163/92158 et seq.; Lighthorne Accounts, Shakespeare's Birthplace, Stratford-upon-Avon, Willoughby de Broke MSS., 672a et seq.; *Ministers' Accounts of the Warwickshire Estates of the Duke of Clarence, 1479–1480*, ed. R. H. Hilton, Dugdale Society, 1952.

champ estates that in the late fourteenth and fifteenth centuries, landowners were prepared to spend money not only on the maintenance of equipment and buildings on the demesne, but on the houses of tenants. A regular item in the accounts of the manor of Earls Croome was *custus domorum tenencium in villa*, and this is found also at Lighthorne and Tanworth (another Warwickshire manor of the Beauchamps). While not unknown, this sort of expenditure is not often found on estates during the (so-called) period of high farming. Provision by landlords of assistance in building and repairs—chiefly great timber—was, of course, a normal condition of leasehold tenure in the later Middle Ages. The earls of Northumberland seem to have regularly provided worked timber for tenants' houses in the fifteenth century, and probably for customary as well as for leasehold tenants.[34] More than half ($£35$) of the not inconsiderable expenses on buildings, fences, ditches, and ponds recorded in the Fountains Abbey (Yorkshire) Bursar's account of 1457–8 was on tenants' houses and barns.[35] Abbot Yatton of Evesham, whom we have already mentioned, is recorded by the chronicler as having spent considerable sums on building *pro suis tenentibus*.[36] Edington Priory was spending up to $£10$ on housing for individual tenants in the fifteenth century on its Berkshire manor of Coleshill.[37] This investment in tenants' buildings is found too on some of the Duchy of Lancaster estates, when these, though separately administered, were in the hands of the Crown. From the 1440s, throughout the period of the civil war, and into the period of relative calm under the Yorkists, the Lancaster estate administration on its Staffordshire manors of Tutbury, Barton-under-Needwood, Marchington, and Rolleston, was regularly spending money on repairs to customary tenants' houses and other buildings. This by no means accounted for all of the investment, however, money was also spent on fencing, drainage, the upkeep of mills and other buildings. Although

---

[34] *Fifteenth Century Bailiff's Rolls of the Earls of Northumberland*, ed. J. C. Hodgson (Surtees Society), 1921.

[35] *Memorials of Fountains Abbey*, ed. J. T. Fowler (Surtees Society), 1918.

[36] *Evesham Chron.*, pp. 304–5.

[37] R. J. Faith, 'The Peasant land market in Berkshire' (unpublished Ph. D. thesis, University of Leicester, 1962), p. 230.

this investment was as low in one or two years as 1 per cent of receipts, it frequently rose much higher, especially on selected manors. In some years, the amount invested was much greater than the cash liveries paid out from the manors. This, it must be remembered, was at a time when there was no demesne kept in hand on the Duchy estates. Irregular though investment expenditure may have been, it was very high in some years, and high for a sustained period at Tutbury.[38]

The number of calculations we have made from sample estate accounts is not, of course, in any way sufficient to prove without

TABLE 4.  *Lancaster Manors in Staffordshire 1440–1485*

| Year | Barton (a) Investment as per cent of receipt | Barton (b) Investment as per cent of cash livery | Rolleston (a) | Rolleston (b) | Tutbury‖ (a) | Tutbury‖ (b) |
|---|---|---|---|---|---|---|
| 1440–1 | 20 | 26 | — | — | 28 | 40 |
| 1444–5 | 1·5 | 2 | 21 | 28 | 16 | no livery |
| 1445–6 | — | — | 2·5 | 3 | no details | |
| 1448–9 | 2·5 | 2·5 | — | — | 3 | 56 |
| 1458–9 | 3·5 | 4 | — | — | 1·5 | 12 |
| 1459–60 | no details | | no details | | 2·5 | 16 |
| 1460–1 | 3 | 6 | — | — | 14 | 24 |
| 1462–3 | 5·5 | 5·5 | 5 | 6·5 | 60 | 395 |
| 1463–4 | — | — | — | — | 16 | 27 |
| 1475–6 | 61* | 203 | 17 | 22 | 12 | 85 |
| 1476–7 | no details | | 24‡ | 20 | 22 | 131 |
| 1478–9 | 15† | 20 | 51 | 2,400§ | 29 | 154 |
| 1480–1 | — | — | — | — | 4 | 9 |
| 1481–2 | — | — | — | — | — | — |
| 1482–3 | 7 | 4 | — | — | — | — |
| 1484–5 | 2 | 2·5 | — | — | — | — |

\* If expenditure on hunting lodge is omitted, 26 per cent and 86 per cent.
† Including hunting lodge.
‡ If expenditure on castle is omitted, 6·5 per cent and 5 per cent.
§ Hunting lodge.
‖ The Tutbury figures do not include expenditure on the Castle.

[38] I have to thank Miss J. R. Birrell who has calculated these figures from Duchy of Lancaster accounts which she is using for a study of the Duchy estates.

doubt that in the fifteenth century landowners were contributing to capital formation in their estates to a greater extent than was possible in the conditions of over-exploitation of the thirteenth century. The figures are quoted in order to question the assumption that the later middle ages was one of slackening capital formation as compared with the feverish and overpopulated thirteenth century. An important criticism however could be made of any conclusions about *increased* capital formation in the fourteenth and fifteenth centuries based on the few figures already quoted. If this period was one of falling landlord receipts and profits, and of rising labour costs and prices, a rising proportion of expenditure in building and equipment could in fact conceal a fall in the physical volume of this type of capital formation. A continuous series of accounts for the Priory of Finchale, a cell of the Cathedral Priory at Durham, illustrates the problem.[39]

The accompanying table is given in order to show how a rise in the proportion of income spent on capital expenses could be compatible with a fall in the actual volume of the real values created. But lest this table should be taken to justify existing assumptions about a low level of capital formation in the later Middle Ages, the following points should be made.

1. The pre-Black Death annual average expenditure on building is based on three surviving accounts only.

2. Capital formation after the middle of the fourteenth century took place in a numerically reduced society where much less land was under cultivation than at the end of the thirteenth century. If it were possible to estimate capital investment per head of population or per acre, the later Middle Ages might, in spite of statistics indicating economic contraction, appear as an era of greater investment than the thirteenth century.[40]

---

[39] *The Charters of Endowment, inventories and account rolls of the Priory of Finchale*, ed. J. Raine (Surtees Soc.), 1837.

[40] This applies to England particularly. The European wars probably involved considerable destruction of capital resources, especially livestock. See the interesting figures for part of Normandy in A. Plaisse, *La Baronnie du Neubourg*, 1961, p. 323. Professor Perroy has stressed this important difference between England and France in his discussion of wage history, 'Wage Labour in France in the later Middle Ages', *EcHR*, 2nd ser. viii. 2, 1955.

TABLE 5.   *Finchale Priory 1346–1481*

| | Annual average expenditure on animals, building and equipment as per cent of total receipt. | Annual average expenditure on buildings. | Building expenditure divided by an index of building wages and prices. |
|---|---|---|---|
| | | £ s. d. | |
| 1346–9 | 9 | 19.9.0 | 18 |
| 1354–60 | 12 | 8.6.1 | 5·5 |
| 1360–9 | 9/20★ | 23.14.0 or 17.15.0 | 11·6/15·5★ |
| 1372–80 | 17 | 26.11.4 | 16·7 |
| 1390–99 | 12 | 22.15.0 | 14·5 |
| 1402–10 | 8 | 13.16.0 | 8 |
| 1410–20 | 11 | 16.16.5 | 10·8 |
| 1422–30 | 11 | 15.6.7 | 8·8 |
| 1430–9 | 11 | 16.1.0 | 9 |
| 1439–50 | 18 | 18.0.0 | 10 |
| 1457–60 | 23 | 23.0.0 | 12·3 |
| 1461–71 | 14 | 12.15.0 | 7 |
| 1471–81 | 13 | 17.18.0 | 9·6 |

★ The lower of the two figures results from the exclusion of very heavy church building expenses

3. The leasing of the demesnes on the Finchale estates began in 1354. By 1400 the only land directly cultivated by the monks was in the immediate neighbourhood of the Priory.

The Finchale figures resemble those others cited from some accounts of the late fourteenth and fifteenth centuries. Let me again emphasize that these few examples, chosen at random, are not offered as proof of a maintenance or increase in capital formation in the late medieval period. In view of the probable existence of regional differences and differences of landlord policy, many more estates would need to be studied. The figures are offered as a suggestion about lines of investigation. I would, however, stress one further matter. Even if it were concluded that the increase in prices and wages after 1350 cancelled any apparent increase in cash expenditure on buildings, equipment etc., the increase in this expenditure as compared with the liveries to the lords of estates would seem to indicate more willingness on their part to reinvest their profits than was the case in the thirteenth century. This was unlikely to be the result either of a greater understanding of economics or of a soberer way of life.[41] It was rather the result of the same factors which caused the contemporary fall in rents and rise in wages—a change in the land:labour ratio. In other words the creation of estate capital was as much the result of tenant demand as of landowners' inclinations.

The evidence we have presented is derived from the estate accounts of wealthy landowners. An investment of not more than 5 per cent of total income in buildings, stock and equipment seems to have been common in the thirteenth century and for various reasons (including rising costs) this proportion seems to have increased noticeably in the post Black Death period. The impression of 'lavish ploughing in' of profits would seem, to say the least of it, somewhat exaggerated. But capital formation obviously need not only come from the profits of the big estates. What contribution was made by obscure freeholders and customary tenants?

Here we are faced with the problem of rent and capital formation seen from its reverse side. Hitherto we have considered rent (among other sources of landowner incomes) as contributing to capital formation. We now have to consider rent as a hindrance to capital formation.

In some respects the situation of the English peasants at the end of the thirteenth century was very similar to that found in France and in the lands of the Empire.[42] The growth of population, of a market in land and of social differentiation had resulted in an extreme fragmentation of peasant holdings, so that in the English villages as in those in other European countries there was a con-

[41] Cf. the remarks by K. B. MacFarlane in 'The Investment of Sir John Fastolf's Profits of War', *Trans. Royal Hist. Soc.*, 5th Series, vii, 1957, pp. 107–8.

[42] The fragmentation of the manse is a familiar theme and its bibliography will be too familiar to the readers of this paper to need repetition here. I suspect that the multiplication of small holdings was even more serious in parts of France and the Empire than in England. I conclude this from M. Carabie's work on Normandy, that of M. Génicot on Namur, of M. Duby on Burgundy, and M. Dollinger on Bavaria. The fragmentation of Italian peasant holdings seems to begin much earlier than it did north of the Alps.

siderable proportion of peasants who were living on dwarf holdings hardly sufficient to maintain life. E. A. Kosminsky's analysis of the *Rotuli Hundredorum* of 1279–80 shows, in four east midland counties, up to 57 per cent of unfree holdings and up to 80 per cent of free holdings to have been less than eight acres in size. Manorial records of the same period show the same sort of majority of small holders in the village populations, especially in those old settled villages where there was no room for further expansion. More than half of the peasant population in twelve of the Bishop of Winchester's manors had in the South of England ten acres of land or less. In the west the Bishop of Worcester's great survey of 1299 shows a diminution in the average size of the standard family holdings as well as a multiplication of dwarf holdings. The impoverished small holders in some villages constituted between a third and a half of the total tenant population.[43]

The thirteenth-century village community did not of course consist entirely of poor small holders. There were a few substantial freeholders, as well as villeins with holdings of thirty or forty acres. The hard core of the village tenantry tended to have holdings fluctuating around the half yardland—in the Midlands about 12–15 acres of arable. These were by no means substantial persons and were almost certainly as underequipped with livestock, buildings, and tools as they were with land. The principal (and extremely rare) sources which tell us about peasant livestock are the few surviving records of movable goods on which the fractional subsidies of the late thirteenth and early fourteenth centuries were based. It is certain that most of the small holders did not pay this tax, because the value of their movable goods was too low for them to be included. Comparisons of subsidy payers with manorial rentals suggests that it was only the middling and richer tenants who were assessed. Even so we find that in the Barford Hundred of Bedfordshire in 1297, 85 per cent of the taxpayers had either no or one draught animals, while in the three

---

[43] E. A. Kosminsky, *Studies in the Agrarian History of England in the Thirteenth Century*, 1956, pp. 216 and 223; Winchester figures are from Dr. J. Z. Titow's unpublished thesis on the Winchester estates; Worcester surveys are printed in *The Red Book of Worcester*, Worcester Historical Society, 1934–50.

hundreds of Barford, Biggleswade, and Flitt, 90 per cent had no or one milking cow. In the Suffolk Hundred of Blackbourne in 1283, 75 per cent of the taxpayers had no or one draught animal, and 47 per cent had no or one milking cow.[44] These were the essential animals for subsistence in what (as far as the peasants were concerned) was essentially a grain-producing economy. Livestock would obviously come first in the stocking of the peasant holding. Where these were so scarce, it is not likely that much would be spent on other factors contributing to capital formation.

Local overpopulation and the diminution of meadow and pasture in relation to arable are partial explanations of the shortage of livestock, and (one assumes) of other forms of capital. Another reason must have been the burden of rent and other payments on the peasant holding. The calculation of a peasant budget at this time is, of course, extremely difficult, made all the more difficult because we do not know the number of persons in the average peasant household. A half-yardlander with eight acres *under crop* on the Bishop of Worcester's manor of Kempsey in 1299 would perhaps have for sale, after allowing for tithe and family subsistence, enough grain to bring in 12s. or 13s. at the average prices obtaining at that period. His rent consisted of 5s. 6d. to be paid in money and 10s. 6d. worth of labour services. The income of the household might be increased by small sales of poultry or by wages brought in by a son. This might pay for tallage, amercements, taxes, and what had to be bought from outside. But if the tenant had to pay a money rent instead of doing the labour services, as was very likely, his cash reserves would be very small, if existing at all.[45]

Other tenants on the Bishop's estate might be better placed. The holder of a yardland of 26 acres at Hampton Lucy in 1299

---

[44] *The Taxation of 1297* (Publications of the Bedfordshire Historical Record Society, xxxix) ,ed. A. T. Gaydon, 1959; *A Suffolk Hundred in 1283*, ed. E. Powell, 1910.

[45] See *Red Book of Worcester*, p. 66. For a household of four I have allowed for subsistence 4 qu. of wheat and 2 qu. of barley, leaving for sale 1 qu. 3 bs. wheat, 2 qu. 6 bs. rye and 2 qu. 4 bs. barley. I have assumed yields of 9 bs per acre of wheat and rye and of 15 bs of barley. The Kempsey sowing rate was 2½ bs of wheat and rye per acre and 6 bs of barley. The subsistence requirement is very

paid a rent of 3s. 11d. in money and owed labour services valued at 11s. 2d. The custom on the demesne here was to sow half of the acreage, so assuming that tenants followed the same rule, the typical yardland would have 13 acres under crop. After subsistence grain had been kept back he would have enough for sale which might bring in 18s. (at 5s. per quarter of wheat and 3s. per quarter of barley). His grain sales more than cover his rent, but only by 3s. 11d. If he had poultry or eggs for sale, and a son earning wages, he might survive rather better than the Kempsey half-yardlander.

Rents, of course, varied very considerably from place to place, and even within the same village. To compare rents per yardland or even rents per acre is misleading unless we know something about the rotation system. An arable acre which was cultivated only once in two years was clearly worth less than one which could be cropped twice in three years. The rents which were put down in the rental did not, moreover, necessarily constitute the full burden of rent. As competition for land increased, landowners in effect raised rents by charging heavy entry fines whilst leaving the customary rent payable at the three or four traditional terms in the year unaltered. As late as 1346–7 the entry fines charged on tenants taking up lands on sixteen manors of the Bishop of Winchester's estate was nearly a third of what was paid in rent in the same year. Sixty years earlier (1284–5) on six episcopal manors entry fines brought in as much as rent. On the Bishop of Ely's estates these fines could range from 1s. to 35s. an acre.[46] If we add annual aid or tallage to the figure of rent, then on the large estates where the power of the lord was great, the nominal assize rent might be far from representing the real burden of rent on the peasant holding. The hypothetical case from Kempsey shows that a rent of 1s. an acre charged on a half yardland of twelve to fifteen acres was a burden that could only be

difficult to estimate. Mine is partly based on provisions for the subsistence of retiring tenants recorded in court rolls. It roughly conforms with M. Goubert's estimate of 18 quintals of wheat for a peasant family of 6 in the seventeenth-century Beauvaisis. Some half yardlands at Kempsey clearly contained only 6 acres. Most of them, including that analysed had, I think, 12 acres of arable land.

[46] A. E. Levett, *The Black Death on the Estates of the Bishop of Winchester*, 1916, Appendix; E. Miller, *The Abbey and Bishopric of Ely*, 1951, p. 139 n.

sustained if prices and yields were reasonable and if some of the labour services could be performed rather than paid for. Certainly nothing would be left for capital formation.

This situation did not apply to all tenants nor at all times. We know that even during the hardest years of the thirteenth and early fourteenth centuries, when mortality may have been as high as 70 to 75 per thousand,[47] there were those who prospered in the countryside without being estate owners. For the most part we know them only as seen through the documents of the landlord—his rentals, court rolls, and cartularies. Consequently we do not know how they spent their profits. But chance has preserved the estate book[48] of a wealthy freeholder of Northamptonshire, Henry of Bray, a man without seigneurial power, and seemingly without the pretensions of even the lowest members of the squire-archy. This estate book, like the more grandiose cartularies of the big estates, contains mainly copies of deeds of title to lands and rights. But it also contains an estimate of Henry himself of his building expenses, year by year, over a period of twenty-two years (1289–1309). These expenses average £4 6s. 7d. a year. I have excluded money spent on buying land, which he includes, on the grounds that such purchases do not contribute, normally, to capital formation. But he does not give his expenses on livestock, or on hedging, ditching, or agricultural equipment. In other words, £4 6s. 7d. is a minimum figure. His income consists of nearly £11 in rent from various tenants and in the profits from an arable demesne of some 250–80 acres. We are given no indication of what these profits were. If he had 180 acres under crop he might get a net gain of 1s. an acre, that is £9. We do not know what livestock he had, but I think that his annual income from his rents and demesne would certainly not have exceeded £25, probably not £20. His investment therefore was between a quarter and a fifth of what he received. This proportion compares very favourably with that found on the big ecclesiastical estates during the same period.

[47] M. M. Postan and J. Z. Titow, 'Heriots and Prices on Winchester Manors', *EcHR*, 2nd ser., xi, 3, 1959.

[48] *The Estate Book of Henry de Bray*, ed. D. Willis (Camden Society).

Lower down the social scale from Henry of Bray were the wealthy customary tenants. Although the rich villein is by no means a purely late medieval phenomenon, he stands out (especially in the period after the Black Death) because he exists in a very different economic and social environment from that of the eleventh to thirteenth centuries. Among the principal changes in the late medieval environment must be counted the fall in rents from land in the narrowest sense as well as of other items of seigneurial income, such as entry fines, heriots, tallage, and amercements in the manorial courts, which in the previous era of lordly economic predominance had sliced off the meagre surplus of the tenants.

The well-to-do villein leaves no accounts, so we know virtually nothing of his expenses. The manorial documents tell us about his landed holdings of course, but it is only by pure accident that we find details of his income. A case in point is provided by the account rolls of the Bishop of Worcester's manor of Hampton Lucy. The reeve of the manor, Walter Shayl, absconded from the manor in June 1377. He was tenant of a yardland which paid a rent of 13s. a year (as against 14s. 1d. in 1299), though as reeve he had been pardoned this rent. He was, however, cultivating a good deal more ground than his official holding, for according to the reeve's account in the year following his departure he had had 33 acres under crop. Since the yardland was only 26 acres, and probably only a half, at most two-thirds, of this would be cropped, it is clear that in one way or another he had acquired land for himself for which he had not accounted in his last year of office. The grain from Shayl's confiscated land was accounted for in the year after his flight separately from the demesne grain as shown in Table 6.

If there were a two-course rotation at Hampton Lucy and Hatton, Shayl must have had some 66 acres of arable, a sizeable peasant holding. As far as can be seen from the account of the previous year, he was only paying 1s. rent, apart from that owed from his own yardland (of 26 acres), which he was pardoned because of his office. Had he been able to sell his grain, less the seed needed for the next year, at the current prices, he would

TABLE 6.   *Hampton Lucy 1377*

| Grain | Shayl's acreage | Crop | | Demesne sowing rate per acre | Demesne yield★ | Shaye's yield (assuming demesne sowing rate) |
|---|---|---|---|---|---|---|
| | | qu. | bs | bs. | | |
| Wheat | 8 | 8 | | 2 | 6·5 | 4 |
| Rye | 5 | 6 | 1 | 2 | 5 | 4·9 |
| Drage | 12 | 20 | 2 | 4 | 4·5 | 1·7 |
| Pulse | 7 | 5 | | 3 | 4 | 1·9 |
| Oats | 1 | 1 | | 4 | 4·5 | 2 |

★ Expressed as a multiple of the amount sown, i.e. a yield of 6·5 bs of wheat for every b. sown, and so on.

have made £3 6s. 4d. If he had kept 6 quarters of wheat for subsistence, he would have made £2 6s. 4d. (wheat was cheap, being 3.4 a quarter this year). As reeve he would apparently pay very little rent, certainly not the full 6d. an acre which was the rent paid for customary land at this time.

That there was a fall in the general level of rent in England between the middle of the fourteenth and the end of the fifteenth century is agreed by most economic historians. It is also common ground that although a considerable amount of arable land went out of cultivation, the amount of land still cropped was sufficiently abundant to permit a general increase in the average size of peasant holdings. At the same time, terms of tenure tended on the whole to favour the tenant rather than the landowner. It has already been suggested above that one of the results of the favourable bargaining position of tenants was that landlords were prepared to spend more money on tenants' houses and other buildings. But what did the tenants themselves, in conditions where they might be able to save out of increased incomes, contribute to capital formation?

There seems little doubt that one of the most important ways in which the late medieval English peasants contributed to capital formation was in the building up of the country's herds of cattle

and flocks of sheep. Change in the balance of land use in the fifteenth century is of course quite an ancient commonplace in
English economic history. Abandoned arable went to grass in
different ways. Long before enclosing landlords were attempting
by fraud or force to evict arable farmers (a phenomenon of the
late fifteenth and early sixteenth centuries) some entire settlements
were abandoned and their arable fields turned into pasture.[49] In
villages which survived the least fertile arable, often that which
had been mostly recently assarted, was allowed to revert to
pasture. In addition, within the still cultivated fields, some of the
ridges were allowed to grass over. In these ways the acute shortage
of pasture, which caused some of the fierce conflicts over common
rights in the thirteenth century, was ended, and peasant livestock
could be built up.

The difficulties of documenting this increase are well known.
When rich peasant demesne lessees took over landlords' flocks, the
leasing is recorded. But this was simply a transfer of management,
involving no increase. The only type of evidence for genuine
peasant increases in livestock is in court records, and is indirect. It
chiefly consists of records of prosecutions in the manor courts.
These prosecutions were of trespasses by peasant sheep and cattle
on growing crops and of the illegal overstocking of common
pastures. Other evidence includes the imposition of restrictions
(stints) on the number of animals each tenant was allowed to put
on the commons.[50] This type of evidence has frequently been
quoted, but mostly to show examples of the size which individual
peasant flocks could attain.[51] Sceptical historians who doubt the
existence of economic recovery before the last quarter of the
fifteenth century argue that evidence about prosecutions may
do no more than indicate improvements in manorial administration. The only way in which some satisfactory conclusions can be

[49] A number of small Cotswold villages which had combined sheep with corn
husbandry were deserted in the second half of the fourteenth century. Their arable
land had always been surrounded by extensive pastures, and were henceforth
absorbed back into them.

[50] Direct evidence, such as that contained in probate inventories, does not become sufficiently abundant until the beginning of the sixteenth century.

[51] Cf. my article in vol. iii of the *Victoria County History of Leicestershire*, 1954, p.
191.

reached is by a systematic examination of a large quantity of this type of evidence in a carefully delimited region. Where this has been done, the results seem to confirm the old view that peasant stock-rearing was on the increase. A systematic investigation of this type has been made for the county of Worcester.[52]

Court records for 27 villages in this county have been examined, in 19 of which the earliest entries are of the fourteenth century or earlier. The earliest prosecution for overstocking is in 1349. But in the majority of villages the first prosecutions for overstocking come between 1390 and 1465. In all 18 villages where stints were imposed, the first imposition was in 1399 or after. The impression of peasant flocks and herds of increasing size which are derived from prosecutions and stints is reinforced by records of prosecutions against tenants who put the overflow from flocks of graziers in neighbouring villages on their own common pastures. It is also supported by evidence from the court records of the little town of Halesowen in the north of the county, where, in the second half of the fifteenth century, there is a sudden spate of regulations controlling the activities of butcher-graziers.[53] The growth in importance of this group of victuallers is found also in fifteenth-century Coventry.[54] The evidence for an increase in stock-raising in fact points to the raising of cattle for meat as well as of sheep for wool. Since the tenants who were prosecuted for overstocking would probably be among the biggest graziers, the numbers in the flocks and herds involved cannot give us any idea of the general distribution of animals among the village population. However, flocks of about 100 sheep, and occasionally of over 200, are found,[55] whilst cattle herds of a score, more or less, were not uncommon.

---

[52] The figures which follow have been calculated by Mr. R. K. Field and are quoted from his unpublished Birmingham M.A. thesis 'The Worcestershire Peasant in the Later Middle Ages', 1962.

[53] This is a town set in a rural manor. The Halesowen manorial records provide abundant evidence of overstocking. Between 1431 and 1509, 189 individuals were prosecuted and fined for overstocking.

[54] See p. 169.

[55] In the Bedfordshire hundreds of Barford, Biggleswade, and Flitt in 1297, three-quarters of the tenant sheep flocks contained fewer than 10 animals. Only about 7 per cent of the flocks contained more than 20. A. T. Gaydon, op. cit.

It cannot be said, of course, on the basis of this indirect evidence, that any over-all decline in the size of landlords' herds and flocks was compensated for by an increase in tenant stock-raising, whether by peasants within the normal framework of the village community, or by capitalist graziers taking enlarged pastures on lease. All the same, in view of the importance of livestock in the capital resources of the medieval economy, it is essential to draw attention to the probability that in the later Middle Ages this may have been a vital peasant contribution to capital formation. And since in countries over which wars were fought, livestock was probably the most vulnerable element in the agrarian economy, relatively tranquil countries like England which were able to build up livestock resources may have had a vital advantage in the early stages of the economic expansion of modern times.

This paper has concentrated on the topic of the relation between income and investment in rural society. This is not only because the English evidence is mainly that from the estates of the lay and ecclesiastical landowners, but because of the primary importance of capital formation in agriculture. For many historians, how-ever, it is hardly possible to consider capital formation in medieval England without paying attention to developments in towns, and to capital formation in industry. For these topics, the evidence is much less abundant than that which has already been sampled. In particular, although something can be said about urban and in-dustrial growth, the contribution of rent to that growth is much more difficult to trace than in agriculture. The following remarks, therefore, are intended to do no more than to pose some of the problems.

It must be borne in mind that in England the most significant developments in capital formation in industry took place in the country rather than in the town. The application of water power in the textile and metal industries is the chief feature here, and followed naturally on the earlier development of the grinding of corn by water power. Professor Carus-Wilson's pioneer article on the development of the water fulling mill quoted a number of examples of these mills in the thirteenth century, and any his-torian acquainted with local historical sources knows that the number that she has listed could be vastly increased.[56] As in the case of water mills, the fulling mill was a seigneurial monopoly. Most of the mills, therefore, for which we have evidence are seigneurial mills, initially financed from landowner incomes. But we do not know how many mills were built by others, including the fullers themselves. I will quote an example of a type of evidence which is found in many different parts of the country. The regular presentments in the Abbot of Pershore's manor court at Hawkesbury, Gloucestershire, in the last decade of the thirteenth century, of tenants who had their cloth fulled at mills other than the lord's suggests that these non-seigneurial mills might have been fairly numerous.[57]

Nor is it possible to estimate the contribution made by the lessees of seigneurial mills to the formation of this important element in the country's capital resources. It is well known that the lessees were responsible for a substantial proportion of repairs and maintenance. In the long run, then, even if the initial investment in fulling mills had come out of landlords' rent income, their continued existence may have depended largely on the reinvestment of profits from production by the lessee. But this must have varied from time to time and from place to place. Professor Carus-Wilson, in the most substantial contribution yet made to the history of growth in the late medieval textile industry, is able to point to rising rents paid by lessees of fulling mills in the Stroud valley in the fifteenth century, but because of the defects of manorial documentation is unable to indicate whether the money invested in buildings and machinery came from tenants or from landlord or, if from both, in what proportions.[58] In some records, however, some indications of responsibility for costs are given. For example, two new fulling mills on the Staffordshire estates of

---

[56] In the reprint of her article 'An Industrial Revolution of the Thirteenth Century' (first published in the *EcHR*, xi, 1941) in *Essays in Economic History*, i, 1954, she adds further evidence, but still further examples turn up regularly as fresh sources are examined.

[57] PRO, SC2/175/41, 42.

[58] 'Evidences of Industrial Growth on some Fifteenth Century Manors', *EcHR*, 2nd ser. xii, 1959 (reprinted in E. Carus-Wilson (ed.), *Essays in Economic History*, ii, 1962.

the Duchy of Lancaster at Uttoxeter in 1418 and at Tutbury in 1445, were built at the expense of the lessee of the site (the king, however, providing timber at Tutbury and a £2 subsidy). The costs of these mills are not known, but they could have been substantial: a fulling mill to be built at Chartham in Kent in 1437, according to a contract between the Prior of Canterbury Cathedral and two millwrights, was to cost 22 marks (£14 13s. 4d.) for the skill and labour of the craftsmen, apart from the cost of the material.[59] Some textile entrepreneurs were capable of providing such sums,[60] but clearly in many cases landowners must have continued to provide some of the initial capital from their rent incomes.

Capital investment in the mining and metal industry was low before the fifteenth century. The mining of iron, coal, tin, and lead was done by small groups of privileged men, who might have certain obligations to the king or the lord of the soil, but rather in return for the right to dig than as a return on capital invested.[61] The early iron bloomeries, located close to the source of the ore and of the fuel (charcoal), can have cost very little to make, and many of them were itinerant. Landowners may have played an important part in making woodland available for charcoal-burning and in providing the ore, but there is little evidence that there was much investment of landowners' rent income in the 350 or so ironworks which are assumed to have existed in the latter part of the thirteenth century.[62] As is now well known, the enlargement of the capital needed in the mining and metal-processing industries took place mainly from the fifteenth century onwards. The application of water power to the smelting of iron, that is in the operation of the bellows, may have occurred

[59] Cited by L. F. Salzman, *Building in England down to 1540*, 1952, p. 509.

[60] e.g. William Heyne of Castle Combe. Cf. G. Poulet Scrope, *History of Castle Combe*, 1852, and Carus-Wilson, *op. cit.*

[61] The bibliography to J. U. Nef, 'Mining and Metallurgy in Medieval Civilisation', *Cambridge Economic History*, ii, 1952, needs much supplementation for England, e.g. H. P. R. Finberg, *Tavistock Abbey*, 1951, for the Devon stannaries; C. E. Hart, *The Free Miners of the Royal Forest of Dean*, 1953; M. S. Giuseppi, 'Fourteenth century accounts of ironworks at Tudeley, Kent', *Archaeologia*, lxiv, 1913; G. S. Tupling, *Economic History of Rossendale*, 1927, etc.

[62] H. R. Schubert, *The History of the British Iron and Steel Industry*, 1957, p. 109.

in the *grossae fabricae* of the thirteenth century, but there is no proof until after the Black Death. It added the costs of a water mill to the bloomery construction costs, which themselves may have increased, for example with an increase in the size of the bellows. A mill and bloomery complete with tools, made for the Bishop of Durham at Bedburn in Weardale in 1408 cost some £10, excluding the cost of the timber. But its annual output was 7 or 8 times that of the average bloomery which was not assisted by water power. In the fourteenth century the Bishop of Durham's bloomeries had been farmed, and the experiment in direct exploitation following the building of the bloomery mill did not last long. But here, nevertheless, is a clear example of the contribution of rent income to capital formation which is worth adding to other indications of capital investment in the fifteenth century.[63]

A presentation of the problems of rent and capital formation would not be complete without a reference to urban ground rent. The subject has been touched upon by historians interested in the origins of the medieval urban patriciate, and today opinion would seem to be swinging back, in reaction against Pirenne, to Sombart's view that rent was an important element in the income of the urban ruling groups of the eleventh and twelfth centuries. But so interesting and abundant are the records of commerce and crafts in European towns between the twelfth and fifteenth centuries, that the question of rent income has receded to the background. It is true that many historians have commented on the investment of trading profits in landed property, both for status and security. But this has resulted from investigations of the real property holdings of individuals whose primary role was other than that of a *rentier*.[64] Are there any indications that the contrary movement took place, that rent income was the source for capital formation in the sense defined? The study of merchants' or manu-

[63] G. T. Lapsley, 'The Account Roll of a Fifteenth Century Iron Master', *English Historical Review*, xiv, 1899, 509–29; Schubert, op. cit., p. 140.

[64] I think of such studies as F. C. Lane, *Andrea Barbarigo, Merchant of Venice*, 1944; G. Espinas, *Les Origines du Capitalisme*, i: *Sire Jehan Boinebroke*, 1933; S. L. Thrupp, *The Merchant Class of Medieval London*, 1948; A. Sapori, 'I mutui dei mercanti fiorentini del trecento e l'incremento della proprietà fondiaria', in *Studi di storia economica medioevale*, 1946.

facturers' accounts with this end in view would encounter the difficulties already mentioned with regard to agricultural investment, the difficulty of distinguishing whether the capital invested came from rent or production income. Another approach is also possible. There are a number of medieval town rentals, and from some of these some estimate might be made of the social groups which were the principal holders of rent-yielding property, and of the extent to which their holdings gave them an income enabling them to invest in productive enterprise. The chief difficulty in making this sort of investigation is that rentals rarely comprehend the whole of the rent yielding property in a town owing to the multiplicity of principal landlords. Another difficulty is that rentals by no means always give full information about sub-tenants, that is, the actual occupiers who contribute the biggest sums of rent.

Simply by way of example I will quote some figures derived from a few English town rentals.

The first figures are not from a rental in the normal sense of the term. They are from a tallage of the town of Bristol in 1312, which was assessed both on movable goods and on rent income.[65] Although the return is incomplete, and the assessment was made at a time of political and social upheaval in the town, it clearly covers much of the town's rentable property, some 1,230 tenancies. Furthermore, an assessment of rents as income for taxation may, in spite of evasions, give more complete information about rent income than a landowner's rental which might not record high rents paid by sub-tenants. According to the tallage, there were 372 owners receiving rent, 41 being ecclesiastical institutions. There was little concentration of real property in the hands of individuals. Only 23 of the 372 landowners had an income of more than £5 from their property, and only six had more than £10. Three of these six were ecclesiastical institutions, of which St. Augustine's Abbey with £35 was the wealthiest. Three men had rent incomes of £12, £16 and £22 respectively. These were fairly substantial incomes. But they were not large enough indi-

---

[65] E. A. Fuller, 'The Tallage of 6 Edward II and the Bristol Rebellion', *Trans. Bristol and Gloucester Arch. Soc.*, 1894–5.

vidually, and there were not enough of such rent incomes to provide for a significant contribution to capital formation. The example of one of Bristol's most famous merchants in the next century, William Canynges, suggests that such men were more likely to use the income from accumulated real property for pious foundations.[66]

Royal officials, in 1279–80, drew up what were in effect detailed rentals of towns and villages in a number of counties. The finished returns are known as the *Rotuli Hundredorum*. Among these the record of the growing town of Coventry has survived.[67] Here was a town whose expansion seems to have been almost entirely a function of industrial and commercial growth, for it was a centre neither of secular nor of ecclesiastical administration. The 1280 survey shows that there had been a considerable subdivision of older burgage tenements, an aspect, of course, of an increasing population and a market in lands and tenements. At this date there were about 500 persons (that is presumably heads of households) and institutions (mostly religious) who either occupied or otherwise had rights in real property in the town. There were about 700 separate properties in which one or more families could live. Clearly there must have been many unrecorded sublettings. However, in spite of this indication of a market in real property, there was surprisingly little concentration of ownership.[68] Only 16 persons held more than the equivalent of five burgages. No religious house or similar institution (apart from the Priory as chief lord) held even as many as five burgages. Those who had the largest real property holdings could hardly have derived much of a living from them, let alone have a surplus for investment. One of the biggest property accumulations was held by a clerk, Mr. Richard Burton. It consisted of 9 burgages, 7 crofts, 4 water mills, 9 cottages and a curtilage. Some of the

---

[66] E. E. Williams, *The Chantries of William Canynges in St. Mary Redcliffe Bristol*, 1950. Dr. W. G. Hoskins has noticed the impermanence of medieval merchants' accumulations of real property, 'English Provincial Towns in the Early Sixteenth Century', *Trans. Royal Hist. Soc.*, 5th Ser., vi, 1956.

[67] Leigh MSS., Shakespeare's Birthplace, Stratford-upon-Avon.

[68] That is, under the chief lord, the Cathedral Priory, which had bought out the other lord, the Earl of Chester's successor.

burgages were further subdivided and sublet as 27 cottages, 18 curtilages, and an oven. The net rent income from this property was £2 16s. 8d.[69] Another property owner, Peter Baroun, who had 17⅓ burgages and two cottages, had a net rent income of £1 19s. 2d. There were a few other property accumulators with similar holdings, but none with more. Only 16 persons held more than 5 burgages.

This situation was much altered by the fifteenth century. It is true that there seems little evidence of greatly increased individual real property holdings. According to a rental of 1411 of the Cathedral Priory, the two biggest property accumulators, John Preston, draper, and Robert Shipley, merchant, held about a dozen tenements each. Their net incomes from this property cannot be calculated but could not have been very great. No other persons approached this number of holdings from the Priory.[70] On the other hand institutional property holding had developed considerably. By 1486, for instance, the Holy Trinity Guild, Coventry's most powerful institution, had between 350 and 400 tenants, many of them the leading merchants of town and guild, who thus appear as rent payers rather than as rent receivers.[71]

The county town of Gloucester had also by 1455 developed a structure of real property ownership where institutions rather than individuals predominated.[72] At this date there were some 580 properties of different types in the town. Monasteries owned some 270, town churches, chantries and religious guilds had about 100 and the stewards of the town between 25 and 30. Individual property owners were comparatively insignificant. The most important was a lawyer, Thomas Deerhurst, with 18 tenements and 9 cottages. Only 10 individuals owned more than 10 tenements. Net rent incomes cannot unfortunately be calculated. The rental was drawn up to record an ancient obligation called 'land-

---

[69] That is, after Burton had paid his rents.

[70] This contrasts with a property owner of 1522 who had 50 houses and a rent income of £41. Hoskins, op. cit., p. 11.

[71] The Priory rental is PRO, Exchequer K. R. Misc. Books, no. 21; *Records of the Holy Trinity, Coventry*, ed. G. Templeman (Dugdale Society, 1944).

[72] *Rental of Houses in Gloucester, 1455*, ed. W. H. Stevenson, 1890.

gable', and the real rents were given for houses in only one street. But there could have been no significant personal income from urban rents.

Another county town, Warwick shows a similar lack of individual accumulation of real property. The returns of 1280[73] for this town show only one sizeable individual property owner, Thomas Payn, who bore the unofficial title of 'mayor'. He held a dozen burgages for low rents from the Earl of Warwick and from various ecclesiastical landowners, as well as three of which he was chief lord. Although the rent he received from sub-tenants was nearly four times as great as that which he paid out, his net rent income was somewhat less than £2. No other landowner, apart from the Earl of Warwick himself and the Collegiate Church of St. Mary, had anything like as much property as Payn. By the end of the fifteenth century, the rentals of the Earl and of the Collegiate Church, the two principal ground landlords, show a similar lack of concentration of urban real property. The biggest accumulator was John Huggeford, Esq., member of a family which for many years had been serving the Earls of Warwick as administrators. He held 10 burgages, 8 messuages, 3 cottages, 2 barns, 2 gardens and half a dozen unoccupied sites of the earl,[74] and possibly a few properties of St. Mary's church. The net income he got after subletting is not known, but it could not have been very impressive.

These few examples are quoted rather as types of material for considering the role of urban rents in the economic life of the country, than as proving any general thesis. However, it is difficult not to emphasize that this evidence would suggest that accumulations of urban real property were not great, except in the case of religious or social institutions; that the owners, whether individuals or institutions, tended not to be among the investors of the period; and that in any case the net incomes derived from these real property holdings were not substantial. It may well be that evidence from other towns will give different results. The towns quoted are, however, fairly characteristic of their type.

[73] PRO, Exchequer KR Misc. Books, no. 15.
[74] PRO, DL 43/9/21.

Let me sum up the ideas about rent and capital formation expressed in this paper. First, as to the method. Using the English evidence it is very difficult to distinguish the contribution to capital formation of rent income from that of the profits of production. The chief reason for this is that evidence about capital formation comes mainly from estate accounts and these are at their most informative precisely at the period when production constituted a large part of landowners' incomes.

Second, it would appear that when landowners seemed to be most directly interested in production, that is, in the thirteenth century, their interest did not seem to go beyond the exaction of the maximum profit. The *idea* of reinvesting profit for the purpose of increasing production seems to have been present in few minds if any. In *practice* the minimum rather than the maximum seems to have been spent on those goods which go towards capital formation. Recalculation of figures from some church estates (Canterbury Cathedral for example) might show that I have somewhat underestimated the level of investment, but would still hardly justify comparing them with modern industrial enterprises.

Third, the high level of rent and other demands made by landowners of tenants seems to have severely restricted capital formation by this class, although natural conditions (shortage of pasture) must also be blamed. But it is possible that large free tenants and lesser gentry may have contributed a higher proportion of their incomes or profits to capital formation than the great secular or ecclesiastical magnates. Such persons did not have the same wish or opportunity for conspicuous waste as the barons, but were not as hard pressed financially as the customary tenants. Unfortunately these smaller men have left hardly any records.

Fourth, the changed economic and social conditions after the middle of the fourteenth century operated in favour of tenants as against landlords. Changes in land use made possible a build-up of peasant flocks and herds. Lower rents and other demands left greater surpluses in tenants' hands. In addition, tenant pressure on landlords, whether conscious or whether operating as a result of the changed land:labour ratio, caused landlords to invest a greater *proportion* of their incomes in building, including tenants' buildings. The physical volume of investment may not have been greater than in the thirteenth century, but it may well have been greater per head or per acre in use.

These points all refer to the agrarian economy. A very brief consideration of industrial and urban aspects of capital formation leads to the following suggestions. First, the landowner contribution to the initial outlay on mills etc. may have been exaggerated. Corn millers, fullers, miners, smelters and others may have built for their own use. Furthermore, lessees of seigneurial mills etc. were obliged by the terms of their tenure to contribute more or less substantially to repairs. Capital formation from this source would therefore come out of production income rather than from rents. Second, there seems to be no reason to suppose that urban rent contributed anything substantial to capital formation. Trading and industrial profits were invested in urban rents rather than the other way round.

These ideas are put forward on the basis, so far, of insufficient evidence. It is hoped, however, that they may serve to provoke discussion, and perhaps suggest a new way of analysing familiar evidence.

# XI

# Lord and Peasant in Staffordshire
## in the Middle Ages*

*The Earl Lecture, delivered at the University of Keele on 28 November*
*1969*

In the Middle Ages, in a primarily agricultural county,[1] the relationships between the two principal classes, lords and peasants,
necessarily embrace much of the social history of the time. These
relationships changed a great deal during the course of the Middle
Ages. But it is hardly possible, in our restricted compass, to
describe the changes adequately. I have consequently decided to
examine them as they are revealed in the documentary evidence
of the early fourteenth century. At this time, on the eve of the
demographic collapse of the second half of the century, the characteristics of Staffordshire rural society, which had resulted from at
least two centuries of economic expansion, had attained some
degree of definition.

For lack of any existing general survey of the principal distinguishing features of Staffordshire lords and peasants of this
period, any study of their relations must be preceded by an
examination, however brief, of each class.

## LORDS

A useful starting-point for a general view of the lords of Staffordshire in the first half of the fourteenth century is a list of landowners which was made in 1337 for fiscal purposes. In that year,

---

* Reprinted from the *North Staffordshire Journal of Field Studies*, x, 1970, 1–20.

[1] Neither Stafford nor Newcastle had more than 2,000 inhabitants, possibly
fewer than 1,500. Stafford merchants in 1337 contributed £5 to the tax which is
referred to below. Lichfield merchants paid £4, those of Newcastle £2 10s. 0d.
Merchants' contributions from other towns were very small.

having decided to make war on France, Edward III necessarily had to consider the raising of money for his armies. The English monarchy already had many fiscal devices at its disposal, but one of the most important, the raising of a subsidy of a tenth and a fifteenth on movable goods, could only be done with the agreement of lords, knights, and burgesses in parliament. In July, when Edward told the council of magnates of his plans, there was some urgency, and perhaps even some uncertainty, as to whether a parliament, to be summoned for September, would give him what he wanted. It was decided that negotiations would be initiated at a county level. Writs, therefore, were sent to sheriffs ordering the assembly of clergy, nobles, merchants, and other rich men to discuss grants of money. In the event, the enterprise did not go far. Few county assemblies seem to have met. Among those which did meet was an assembly of the clergy, lay notables, and merchants of Staffordshire.[2]

These met at Stafford in the second week of September. The clergy were asked to help first, and agreed to do so. Owing to short notice, only a few lay notables were present, so a week's delay was allowed to enable more of them to be mobilized. A week later, enough turned up to make the negotiations worth while. At their own request, they broke up into discussion groups according to their social status (*in suis gradibus*); that is knights and lords of villages deliberated together, separately from the merchants. The knights and lords eventually agreed to pay 1s. in the pound of landed revenue. on the basis of an extent which had been made in Edward II's eighteenth year (July 1324–July 1325). A copy of this was in the possession of Sir Philip de Somerville of Wychnor. The extent must have been the basis of the list of Staffordshire landowners in 1337 with valuations of their landed property which provides the first over-all impression of the hierarchy of landed society of the county.[3] The values allotted to each individual are obviously purely conventional as well as being, no doubt, considerably underestimated. The fact that the

---

[2] J. F. Willard, 'Edward III's negotiation for a grant in 1337', *Eng. Hist. Rev.* xxi, 1906.

[3] PRO, SC 12/1/32.

extent was accepted as a basis for assessment by the assembled gentry suggests that they themselves accepted the gradations within the hierarchy of wealth which it expresses.

A preliminary observation must be made. This list is clearly not complete. Apart from the fact that seven names are illegible in the manuscript, the names of some important county families are missing, omissions which cannot be explained simply on the grounds that they have lands in other counties, for this is also true of many on the list. At least 35 important family names are not mentioned. Even if we imagine that seven of these would be revealed if it were possible to read the illegible names, we are still left with 28 missing families, of whom the most important names are Basset, Camville, Gresley, Okeover, Trussel, and Wrottesley. However, the list does contain 104 names, so we have between three-quarters and four-fifths of the Staffordshire gentry arranged in hierarchal order, sufficient to give us some indication of the structure of the class.

There are six grades of annual values, ranging from £100 per annum to £5 per annum, the intermediate stages being £40, £20, £10 and 10 marks. Earl Henry of Lancaster is at the top of the list, his lands being valued at £100 and after him his son, Henry of Grosmont, Earl of Derby, whose valuation figure is illegible. The Lancastrian estate was that which had been virtually confiscated from the unfortunate family of Robert Ferrers, Earl of Derby, as a punishment for his support of Simon de Montfort during the Barons' Wars. In Staffordshire the estate comprised a substantial portion of the Honour of Tutbury, consisting of manors and forests in the east-central part of the county, together with the town and castle of Newcastle-under-Lyme in the north-west.[4] Those who were assessed at £40 (13 in all) include the baronial families in the county of whom the most important were Stafford, Audley, Sutton of Dudley (successor by marriage to the Somerys), and the dispossessed Ferrers with their seat now at Chartley. This group also included wealthy gentry not of ba-

---

[4] J. R. Birrell, *The Honour of Tutbury in the Fourteenth and Fifteenth Centuries*, M.A. thesis, University of Birmingham, 1962, and 'The Forest Economy of the Honour of Tutbury', *Birmingham Univ. Hist. Journ.* viii, 1962, 114–34.

ronial status, such as Swynnerton and Somerville and the *nouveau riche* lawyer, William of Shareshull.[5] On the other hand, the middle group of 30 families assessed at £20 includes Sir Thomas de Furneval, husband of an heiress to the Staffordshire portion of the now dispersed Verdon barony, with its seat at Alton. He did receive a baronial summons to Parliament. However, for the most part this group is made up of such well-known gentry family names as Pype, Trussebut, Legh, Wasteneys, and Stafford of Bramshall. Among the 17 families assessed at £10 are also well-established names, such as Rydware, Mauvesyn, Meynil, and Bagot, while even two of the three assessed at 10 marks bear names also found in the higher-paying ranks—Meynil and Doyley. Finally, there is the most numerous group, containing 39 names. Of these lords of villages, assessed at £5, many were from obscure local families, but there was a sprinkling of better-known names such as Hugford, Rolleston, Stafford of Pype, Coyne of Weston.

At this time knighthood was a social distinction, apart from its military implications, though many men thought it to be too expensive to acquire. Of the 104 men on the 1337 list, 35 were knights. They are not altogether concentrated at the top end of the social scale. Of the £10, £20, and £40 groups about half of the men in each were knights. None of the three assessed at 10 marks was a knight, and out of the 39 assessed at £5 only two were knights. This should warn us not to regard the county gentry and the knights as being synonymous. Some of the *domini villarum* might put off being dubbed as long as possible rather than rushing to acquire this honour when of age. Many never bothered. There were, however, changes of fashion. Knighthood blossomed somewhat under the influence of successful wars in France, with profits to be made from wages (higher for knights than for men-at-arms), ransoms, and, of course, loot. A study of the plea rolls during a 10-year period in the middle of the war with France (1341–51) reveals some 60 Staffordshire men who acquired the title of knight.[6] At least 90 members of Staffordshire gentry families, whether knighted or not, went off to France in the first 10 years

[5] B. Putnam, *The Place in Legal History of Sir William Shareshull*, 1950.
[6] *Collections for a History of Staffordshire* (C.H.S.), xii, 1891.

of the Hundred Years' War, judging at any rate by the pardons they acquired to cover their period of foreign service.[7]

Lordship was not only exercised in medieval England by barons, knights, and other lay landowners. Ecclesiastical landowners constituted a substantial and active element in this class. It would be a mistake to confuse their social role entirely with that of the lay nobility, if only because of the sacerdotal function which, through the distribution of the sacraments, made them so essential to the medieval believer. On the other hand, it cannot be assumed that as lords and landowners their ecclesiastical position and training softened in any way their attitudes towards the dependent peasantry. If anything, the reverse was the case, as is illustrated in a thirteenth-century conflict between the Abbot of Burton and his tenants of Abbots Bromley, when the Abbot denounced as particularly detestable to God and man those serfs who presumed to implead a prelate of the Church in the public courts before the secular power.[8]

The ecclesiastical hierarchy at all levels tended to mirror that of secular society. In Staffordshire, the principal ecclesiastical magnate was the Bishop of Coventry and Lichfield, with considerable estates in the villages and forested lands in the south-east of the county. Monastic landowners, in particular those of the Benedictine order, were, however, less important than in some counties where a deeply rooted position in landed society was based on the continuous possession of estates and domination over the peasantry going back to early Anglo-Saxon times. In Staffordshire the oldest Benedictine house was that at Burton, founded in 1004 and endowed adequately, though by no means lavishly, with landed property. Its records do not allow us to calculate its income in the early fourteenth century nor even very satisfactorily from the valuation of Pope Nicholas IV in 1291. However, on the eve of the dissolution of the monasteries, its income was much less than half of that of Evesham Abbey, less than a quarter that of Bury St. Edmunds, less than a seventh that of Glastonbury.[9] And the next two biggest monastic landowners in Staffordshire, the

---

[7] *C.H.S.* viii, 1887.　　[8] Burton Abbey Cartulary, *C.H.S.*, v, 1, 1884, 65.
[9] A. Savine, *English Monasteries on the Eve of the Dissolution*, 1909, Appendix.

Benedictine priory of Tutbury and the Cistercian Abbey of Dieulacres, each had less than half of Burton's income. The remaining 16 religious foundations in Staffordshire, almost all founded in the twelfth century, had small estates and were in no position to impose themselves on the countryside as the bishop and the lay lords were able to do.

The clerical presence was, however, by no means negligible on the secular side. An interesting feature of the county was the number of collegiate churches under royal patronage. Apart from the cathedral chapter itself, presided over by its dean, there were deans with colleges of clergy at Wolverhampton, Tettenhall, Penkridge, St. Mary Stafford, and Gnosall, all with landed endowments. In the case of the deans of Wolverhampton these led to a dispute with the peasants on their estates which was prolonged over more than half a century, and which entirely resembles similar disputes on both monastic and lay estates. As to the parish clergy, their position varied considerably according to their degree of absenteeism, their social origin and their local endowment. One has the impression from the public records that they were intimately involved in all the affairs, legal and illegal, of the county gentry to whom many of them were related. This intimate relationship is typified in the latter part of Edward II's reign by the pitched battles which took place between the gentry families of Ipstones and Brompton over the question of whose kinsmen should be the parson of the parish of Church Eaton. As in most quarrels of this type each side brought in supporters, many of them leading members of allied gentry families, so that in the end nearly 70 persons were accused of taking part in this family and ecclesiastical fracas.[10]

Landed society, then, in early fourteenth-century Staffordshire, was led by two magnates, one lay, one ecclesiastical, that is the Earl of Lancaster and the Bishop of Coventry and Lichfield. The focal points of the Earl's estates were the two boroughs of Tutbury and Uttoxeter. Each of them was to some extent an agricultural settlement as well as a market town. Tutbury's burgesses owed

---

[10] T. Tanner, *Notitia Monastria*, 1744, D. Styles, 'Early History of the King's Chapels in Staffordshire.' *Trans. Birmingham Archaeol. Soc.* lx. *C.H.S.* x, 1889, 62, 66.

haymaking services in the Earl's meadows, and sales of grain and stock constituted a significant item of the Earl's revenue. At Uttoxeter there were arable and meadowlands in demesne of more than 400 acres. The Earl's other borough, Newcastle-under-Lyme, was separate from the rest of the Staffordshire lands. There was a castle here, a coalmine and an iron mine, some meadow land, and a substantial number of agricultural tenants. Then there were three big manors in the rich valleys of the Dove and Trent—Rolleston, Marchington, and Barton-under-Needwood. These manors and manorial boroughs all produced a considerable income. The special feature, however, of the Lancastrian estate, was that it included the Forest of Needwood. This was divided into the five wards of Tutbury, Barton, Marchington, Uttoxeter, and Yoxall, and yielded a substantial income from rents, pasture fees, hay sales, and profits of the forest courts (*wodemotes*). Within the forest were also the two settlements of Agardsley, to be renamed 'Newborough' with its 101 newly-founded burgages, and Hoarcross nearby with few old-established tenements, but with a considerable number of new lettings of demesne. It is necessary to add to these some half-dozen hamlets within the forest or included within the manors already mentioned.[11]

The bishop's estate was a much more complex affair even than that of the Earl (which was only the Staffordshire portion of the Honour of Tutbury). In addition to Lichfield itself, the bishop had seven main manors. Haywood, Baswich, Longdon, Brewood, Rugeley, Cannockbury, and Eccleshall, with tenants in a whole number of lesser hamlets. For example, apart from the men of Lichfield and Longdon, the bishop's tenants from 16 lesser settlements owed suit of court to his view of frankpledge at Lichfield. There were separate courts in Eccleshall, Rugeley, and Cannock, and it seemed to be generally admitted that the bishop had hundredal jurisdiction in all of his manors, not to speak of free warren and the profits of some half-dozen markets and fairs. This estate was much influenced by its situation in a heavily wooded area (the forest of Cannock), as we shall see when we come to consider characteristics of its peasant tenures. Apart from this, the manors

[11] PRO, DL 29/1/3.

which comprised the estate had many features normal for the period—demesne lands, tenants owing labour services, manorial jurisdiction, and seignorial control over access to the commons, such as pastures and fisheries.[12]

Although the territorial and political influence of the Earl and the bishop within the county was considerable, it was not overwhelming. Apart from the fact that their estates were rather localized, they obviously had many interests outside the county. The Earl's estates were scattered widely over the Midlands, the Welsh Marches and the North. His political interests were focused on the centre of government rather than on the periphery. The same might be said of the bishops, whose territorial interests were not so wide, but who at this period were promoted civil servants with national rather than local preoccupations. What of the middle ranks of the baronage with important estates in the country? The Audley family is typical. Their lands were concentrated in the north-west of the county. Their castle was at Heighley near Audley, to which a small amount of arable land, woodland and pasture was attached. But their manors in the villages of Audley, Betley, Endon, Horton, Tunstall, and Alstonfield were not organized on the principle of an organic connection between demesne and tenants. The Audley's had a considerable number of tenants over whom they had jurisdiction, but apart from the marginal case of Alstonefield (in which there were several other manorial lords) they seemed to have had no interest in agricultural production. On a smaller scale, they resembled the Earls of Lancaster in that their interests were not exclusively within the county. They had some four or five manors in Shropshire, a manor and lands in five Cheshire villages. Perhaps their great days as lords of the March were over, but their interests still lay in that direction. Both of the wives of James Audley (1312–86) came from Marcher families (Mortimer of Wigmore and Strange of Knockin).[13]

---

[12] Stafford Record Office (SRO), D1734 J2268, Survey of the bishop's estate, 1298. I wish to thank Miss J. R. Birrell for allowing me to consult her transcript of this and other documents. Aspects of the bishop's franchises are also described in *Placita de Quo Warranto (PQW)*, ed. W. Illingworth, 1818, 705–20.

[13] Audley inquisitions *post mortem*, *C.H.S.* N.S. ix, 1906, xi, 1908; *Complete Peerage*, i, 1910, 339–40.

Other baronial interests in Staffordshire were also, for various reasons, rather weak. The barons of Stafford, however prestigious their origins, however brilliant their future, were not at this time particularly rich or influential, as could be guessed from the marriages in late thirteenth and early fourteenth centuries into such middling local families as Langley, Bassett of Drayton, and Hastang of Chebsey. Ralph (1301–72), who improved the family's fortunes and was made an earl in 1350, probably did so by being away from Staffordshire in the king's wars and at court, where he was Steward of the Household and a founder of the Order of the Garter. The important Verdon family became extinct in the male line in 1316, and its castle at Alton was taken over by the husband of one of the heiresses, Sir Thomas de Furneval. In any case the Verdons had many interests in other Midland counties than Staffordshire. In the far south of the county, the powerful Somery interests, centred on Dudley castle and a group of manors on the Staffordshire—Worcestershire border, were divided between co-heiresses in 1322, one of whom took Dudley and the Staffordshire lands to John Sutton of Malpas (Cheshire). Sutton of Dudley, to some extent, filled the role of Somery. Other baronial families were of relatively little weight, a situation reflecting rather minor territorial power in the country. The Ferrers of Chartley had perhaps hardly recovered from their dispossession in favour of the Lancastrians and showed more interest in their property outside the county than in their Staffordshire holdings. Bassett of Drayton had only three manors in the south of the county, and whatever role Ralph Bassett played as a royal official in England and Aquitaine, he was not noticeably active in county affairs.[14]

Probably the members of the landowning class with whom the peasants came most into contact were the gentry at lower than baronial level. These were the men who did most of the work of local administration, as sheriffs,[15] as keepers of the peace, as tax assessors or commissioners of array; on the other hand it was

[14] *Complete Peerage*, ii, 1912, 2–3, and v, 1926, 305–13, and xii, 1, 1953, 173–7; Verdon and Basset inquisitions, *C.H.S.*, 1913.

[15] Henry of Grosmont was sheriff from 19 to 35 Edward III, but, like the other (rather few) high ranking sheriffs of the time, exercised his office through a deputy.

they who rode about the countryside, poached in the parks and forests of the crown and the magnates and generally contributed to that 'air of turbulence' which some historians once believed to be mainly characteristic of the fifteenth century.[16] They differed considerably, as we have seen, with regard to their landed wealth. Philip de Somerville, knight, assessed at £40 in 1337, was lord of Alrewas and Wychnor, his main possessions, and had land at Tunstall, Newbold, and Curborough. This family's interests appear to have been entirely based in Staffordshire. It is best known of course, because of the survival of the Alrewas court rolls, but on the whole seems to have played a quiet part during our period—except that a Roger de Somerville in 1314 had to obtain a pardon for his support for Earl Thomas of Lancaster. Contrasting, in different ways, were the Shareshull and Swynnerton families, both also assessed at £40 in 1337. Sir William Shareshull, the lawyer, from obscure beginnings had, by that date, acquired Shareshill and Patshull, and by marriage and purchase, lands in Oxfordshire and Shropshire as well. The main line of the Swynnerton family, prominent in Staffordshire as Shareshull was to become in England, was mainly based on the manor of Swynnerton, but with lands and rents in half a dozen other villages, some acquired from the king from the confiscated lands of the elder Despenser.[17]

Many of the gentry, though owning few manors, had, like Shareshull, land in more than one county. The Beysin family, assessed at £20 in 1337, had land in Ashley, and Water Eaton, and also in five Shropshire villages. The Bromptons, who were involved in the dispute about the incumbency of Church Eaton, held a manor there, another at Longford in Shropshire, and some land in Oxfordshire. The rival family of Ipstones held Ipstones and Foxwist (of the Verdons), lesser pieces of land in four other

---

[16] N. Denholm-Young, *History and Heraldry*, 1965. HAHAHA

[17] Evidence for the presence of the gentry in the villages is to be found in the *Nomina Villarum* of 1316 (*Feudal Aids*, v, HMSO, 1908) and in the 1332 subsidy (*C.H.S.*, x). *C.H.S.*, 1907 and 1910 for Somerville and Alrewas; *C.H.S.*, viii, 31, for Roger de Somerville's pardon; Putnam, op. cit., for Shareshull, Swynnerton inquisition in *Calendar of Inquisition*, viii, HMSO, 1913, no. 180 and no. 268 (lesser branch of the family).

places from the lord of Cheddleton, another piece of land and a mill from the lord of Kingsley, half of the hamlet of Castern, and a quarter of the manor at Blymhill. The land was valued at £18 in an inquisition *post mortem* of 1293, but only at £5 for taxation purposes in 1337.[18] This fragmented tenure, probably the consequence of piecemeal acquisition, is characteristic of the lesser gentry. Unfortunately, these lesser families tended to leave fewer private records than the big estate owners. What they did leave were mostly deeds of title rather than records of estate administration. Their names bulk large, however, in the legal records of the time, as litigants, as jurors, and not seldom as defendants in cases of felony.

## PEASANTS

By peasants I mean members of rural communities in possession of a family holding. This holding was worked in order to provide the subsistence, derived from cereals and animal products, necessary to keep the family alive and provide from year to year the necessary seed and young animals to repeat the cycle of production. Small holders, part-time artisans, even landless labourers, in a society of this type should also be included among the peasants because not only were they members of village or hamlet communities, but very often belonged to peasant households. At the top end of the social scale in peasant society, there were well-to-do families who seemed to merge into the ranks of the lesser gentry. But they were few, and quite apart from economic differences, the style of life, not to speak of the aspirations of poor gentry and rich peasants, had few resemblances. There was for instance, a clearly recognizable group of free tenants of gentry status on the bishop's estate in 1298, with names such as Camville, Handsacre, Tamenhorn, Heronville, Pype, Doyli, Giffard, Harcourt, Swynnerton, Hastang. Although some might be holding a complete village or hamlet as a quarter, half or whole knight's fee, others seemed to be holding ordinary free tenures such as the two yardlands for 4s. a year and the service of one-eighteenth of a knight's fee, which John of Swynnerton had at Sugnall. But these

[18] Beysin, Brompton and Ipstones inquisitions, *C.H.S.*, 1911.

men are in practice easily distinguishable from the peasant free-holders on the bishop's estate, although the market in free land had certainly brought many parcels of socage land into gentry possession which they either sublet or took into demesne.

Although the majority of Staffordshire manors were owned by rather obscure lords, our best evidence about peasant tenants comes inevitably from the estates of the larger lay and ecclesiastical owners. These were the people who kept estate records covering considerable areas of land and who have passed them on to posterity. The possibility has to be borne in mind that the structure of such estates differed from that of smaller properties. Researches into the 1279–80 Hundred Rolls suggest that on the bigger estates there would be a relative predominance of the classical type of manorial structure, characterized by a close association of peasant holdings with demesne, and a relatively high percentage of tenants in villeinage. It is the more surprising, therefore, to discover that, even when relying on evidence from the bigger estates in this county, at the beginning of the fourteenth century there was a substantial proportion of free tenure. In calculating the proportions of free tenants which follow, I have included tenants of burgages. Whilst realizing the sharp theoretical distinction both in law and in economy between the burgage and the agricultural socage holding, I have no hesitation in assimilating the two in order to give an impression of the relative weight of freedom and servitude in the Staffordshire of the period. Even in places which were indubitably urban in character, the agricultural element was still strong: and in fact, many of the Staffordshire seignorial boroughs were little more than renamed villages.

The following figures are based on two types of evidence about the manorial personnel—tenants, and *amounts* of money rent paid by them.[19] It is best, of course, to be able to count the

---

[19] SRO, D 1734, J2268, Survey of bishop's estate, 1298; A. Saltman (ed.), *Tutbury Priory Cartulary*, *C.H.S.*, iv, Fourth Series; PRO, DL 29/1/3, Duchy of Lancaster ministers' accounts; Audley inquisitions *post mortem*, *C.H.S.*, N.S. xi, 1908; Verdon inquiry, *C.H.S.* 1913; Two Wigginton inquisitions, *C.H.S.*, 1911 146 and 312; Church Eaton (Adam of Brompton), *C.H.S.*, 1911; Drayton Basset, *C.H.S.*, 1913; Clifton Camville (Geoffrey de Camville), *C.H.S.*, 1911; Lapley Priory, *C.H.S.*, 1913.

number of individual tenants who were free or servile. This can be done for the bishop's estate, for that of Tutbury Priory, and for that of the Audley family. The Lancastrian estate accounts of 1313–14 and a survey of the Verdon estate made in 1327 at the request of the three heiresses, only provide evidence about the amounts of money paid from free and customary (villein) holdings. As will be seen from the Tutbury and Audley figures, the striking difference in the percentages of free tenures and free rent shows clearly that free rents must on the whole have been considerably lower than customary rents. Consequently when we have only the rent payment totals we are entitled to assume that a given percentage of free rent represents a much higher percentage of free persons.

TABLE I. *Tenurial Status on some Staffordshire Estates (percentages)*

| Estate and date | Free and burgage | | Customary (inc. cottages) | Undifferentiated |
|---|---|---|---|---|
| Tutbury Priory 1295 | Tenants | 40 | 60 | — |
| | Rent | 30 | 70 | |
| Bishop of Coventry and Lichfield 1298 | Tenants | 51 | 34 | 15 |
| Audley 1307–8 | Tenants | 42 | 58 | — |
| | Rent | 27 | 73 | |
| Lancaster 1313–14 | Rent | 47 | 14 | 39 |
| Verdon 1327 | Rent | 52 | 26 | 22 |

These over-all figures conceal variations from manor to manor. Surviving descriptions of individual manors illustrate this variety. In some of them there was no servile tenure, in others no free tenure. At Church Eaton in 1315 there was an entirely free tenant population. At Wigginton near Tamworth in 1313 the tenant population consisted of 13 free tenants and 18 sokemen. The term 'sokemen' implies freedom, though in this case their ancestors as recently as *c.* 1249 may have been villein sokemen of the ancient demesne of the crown. At Drayton Bassett, the chief manor of the

baronial family of Bassett of Drayton, more than half of the rent
in 1344 was free rent, indicating an even higher proportion of free
tenure. On the other hand at Clifton Campville in 1308, only four
miles from Wigginton, 90 per cent of the rent was from customary tenants. On the small estate of Lapley Priory (Lapley,
Wheaton Aston, and Marston) in 1339 there were 61 customary
but no free tenants. But in spite of these variations the strong
impression remains that in the borderlands between south Staffordshire and north Warwickshire there was a predominance of
free tenure.[20] Taken in conjunction with the figures calculated
from the estates which provide samples from the north-east, the
north-west, the east-central and south-east parts of the county, it
would seem hardly rash to suggest that certainly more than half of
the peasant families of early fourteenth-century Staffordshire were
tenants of free holdings. It is, of course, true that personal status
did not necessarily coincide with the status of the holding, though
the whole history of the thirteenth century seems to show a
tendency towards the establishment of an identity between the two.
In so far as that identity did not exist, it is more likely that free
men were holding customary tenures than the reverse. If this is
so, it should not alter our impression of the high degree of peasant
free status derived from the figures cited. The principal modifying
feature, if the evidence were at our disposal, would be that the
estate of Burton Abbey might have been a reservoir of servile
tenure in the Vale of Trent.

The predominance of free tenures in Staffordshire at the beginning of the fourteenth century may well have been partly the
result of the fact that there were not, in this county, many of those
old and highly organized estates, particularly monastic estates,
which elsewhere we find associated with servile villeinage. It
must also certainly be due in part to the considerable amount of
wasteland and woodland available for colonization on attractive
terms of tenure, of which free status was a normal component.
Staffordshire was a well-wooded county particularly in the south
and south-east where the episcopal and Lancastrian estates were

[20] R. H. Hilton, *Social Structure of Rural Warwickshire in the Middle Ages*, 1950
(reprinted above, p. 113) for north Warwickshire.

situated. But another factor entered into the situation at this period. Staffordshire shared with the rest of England, and indeed with Western Europe, a considerable growth of population. In a peasant society employing primitive and relatively unchanging techniques in cultivation, the answer to the problem of feeding increased mouths was an extension of the cultivated area. This need for new land was a necessary condition of the colonization process. But if the peasant demand for land led to colonization and in certain circumstances to better conditions of tenure, the same pressures, if land were not available in sufficient quantities, could also lead to the creation of small holdings, perhaps held in free tenure, but not necessarily large enough to provide enough subsistence for the peasant family.

This feature of the peasant economy is one for which it is difficult to provide full proof. We normally rely on estate documents which do not necessarily show what land tenants may have been leasing from other lords than the estate owner, or other peasants. The following figures must therefore be read with this possibility in mind. On the Audley estate in the north-west of the county, there was, according to the inquisitions *post mortem*, a very high proportion of smallholders, reminiscent of conditions in more densely populated counties of the south east. In fact about half of all the tenants on the Audley estate at the beginning of the century had holdings of six acres or less; and a substantial number of these smallholders were free tenants. The Lancastrian material does not enable this sort of calculation to be made, but a surviving survey of the populous Lancastrian manor of Barton-under-Needwood, drawn up in 1327, shows a similar proportion of small holders to that found in the Audley estate.[21] About half of the holdings were under five acres in area.

On the bishop's estate in 1298, according to the very detailed survey of that year, about 40 per cent of the purely agricultural tenants were holding, at any rate from the bishop, very small amounts of land. This average for the estate as a whole conceals considerable variations, from a third in Haywood and Baswich to about two-thirds in Cannock. On some manors, therefore, the

[21] PRO SC. 11/602.

average size of holdings must have been rather higher than on others on the same estate or in other parts of Staffordshire. Many explanations are possible, of which the availability of land is one. Much of the bishop's estate lay in a well-wooded area, and there is considerable evidence of land taken recently into cultivation. But this expansion may have been affected in some places by the restrictions of forest law. Some parts of the Lancastrian estate, those manors in the wooded areas for which we have no figures, may also have had, on the average, larger holdings than on the Trent valley manor of Barton. However this may be, forest peasants had an advantage over those in other areas. These were their pasture rights and their opportunity for gaining extra income from non-agricultural operations in the forest.[22] There are also indications on the Audley estate that a number of Betley free tenants had other than purely agricultural occupations. While one survey presents them as ordinary free tenants, another of nearly the same date refers to many of them as burgesses.

A peasant family's standard of life did not depend entirely on its income. The outgoings must also be taken into account, consisting of the payment of rents and the performance of services for the landowner, as well as of obligations to Church and State. In Staffordshire the position with regard to obligations to landowners seems broadly speaking to be as follows. There was an overwhelming predominance of money rent. In the early fourteenth century, these money rents do not appear to have been high, being normally about 4d. an acre for arable and 1s. an acre for meadow land. Week work such as was found on the Burton Abbey estates in the twelfth century is nowhere to be found in thirteenth-century Staffordshire, not even on the Burton estate.[23] The labour service obligations of peasants were mainly in the form of haymaking and harvest boons together with some carrying services. Even these were often commuted for money payments on such estates as the Lancastrian where the direct exploitation of the demesne

[22] J. R. Birrell, 'Peasant Craftsmen in the Medieval Forest', *Agric. Hist. Rev.*, xvii, 1969.

[23] C. G. O. Bridgeman (ed.), Burton Abbey Surveys, *C.H.S.*, 1916. There are, however, references to a limited amount of week work during part of the year on the bishop's estate in 1298 at Haywood (Survey f. 24v).

was already largely abandoned. Do these facts mean, therefore, that in early fourteenth-century Staffordshire the peasantry was relatively lightly burdened? This might seem to be the situation in an area where customary land owed moderate rents and services and where a majority of the peasants, being free, were paying even lower rents than those mentioned. But such a situation would mean not only a fortunate peasantry, but an unfortunate landowning class. The incomes of landowners depended almost entirely on what was paid over to them, in one form or another, from the surplus product of peasant holdings. How did the Staffordshire landowners face this apparently unfavourable situation? One way in which landowners could recoup the diminishing income from rent was to increase demesne production and sell the goods on the market. This was not, however, a universal remedy, so at the same time they adopted another. As lords they had profitable rights over all serfs which gave them cash returns beyond mere rent payment. These included profits from manorial and other private courts, tallage taken annually, payments for the exercise of rights on the commons, including fisheries, and the profits arising from the monopoly of the mill. Profits from the court naturally included amercements which were imposed as punishments for varying defaults, misdemeanours, and trespasses. Such amercements could arise from the jurisdiction inherent in lordship of the manor as well as in some cases being derived from the exercise of private views of frankpledge. Additionally there were specific consequences of villein condition which (apart from the collection of tallage) yielded an irregular though constant revenue. The most important of these were the heriot paid from a dead tenant's holding the entry fine paid by his successor, and the fines paid to marry off daughters (merchet) or to compound for unchastity (leyrwite).

The evidence of the *Quo Warranto* pleas[24] indicates that the Staffordshire landowners, like those elsewhere in the country, had been reinforcing their jurisdictional rights during the course of the thirteenth century. Their success was uneven and inevitably it was the more influential, such as the bishop and the laymen of

---

[24] *Placita de Quo Warranto*, 1818, 705–20.

baronial status, who made the most gains. The bishop and the Earl of Lancaster established their right to important jurisdictional franchises, including the privilege of return of writs within their estates. At least 21 others claimed to exercise the view of frank-pledge in their own courts and 14 of them also claimed the right to hang on their own private gallows such thieves as were caught red-handed on their estates. Sixteen of the claims for view of frankpledge were admitted immediately by the crown lawyers, the rest being postponed but probably in the end accepted. Since there were some 98 lay lords and 12 ecclesiastical lords listed in the *Nomina Villarum* of 1316 it is clear that it was indeed only a minority which could sustain claims for the most important jurisdictional privileges, even if we take into account some obvious omissions from the *Quo Warranto* investigations. All the same, these claims are pointers to trends which have other echoes.

An obvious way to measure the financial importance of the exercise of lordly power is to calculate the proportions of various sources of income of those landowners who have left records susceptible of analysis. The valuation which was made of the bishop's estate in 1291[25] for the purposes of assessing the clerical tenth, enables us to make a useful breakdown of incomes:

|                               | (per cent) |
| ----------------------------- | ---------- |
| From the demesne              | 15         |
| From rents                    | 47         |
| From the exercise of lordship | 38         |

Similar calculations can be made from the Lancastrian estate account of 1313–14:[26]

---

[25] *Taxatio Ecclesiastica*, 1802, 242 ff.

[26] The demesne profits are almost entirely from sales of timber. An important element in the revenue from the exercise of lordship is profit from mills. I do not regard this as a normal payment for a service provided by the landowner as builder of the mill. I follow continental historians in regarding this as a profit arising from the lord's right to compel tenants to use only his mill and to pay a multure.

|                              | (per cent) |
| ---------------------------- | ---------- |
| From the demesne             | 11         |
| From rent                    | 50         |
| From the exercise of lordship | 39        |

It is only natural, of course, that the two greatest magnates of the county should have been able to extract from their tenants a considerable income derived from the exercise of lordship. Some lesser lords can also be shown to have substantial profits from this source. Tutbury Priory income from its Staffordshire property in 1295 can be divided thus:

|               | (per cent) |
| ------------- | ---------- |
| Demesne       | 13         |
| Rent          | 66         |
| Lordly income | 21         |

The Verdon estate in 1327 shows the following proportions:

|               | (per cent) |
| ------------- | ---------- |
| Demesne       | 26         |
| Rents         | 55         |
| Lordly income | 19         |

Inquisitions *post mortem* are very unreliable for this sort of calculation, since jurisdictional income seems to have been easy to minimize. The inquisition of 1344 on Ralph Bassett of Drayton shows an annual return at the manor of Pattingham under the heading 'Pleas and Perquisities of Courts' of only 3s. 4d. The contemporary Pattingham court rolls give the lie to this, showing a fluctuating income from fines and amercements which often reached one or more pounds a year.[27] Hence the inquisitions which have been used to calculate, for instance, proportions of free and customary rent cannot be used to estimate the financial burden of jurisdictional powers.

The figures just quoted give a lord's eye view of those profits derived from his command over men, which, we have suggested, were considerably increased during the thirteenth century. If we

[27] SRO, D 1807, 1 and 2.

look at the detail of the exactions as they affected the peasant household, our impression that the previous century or so may have been an increase in the exploitation of seignorial power is reinforced. This is particularly the case with the payment of heriot. This death duty, of frequent occurrence in view of the short expectation of life, must have been an important item in estate income, just as it must have been a difficult burden for a peasant economy, notoriously deficient in livestock, to bear. On most English estates the normal heriot was the peasant's best animal or chattel. In Staffordshire, however, we find that an extraordinarily heavy heriot was customarily demanded. The bishop's survey of 1298 goes into considerable detail about servile obligations which include, as heriot, not only the best beast but all stallions, an iron-shod cart, a brass cauldron, woollen cloth, uncut bacons, all pigs except for one sow, and all beehives. The stipulated heriot on the Lancastrian manor of Barton-under-Needwood, surveyed in 1327, was the best beast, all brass dishes, all iron-bound carts and wains, all beehives, all uncut cloth, all horses and foals, all pigs, all uncut bacons, and cash reserves (*thesaurum*).

These, as it happens, were maximum demands. We often read in the court rolls that tenants did not have enough chattels to pay heriots of this weight. Sometimes the lord took no heriot *propter pauperitatem* or *quia pauper*. But he clearly took what he could get, and it was often more than one beast. The Abbot of Burton in 1325 took two oxen, a mare, and a foal from a servile yardland at Winshill. In 1326, on the Audley manor of Tunstall, a 20-acre holding was relieved of a sow, 10 hogs, and a brass pot on the death of the tenant. Nor were these heavy demands confined to the estates of the magnates. John de Heronville, lord of the ancient demesne manor of Wednesbury, in pursuit of long-standing litigation with his tenants, claimed as heriot half of the tenant's pigs, the boar, all male colts, all uncut cloth, the iron-bound cart, and all uncut bacons. The Somervilles of Alrewas only asked for the best beast, but they extended their demands for heriot from their tenants to all the inhabitants of the lordship, whether holding land from them or not. Thus even poor labourers had to pay a heriot which would often be no more than a paltry garment.[28]

It would be a mistake to see this enlarged heriot simply as a relic of the Anglo-Saxon free man's heriot, that is the military equipment, originally granted by the lord and taken back at the vassal's death. Our only detailed survey of peasant conditions in twelfth-century Staffordshire, from the estates of Burton Abbey, has no reference at all to villein heriot and only one reference to a free man's heriot. Furthermore, although thirteenth-century legal theory attributed the ownership of a villein's chattels to his lord— this being the basis of the claim to heriot—it was the villein who accumulated the chattels. There is very little evidence indeed in manorial accounts of expenditure by lords on equipment or live-stock for villein holdings. In other words, this heavy obligation was not ancient but comparatively recent; it was a levy on goods accumulated by peasants, not a claim on stock which lords had leased out with the land.

The evidence does not allow us to see to what extent other servile dues increased in weight over the course of time. We can only indicate the level of various fines over the period with which we are concerned.[29] A substantial item of jurisdictional income came from entry fines, payable by a tenant entering on a villein holding, and analogous to the relief payable by the new tenant of a free holding. The entry fine, however, was arbitrary, whereas the relief was usually fixed at one or two years' rent—the light rent furthermore of the freeholding. Entry fines, though potentially arbitrary, did tend to be related to the current supply and demand situation. For this reason they are sometimes thought not to reflect the power of the lord so much as the bargaining position of the landowner. There is, of course, an element of this. One must remember, however, that the villein, whose physical movements and whose liberty of access to alternative supplies of land were restricted, was not a free agent. There is, therefore, in the level of entry fines an inevitable element of seignorial monopoly. In

[28] SRO, D 1734/2/1/101 and D 0/3; *Trans. N. Staffs. Field Club*, 1924–5, 36–86; C.H.S., ix, 17.

[29] Examples which follow are taken from documents to which reference has already been made.

Staffordshire in the early fourteenth century, fines were often about 1s. an acre, or about three times the annual rent. They could be much heavier. At Pattingham they could reach 2s. 6d. an acre, and in 1314 13s. 4d. was taken for entry to an acre of waste. The Abbot of Burton in 1317 took £4 from a widow so that she could succeed to her husband's yardland in Stretton (probably about 24 acres). A man who wanted to marry this widow and get the holding then had to pay the Abbot another 33s. 4d.

Other fines besides entry fines also combined the tendency to regularity with occasional examples of arbitrariness. In the 1320s the Audleys at Tunstall asked anything between 1s. and 2s. for merchet; the Bassetts at Pattingham up to 4s. (in 1312 for instance). In 1319 the Abbot of Burton took 3s. 4d. from a widow for permission to marry a free man.[30] Examples of other fines which were justified by seignorial right include 2s. paid by a man at Horninglow in 1309 to the Abbot of Burton for permission to put his son to school; 1s. and 5s. paid by men in Tunstall in 1326 for permission to leave the lord's land; an agreement by a Pattingham man to pay 3d. a year for the right to move freely in and out of the lordship. To fines of this type must be added the whole range of amercements for petty offences. Amercements for the same offence could differ widely according to the resources of the offender and the degree of culpability—both factors only occasionally mentioned in the record. The most common offences were trespass by animals, breaches of the assize of ale by village ale wives, default of suit of court, failure to prosecute complaints against fellow tenants, and illegal purchase or leasing of land. Such offences could bring about amercements of anything from 2d. to 6d. More serious offences could only be compounded with higher payment, as, for instance, at Hilton in 1314 when a man was amerced at 2s. for digging marl from the lord's pit.[31] Most of the sums seem trivial, though this is partly an illusion caused by our failure to keep constantly in mind the change in the value of

---

[30] But he took 13s. 4d. from a Stapenhill widow for the same thing in 1368. Was this a symptom of the 'feudal reaction' after the Black Death? SRO, D 1734/2/3/1129 for 1319 and D 1734/2/1/101 for 1368.
[31] SRO, D 1790/0/1/1. The lord was John of Swynnerton.

money: after all 2*d.* was a man's daily wage. By no means trivial, however, was another monetary facet of lordly power, the arbitrary tallage which was taken annually from unfree tenants. Precise details of amounts taken are difficult to come by, even though the obligation was fairly general. But the tallages levied on the bishop's tenants were estimated in 1291 in 4 per cent of his total manorial income or 10 per cent of the total rent income. And on the Lancastrian manors in 1313-14 a tallage amounted to between a quarter and a third of the total of bondsmen's rents.

Where there was inequality of status and obligation, where the free exercise of seignorial fiscal demands had to be confined to the servile minority, friction between lords and tenants was inevitable. Not unnaturally, as in other parts of the country, it frequently developed into claims by the unfree to have the advantages of their more fortunate free neighbours. Conversely, lords were all the more concerned to keep controls and the profits which were inherent in servile villeinage. Hence by 1280, the Abbot of Burton is on record in the courts as saying (through his lawyers) that his villeins owned nothing besides their bellies, a graphic way of expressing the view that a villein had no ownership in his chattels. This statement came after a long and bitter dispute with the Abbey's villein tenants at Mickleover near Derby.[32] The Dean of Wolverhampton, who five years earlier had confiscated his tenants' cattle to force them to pay tallage and pannage and to recognize their villein status, may not have been acting, in law, on exactly the same assumptions—his action could have been the normal process of distraint—but he came rather near to it. Furthermore, his successors were still attempting to prove that their tenants were villeins in the 1350s.[33] Another long-drawn-out process was between the Heronville family and their tenants of the ancient demesne manor of Wednesbury. Already in 1272, 25 of the tenants impleaded John of Heronville for exacting other customs than they were accustomed to render in the twelfth century when the king was lord, but details were not forthcoming at this particular time. The matter was not forgotten, however,

---

[32] Burton Cartulary, *C.H.S.*, v, i, 1884, 81 ff.
[33] *C.H.S.*, vi, i, 1886, 66; *C.H.S.*, xii, 1891, 110.

and in the first year of Edward II's reign a group of four leading tenants (one of them possibly the manorial reeve) was making the same allegations and in consequence suffering from illegal distraint by the lord, the same John as Heronville, knight, now aged about 70.

This Heronville case illustrates clearly what the manorial tenants saw as the advantages of free tenure. The fact that Wednesbury was a manor of the ancient demesne of the crown, in whose court the king's 'little writ of right close' ran, hardly alters the situation. The conditions alleged to have been in existence in Henry II's reign were essentially those of ordinary free tenure, that is a fixed money rent for the yardland of 5s. a year; suit of court twice a year (unless the writ of right was being pleaded, when courts should meet every three weeks); and tallage to be taken, according to the amount of land held, only when the king tallaged his boroughs and his demesne. The tenants accused John of having, in the previous reign, forced them by distraint to do suit of court every three weeks, demanded tallage at his will, high and low, and exacted merchet and other villein customs. John's lawyer made various moves to defeat the plaint but in essence he submitted that the tenants, by very reason of ancient demesne tenure, owed a normal range of villein obligations. In addition to the exactions already complained about, he claimed a biennial view of frankpledge; the obligation on the part of the tenants to undertake reeve's and tithingman's duties; a day's ploughing and harrowing in spring; a day's haymaking; four days' reaping, a penny toll when ale was brewed; pannage; 2s. merchet for marriage in and 3s. for marriage out of the manor; leyrwite (12d.); and the heavy heriot which has already been mentioned. No money rent is referred to, and it is not impossible that the valuation of the exactions would not in fact be more than 5s.—perhaps even less. It was uncertainty, and those aspects of villein tenure which meant that a man was not his own master which produced the conflict—a conflict which incidentally was repeated in similar terms a dozen or so years later on John of Perton's ancient demesne manor of Tettenhall.[34]

[34] *C.H.S.*, vi, i, 60; *C.H.S.*, ix, 1888, 7, 17 and 89.

Heronville and Perton were not wealthy barons. Heronville had land in Tipton as well as in Wednesbury. His grandson John was assessed at only 100s. in 1337. Perton owned the manor of Perton and another manor in Shropshire as well as being lessee of Tettenhall. Assessed at £20 in 1337, the Perton family counts as middling gentry. In fact the peasants may have had more to put up with at the hands of the local gentlemen than from the more powerful absentee lords. Roger of Okeover, lord of Okeover and Ilam, another gentleman of minor importance, is found persecuting a free man, Lawrence of Okeover from Ashbourne, who was probably a merchant. Roger claimed Lawrence as his villein and refused to accept documentary evidence of Lawrence's freedom. The aim seems to have been pure and simple extortion, for having lured Lawrence to Okeover, Roger and his abettors imprisoned him, fined him £10, of which they actually got 13 marks, and made him enter into a bond of £14. This case was won in the King's court by Lawrence who got £70 damages, but who had considerable difficulty in raising it from Roger's property.[35]

We even find one of the great lords protecting customary tenants from local oppression by one of the lesser gentry. Sir Ralph of Rolleston, a knight, was lessee of the Earl of Lancaster in the manor of Rolleston. According to complaints made in the Earl's court held for Rolleston tenants as part of the honour of Tutbury in 1339, this Sir Ralph, as far back as the days of Earl Thomas (died 1321), had bullied two of the bond tenants of the manor into surrendering one and a quarter acres from their holdings in exchange for a couple of old overcoats, so that the tenants who had succeeded to them by 1339 were paying rent for incomplete holdings. Although they had been threatened that if they complained it would weigh against them, they nevertheless petitioned. The Earl instructed the Steward of Tutbury to inquire into the matter, since not only might there be damage to the bondsmen, but prejudice to him as overlord. A jury confirmed the bondsmen's complaint, and the tenant (probably now Thomas

---

[35] *C.H.S.*, x, 1889, 26.

of Rolleston) was told to explain the facts to the Earl's council.[36]

We should remember that these cases of oppression by lords of their tenants are examples which happen to have been recorded. Many episodes probably never resulted in court proceedings. Furthermore, they must be considered against the background of more general violence in which the gentry played a leading part at the expense of the public at large and their own personal enemies in particular. Most of the evidence for this is in the records of the king's court and is therefore couched in conventional terminology which might not adequately describe the events leading up to the episodes which resulted in appeals, presentments, and so on. However, they are all that we have and cannot be ignored, for they show how limited was the influence of the central government or even of the territorial magnates. An interesting example of a violent campaign conducted by a local family against the Bishop of Coventry and Lichfield, and with apparent immunity, occurs in the 1290s. Agnes, described as the lady (*domina*) of Stretton, had seven sons, who were accused of all sorts of lawless activities by local juries of presentment in the Penkridge district. But in particular they broke into the bishop's park at Brewood and molested anybody who happened to be under his protection (*qui se advocaverunt cum episcopo*). With various supporters they waylaid, arrested and beat up the bishop's men on their way to the fair at Penkridge. The reasons for this enmity are obscure, but it is worth noting that Bishop Walter Langton eventually acquired the manor, except for Agnes of Stretton's dower. The succession to her first husband's lands is difficult to follow, but her second husband, Robert le Champion, seems to have been in collusion with his stepsons in their attack on the bishop's property. It is not inconceivable that the bishop was already, before the end of the thirteenth century, beginning to buy up the manor. Rivalries over landed property must have lain at the back of many of the family feuds of the period.[37]

---

[36] PRO, DL 30/1607/109. Thomas of Rolleston appears in the 1332 subsidy assessed in Rolleston at 100*s*.

[37] PRO, JI 809; *Victoria County History of Staffordshire*, iv, 1958, 164–5.

Probably not all the disturbances which involved the local gentry would have the simple explanation of conflict over property. Some episodes which appear in the courts, usually as a result of presentments by local juries, give the appearance of being part of ancient feuds between families whose original cause was perhaps forgotten, but whose momentum was maintained by assaults, killings and revenge outside the law. Inevitably, at periods of more general political disturbance, the feuding families tended to line up on opposing sides. Such seems to have been the case in the reign of Edward II, when the Swynnerton family supported the king and the Staffords (of Bramshall and Sandon) lined up behind the Earl of Lancaster. It is to be doubted, however, whether the Staffords were committed Lancastrians, though the Swynnertons naturally profited from their 'loyal' connection by acquiring profitable offices and immunities. The feud was recognized locally as such by the jury of presentment of the hundred of Tatmanslow, for in 1324 they referred to the support given by the late Countess of Lincoln to Sir William of Stafford and his allies in his quarrel against Sir Roger of Swynnerton. Her support was given, so it was said, in the dispatch of a band of armed men under the leadership of two knights (Sir Peter of Lymesy and Sir Thomas Blauncfront) to lay waste the parks of Sir William of Stafford's enemies. The Swynnerton clan was by no means innocent in these battles with the Staffords, or in other matters. Some of them were accused in 1315 by the widow of Robert of Essyngton of the murder of her husband, possibly arising in this case from a dispute about land in Essington. Others, aided and abetted by Sir Roger, the head of the family, were involved in the abduction of a woman of the Gresley family in 1324. Sir Roger's son Roger killed a royal forester in Cannock, and got a royal pardon in return for service in the king's army in Aquitaine. The Swynnertons in fact, were well able to look after themselves, by stopping the county court in 1314 and threatening the sheriff and Sir William of Stafford who were present. This was done by Sir Roger in the company of some 28 relatives and allies. The incursion into this court was matched by another Swynnerton gang's interruption of the assize justices at Clifton

Campville two years later. Roger, who at the beginning of the reign was alleged to have forced the coroner and witnesses against him in a murder charge to pay some £130 for their temerity, nevertheless was employed in various ways by the crown. For example he was placed on a commission to sentence the king's Lancastrian enemies, and was even made Constable of the Tower of London.[38]

Another violent member of the county gentry was Sir Hugh of Wrottesley, a founder member of the Order of the Garter, some of whose activities remind us how close was the connection during this period between fighting the king's and fighting one's own domestic enemy. In 1337, with 15 followers from Staffordshire, he was in the retinue of the Earl of Salisbury for the Scottish campaign of that year. On his way, however, he and his men paid off some old scores and killed John of Perton whom we have already met as lord of Tettenhall. Sir Hugh had other murders to answer for, including that of the under-sheriff and coroner, Philip of Luttley and Philip of Whitemore (probably a member of the coroner's staff) in 1352. But he was pardoned later because of his service in the king's army in France, and in spite of the possible prejudice against him of the trial judge, Sir William of Shareshull, whose daughter had married John of Perton's nephew. Sir Hugh's half-brother, William of Tetbury, was also involved in these later murders and was also issued with a pardon as a recognition of his service in France.[39]

The examples cited are a very small proportion of the cases which came before the royal justices. It can of course be argued that the use of court records will necessarily over-emphasize the incidence of criminal violence. On the other hand it is still significant that a good deal of this violence was committed by the county gentry to whose hands most of the law enforcement in the counties was entrusted. This paradoxical situation has already been noticed by Professor Putnam in her examination of the career of Sir Hugh of Wrottesley, whose life of violence did not prevent him from sitting as a Justice of the Peace in the county

[38] *C.H.S.*, x, 1889, 3–75 *passim*, for Swynnerton and Stafford rivalries.
[39] *C.H.S.*, viii, 1887, 59; *C.H.S.*, xv, 1894, 84–104.

where his crimes were committed.[40] This general atmosphere must be remembered when one is considering relations between lords and peasants. Apart from specific actions in pursuit of inter-family feuds, the more unruly gentry were also creating general disturbances by their ridings to and fro, their pillaging at markets and fairs, and not infrequently ordinary robbery. The lower ranks of the rural population must have suffered from all this, as for instance when the retainers of Thomas de Furneval of Alton raided barns and byres for livestock and other victuals on the pretext that they had to find provisions for themselves in the course of rounding up the supporters of Earl Thomas of Lancaster.[41] On the other hand it is also worth inquiring to what extent peasants became involved in gentry feuds. Accusations against bands of marauders where names are given frequent mention, in addition to the knights and gentry who were the leaders, not a few obviously plebeian individuals. Were these simply serving men in the gentry households or were wider sections of the tenantry involved? A comparison of legal and manorial records could provide interesting answers to such questions and throw much light on social relationships at the period.

[40] Putnam, op. cit., p. 137.    [41] *C.H.S.*, x, 1889, 53.

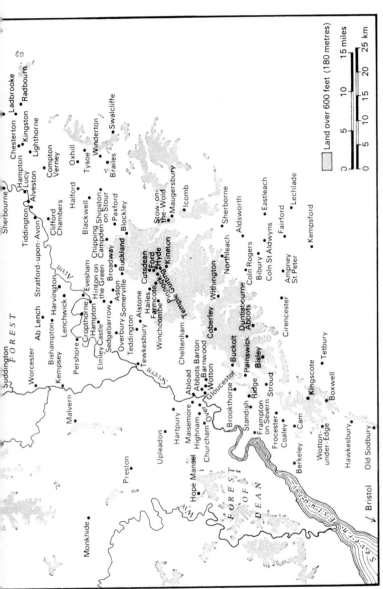

Places in the West Midland Counties mentioned in the text.

# INDEX